The Science of Music

A Practical Look at Music Theory

Allen Van Wert

Library of Congress Control Number: 2024900229
Registration TX-9-527-500

ISBN: 979-8-9907898-0-7

Foreword by Chris Adler
Illustration by Allen Van Wert and Rylie Van Wert
Thanks to my student James Cooper

Author: AllenVanWert.com | Book: MusicTheorySucks.com

Discord: https://discord.gg/3t2Y8mSPrH

Revised Edition 2026

FOREWORD

When Allen Van Wert approached me to contribute to his music theory book, I was both honored and intrigued. As a drummer with limited formal music theory knowledge, I have always admired those who can navigate the intricate landscape of music with such precision and depth. Allen, an extraordinary guitarist and teacher, embodies this expertise. His ability to distill complex concepts into accessible and engaging lessons has inspired countless musicians, including myself.

In this book, Allen bridges the gap between technical mastery and creative expression. Whether you are a seasoned musician or just starting your journey, his insights will enrich your understanding and appreciation of music. As someone who has always felt more comfortable behind the drum kit than the music stand, I can confidently say that Allen's approach makes theory not just comprehensible, but genuinely exciting.

Prepare to unlock new dimensions in your musicality. This is more than a guide, it's a gateway to a deeper connection with your craft. Enjoy the journey.

— Chris Adler
Lamb Of God and Megadeth

Contents

97 min7 sus 4	1 4 5 b7
:root on b7 is sus 2 add 13	1 2 5 6
98 min add 9	1 2 b3 5
99 min add 11	1 b3 4 5
:root on 4 is min 7 sus 2	1 2 5 b7
100 min Maj 7	1 b3 5 7
:root on 3 is aug add 11	1 3 4 #5
:root on 6 is aug add 13	1 3 #5 6
101 sus2 add b13	1 2 5 b6
102 aug maj7th	1 3 #5 7
103 aug 7th	1 3 #5 b7
:root on 3 is aug add 9	1 2 3 #5
:root on #4 is aug add #11	1 3 #4 #5
104 halfdim	1 b3 b5 b7
:root on b3 is flat 5 add b13	1 3 b5 6
105 dim7th	1 b3 b5 6
106 dim add 9	1 2 b3 b5
107 dim add b9	1 b2 b3 b5
108 aug4 add 7	1 #4 5 7
109 aug4 add b7	1 #4 5 b7
110 dom7 b5	1 3 b5 b7
111 b5 add9	1 2 3 b5
112 b5 add #9	1 #2 3 b5

113 5 Note Chords

113 maj9	1 2 3 5 7
114 maj #9	1 #2 3 5 7
:root on 3 is minMaj7add b13	1 b3 5 b6 7
115 maj7 add 11	1 3 4 5 7
:root on 3 is min addb9add b13	1 b2 b3 5 b6
:root on 4 is maj 9 aug 4	1 2 #4 5 7
116 maj7 add #11	1 3 #4 5 7
:root on 3 is min add9add b13	1 2 b3 5 b6
:root on 1 is maj 7 aug 4	1 3 #4 5 7
117 maj7 add b13	1 3 5 b6 7
:root on b6 is majadd#9add b13	1 #2 3 5 b6
:root on 3 is maj add #9 add 11	1 #2 3 4 5
:root on b6 is aug maj #9	1 #2 3 #5 7
118 maj7 aug4 add 13	1 #4 5 6 7
119 maj add 9 add 11	1 2 3 4 5
:root on 3 is aug min b9	1 b2 b3#5b7
120 maj add b9 add 11	1 b2 3 4 5
:root on 3 is maj #9 flat 5	1 #2 3 b5 7

121 maj add 9 add #11	1 2 3 #4 5
:root on 3 is aug min 9	1 2 b3 #5 b7
122 maj add b9 add #11	1 b2 3 #4 5
:root on 5 is min b9 aug 4	1 b2 #4 5 b7
123 maj add #9 add #11	1 #2 3 #4 5
:root on 3 is aug min maj 9	1 2 b3 #5 7
124 maj add 9 add b13	1 2 3 5 b6
:root on b6 is maj 7 b5 add b13	1 3 b5 b6 7
:root on b5 is aug maj 7 add #11	1 3 #4 #5 7
125 dom 9	1 2 3 5 b7
:root on 3 is aug min 7 add #11	1 b3#4#5b7
:root on 2 is flat 5 add 9 add 13	1 2 3 b5 6
126 dom b9	1 b2 3 5 b7
:root on 5 is dim add 11	1 b3 4 b5
:root on b7 is dim 9	1 2 b3 b5 6
:root on 3 is dim maj 7	1 b3 b5 6 7
127 dom #9	1 #2 3 5 b7
:root on 5 is maj add b9 add 13	1 b2 3 5 6
:root on 3 is aug min maj 7 add #11	1 b3 #4 #5 7
128 dom #9 b5	1 #2 3 b5 b7
:root on b5 is min add b9 add 13	1 b2 b3 5 6
:root on b5 is dom b5 add 13	1 3 b5 6 b7
129 dom 7 add #11	1 3 #4 5 b7
:root on b5 is dom b9 b5	1 b2 3 b5 b7
130 dom 7 add 13	1 3 5 6 b7
:root on 6 is min 7 add b9	1 b2 b3 5 b7
131 dom 7 add b13	1 3 5 b6 b7
:root on b6 is aug maj 9	1 2 3 #5 7
:root on 3 is flat 5 add #9 add b13	1 #2 3 b5 b6
132 dom 9 b5	1 2 3 b5 b7
:root on b5 is flat 5 add 9 add b13	1 2 3 b5 b6
:root on b5 is dom 7 b5 add b13	1 3 b5 b6 b7
133 dom 7 add 11	1 3 4 5 b7
134 min 7 add 11	1 b3 4 5 b7
:root on b7 is maj add 9 add 13	1 2 3 5 6
:root on 4 is aug min 7 add 11	1 b3 4 #5 b7
135 min 7 add #11	1 b3 #4 5 b7
:root on b7 is maj add #9 add 13	1 #2 3 5 6
:root on 4 is aug min maj 7 add 11	1 b3 4 #5 7
:root on 1 is min 7 aug 4	1 b3 #4 5 b7
136 min 7 aug 4 add 13	1 #4 5 6 b7
137 min 9	1 2 b3 5 b7

138 min 9 add 11 — 1 2 b3 4 5
139 min 9 add #11 — 1 2 b3 #4 5
140 min add b9 add #11 — 1 b2 b3 #4 5
141 min maj 7 add 11 — 1 b3 4 5 7
:root on 5 is min 9 aug 4 — 1 2 #4 5 b7
:root on 4 is flat 5 add b9 add b13 — 1 b2 3 b5 b6
142 min maj 7 add #11 — 1 b3 #4 5 7
:root on 3 is aug maj 7 add 11 — 1 3 4 #5 7
:root on 7 is maj add b9 add b13 — 1 b2 3 5 b6
143 min maj 9 — 1 2 b3 5 7
:root on 7 is maj b9 — 1 b2 3 5 7
:root on 5 is aug maj 7 add 13 — 1 3 #5 6 7
144 aug minmaj7 add 13 — 1 b3 #5 6 7
145 halfdim 9 — 1 2 b3 b5 b7
:root on b7 is min maj 7 add 13 — 1 b3 5 6 7
146 halfdim 7 add 11 — 1 b3 4 b5 b7
:root on b7 is min add 9 add 13 — 1 2 b3 5 6
147 dim b9 — 1 b2 b3 b5 b7
:root on 6 is dim m7 — 1 b3 b5 6 b7
:root on b3 is flat 5 add #9 add 13 — 1 #2 3 b5 6
148 maj 9 b5 — 1 2 3 b5 7
:root on 7 is min add b9 add 11 — 1 b2 b3 4 5

149 6 Note Chords

149 maj #9 add b13 — 1 #2 3 5 b6 7
150 maj #11 #9 — 1#2 3 #4 5 7
151 maj 11 — 1 2 3 4 5 7
:root on 5 is maj 11 b9 — 1 b2 3 4 5 7
:root on 4 is maj 11 #9 — 1 #2 3 4 5 7
:root on b6 is min b9 add b13 — 1b2b3 5b6b7
:root on 7 is dom 7 add 11 add 13 — 1 3 4 5 6 b7
152 maj #11 — 1 2 3 #4 5 7
:root on 4 is maj 7 add 11 add 13 — 1 3 4 5 6 7
:root on 2 is min 9 add b13 — 1 2 b3 5b6 b7
153 maj 9 add b13 — 1 2 3 5 b6 7
:root on b6 is maj b9 add b13 — 1 b2 3 5 b6 7
:root on b6 is dom #9 add b13 — 1#2 3 5 b6b7
154 min #11 — 1 2 b3#4 5b7
:root on b7 is maj #9 add 13 — 1 #2 3 5 6 7

155 min 9 add 13	1 2 b3 5 6 b7
:root on 6 is maj 7 add #11 add 13	1 3 #4 5 6 7
:root on 4 is halfdim 11 b9	1 b2 b3 4 b5 b7
:root on 5 is dom 11 #9	1 #2 3 4 5 b7
156 min 11	1 2 b3 4 5 b7
:root on b3 is maj #11 b9	1 b2 3 #4 5 7
:root on b7 is maj 9 add 13	1 2 3 5 6 7
:root on 4 is min 7 add 11 add b13	1 b3 4 5 b6 b7
157 min b9 add 13	1 b2b3 5 6 b7
:root on 6 is dom 7 add #11 add 13	1 3 #4 5 6 b7
158 dom #11 b9	1 b2 3 #4 5 b7
:root on #4 is dim add 11 add 7	1 b3 4 b5 6 7
159 dom #9 b5 add 13	1 #2 3 b5 6 b7
160 dom #11	1 2 3 #4 5 b7
:root on b6 is halfdim 9 add b13	1 2 b3 b5 b6 b7
161 dom 9 add b13	1 2 3 5 b6 b7
:root on b7 is min7add#11addb13	1 b3 #4 5 b6 b7
:root on b6 is dom #9 b5 add b13	1 #2 3 b5 b6 b7
162 dom 9 b5 add b13	1 2 3 b5 b6 b7
:root on b6 is min 7 aug 4 add b13	1 #4 5 b6 b7
163 dom 11 b9	1 b2 3 4 5 b7
:root on 5 is maj 7 add #11 add b13	1 3 #4 5 b6 7
:root on 4 is halfdim 11 add 13	1 b3 4 b5 6 b7
:root on b7 is min maj b9 b5 add 13	1 b2 b3 b5 6 7
164 dom 11	1 2 3 4 5 b7
:root on 5 is maj b9 add 13	1 b2 3 5 6 7
:root on b7 is min #11 b9	1 b2 b3 #4 5 b7
:root on 4 is min 7 add 11 add 13	1 b3 4 5 6 b7
:root on b6 is halfdim b9 add b13	1 b2 b3 b5 b6 b7
:root on 3 is halfdim b9 add 13	1 b2 b3 b5 6 b7
165 min maj 11	1 2 b3 4 5 7
166 min maj #11	1 2 b3 #4 5 7
167 aug minmaj9 add 13	1 2 b3 #5 6 7
:root on b7 is dom #11 #9	1 #2 3 #4 5 b7
168 halfdim 9 add 13	1 2 b3 b5 6 b7
:root on 6 is dom b9 add b13	1 b2 3 5 b6 b7
:root on b5 is dim 11 b9	1 b2 b3 4 b5 6
169 halfdim 11	1 2 b3 4 b5 b7
:root on 6 is min7add#11add13	1 b3 #4 5 6 b7

Thank you to my father,
Allen Van Wert Sr.
1951-2025
for inspiring me to dream.

WELCOME

Welcome to my music theory guide. I started writing this when I was about nineteen years old. I had been kept from music college even after earning a partial scholarship on guitar due to my family not having enough money for me to attend. I studied at home with books I got from various colleges and started to notice the same problems in all of them... complexity, redundancy and confusing naming conventions. So I fixed it. Over many years, I made changes to traditional music theory to make it more accurate and logical. This guide shows you what you need to learn in an order that makes sense, with assignments to help you remember the information so you can actually use it.

This is practical music theory for composition, learning songs, and improvisation. My students have had an easier time with this approach for years. It works. Take your time. If something seems confusing, slow down and figure out why. Reread sections when you need to. Most people assume music theory has to be complex because that's what they've been told. It isn't. People just explain it poorly. Relax and experiment with what you learn. Make it fun.

This is about practicing theory you will actually use. This isn't one of those thick textbooks full of details you'll never need. This is less wordy and more useful.

Allen Van Wert

HOW THIS HAPPENED

While teaching group lessons online, I noticed students arriving with questions and confusion about music theory, composition, and improvisation. They were receiving inconsistent information from other sources, and I found myself regularly clarifying these concepts for them. Over time, my students began requesting that I create a theory book or guide they could reference. I had a similar experience on social media, where people asked me to write a music theory book explaining my approach. I tend to explain concepts in ways that reduce confusion rather than add to it. This is that book.

When you look online or in other books, you will find hundreds of scales and thousands of chords listed. These are all contained within the elements presented here. Other authors simply didn't notice they were renaming the same structures, which is why this book offers a more accurate and elegant framework than virtually anything else available.

I named it "The Science of Music" because music theory has lacked consistency and scientific rigor, particularly in its confusing naming conventions and its failure to identify even common scales systematically. My approach prioritizes accuracy and universal truth. I discard misunderstood associations from the past and connect musical elements with objective reality. This allows for a more useful and practical understanding of music as a systematic discipline.

In science, you should be able to predict an outcome, measure with accuracy, and repeat the result every time. This is not exactly how music theory has been handled. We went off the rails at some point and there were some schisms and common sense failures. I feel like students just learn what they are told to learn and never actually test anything. They just assume things are constructed and named as they are for a good reason.

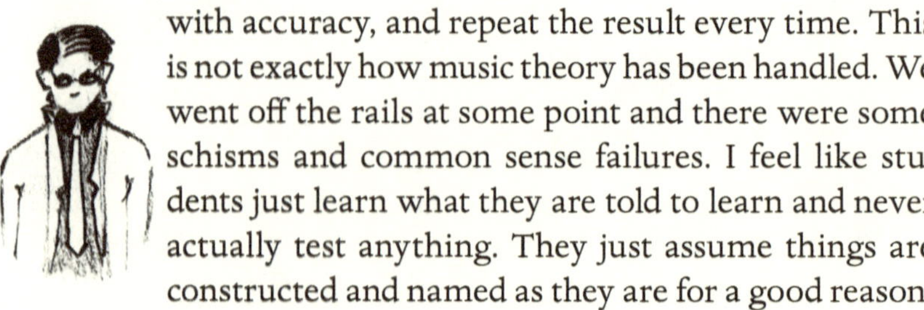

I don't do that. I like to fully understand things and make deeper connections with them. This isn't an entire upheaval of music theory but offers some corrections to its current flaws. This scientific approach doesn't eliminate the artistry of music. There is still magic in the way we combine elements like rhythm, harmony, and melody to create tension and release. Understanding the science simply gives us better tools to create that magic intentionally and consistently.

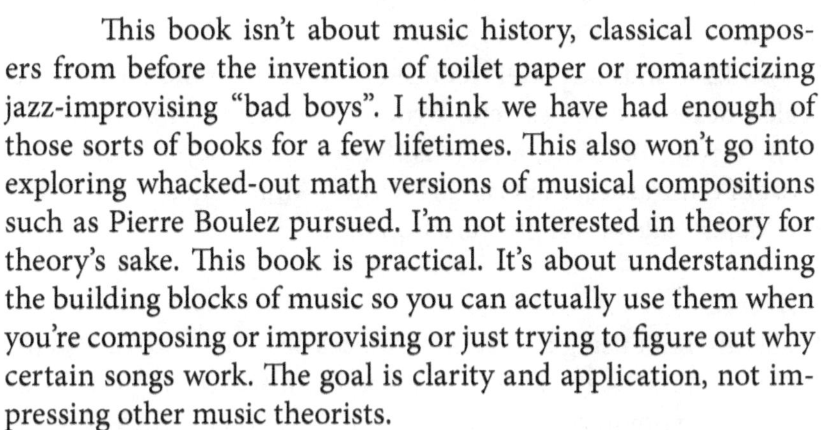

We can be scientists and also wizards. These two combined make a complete musician. You need a systematic approach for associating and testing musical elements like a scientist, but you also need wonder and the ability to create magical moments like a wizard. Light and dark coexist, as do tension and resolution. Be a scientific wizard. Just like Don Herbert. Mr. Wizard. He made science fun and accessible. That's what I'm doing here with music.

This book isn't about music history, classical composers from before the invention of toilet paper or romanticizing jazz-improvising "bad boys". I think we have had enough of those sorts of books for a few lifetimes. This also won't go into exploring whacked-out math versions of musical compositions such as Pierre Boulez pursued. I'm not interested in theory for theory's sake. This book is practical. It's about understanding the building blocks of music so you can actually use them when you're composing or improvising or just trying to figure out why certain songs work. The goal is clarity and application, not impressing other music theorists.

THE STRUCTURE

This won't be a perfect analogy, but if "music" itself were a book, think of it this way... Notes are the letters, Chords are the words, Melodies are the sentences, and Modes are the different personalities of characters you notice within the story.

As you learn from each section in this book, it's easy to lose sight of why you are learning a particular thing or how it fits into the overall system. You can reference this "map" to see how everything relates.

MUSICAL ALPHABET

There are 12 sounds/frequencies we identify as notes. This is our musical alphabet.

SCALES

Those 12 sounds are often reduced to a set of 7 notes. These are scales. Scales are the skeletal structure we extract melodies and chords from. Basically, a scale is the specific group of notes that most of our musical material fits within. Almost all scales are just the Major Scale or a slight variation of it.

INTERVALS

Scales are built using universal distances between notes called intervals. Intervals are universally applied distances regardless of the starting point, so it is much better to use them when describing scales and chords rather than attempting to memorize hundreds of variations. They are simply how we label the distance between two notes.

MAJOR SCALE

The most important scale is the Major Scale. We build, name, and identify all other scales and chords by comparing their intervals to the natural Major Scale's intervals (starting from the same root note). By the way, the term "Key" is just the Major Scale's root note. It's just another way of saying which Major Scale we are currently using.

CHORDS AND CHORD PROGRESSIONS

Chords are typically built by starting on a scale note and skipping every other note. We name them based on their universal intervallic structure. We start with 3-note chords (triads) and then extend them into 4, 5, and 6-note chords. It is useful in composition and improvisation to know exactly which chords emerge from which scales. We group these into a "chord progression" and use Roman numerals or Nashville numbering so the pattern is universally adaptable and easy to memorize.

MELODY

Melody is a musical phrase that we identify as a single moving entity. Melodies tend to land on notes contained in the current chord, so they generally stay within the same scale as the chords. If a melody contains notes outside the scale on weak beats, we call them chromatic passing tones. If a chord falls outside the scale, the melody usually follows it by including a note from that new chord.

TONAL CENTER

While listening to music, we compare everything we hear to one specific note that feels like the "home" or the most important note. This is our tonal center.

MODE

The tonal center's position within the scale will cause us to hear certain qualities we can remember, predict, and label. These are modes. Modes are simply how our brain experiences the scale based on which note feels most important.

RHYTHM

Rhythm is an underlying pattern or loop composed of strong and weak beats. Anything that takes place on a strong beat is naturally perceived as more important.

If you ever feel confused about what you are learning, just go over the above "map" and it might help remind you where you are in the scheme of things.

Here is a diagram where I use random images as place-holders for frequencies/notes in music. Here is how we structure a scale and some chords from it. This will be shown in detail later on, but it is nice to have an abstract graphical overview for some types of learners.

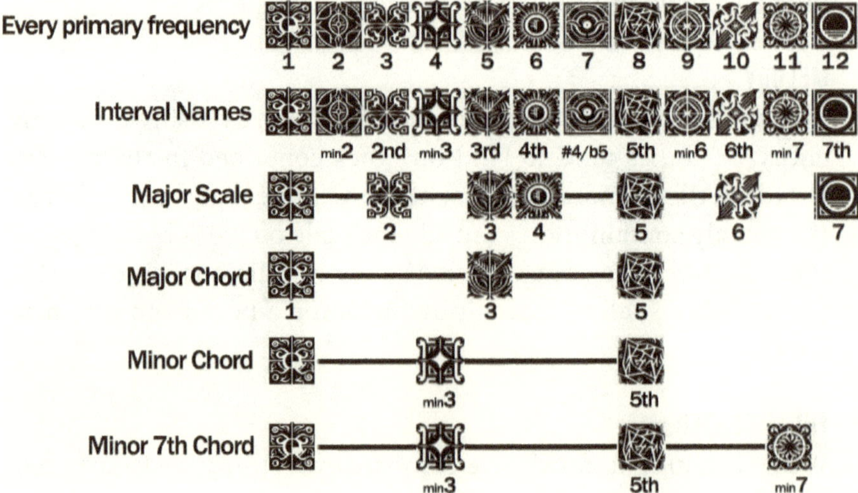

THE MUSICAL ALPHABET

Starting with the basic alphabet, there are seven letter names in music.

A B C D E F G

However, there are actually twelve notes in music. This is because most of the letter names above contain notes between them called Sharps or Flats. We use symbols to indicate these "in-between" notes.

Sharp (#): Means the note is one step higher.
Flat (b): Means the note is one step lower.

Here is where it gets confusing, A# and Bb are the exact same sound and the same note for the current tuning system we use. I consider this a flawed system. A Better Way? (Hypothetically) Look at how the traditional system compares to a logical system that accounts for the reality of the 12 letter names (rather than the historical perspective of just 7).

Note #	Logical (A-L)	Traditional (Current)
1	**A**	A
2	**B**	A# / Bb
3	**C**	B
4	**D**	C
5	**E**	C# / Db
6	**F**	D
7	**G**	D# / Eb
8	**H**	E
9	**I**	F
10	**J**	F# / Gb
11	**K**	G
12	**L**	G# / Ab

If I could use a time machine to go back and correct this fundamental oddity, I would simply use the first twelve letters (A through L) and omit sharps and flats entirely. One big advantage to using a 12-letter name system is that we wouldn't have the "EF" and "BC" anomalies where there is no sharp/flat between letters. These anomalies cause a big slowdown for students learning how to construct scales and chords. Interestingly, a computer program I hand coded years ago (before AI existed) to list associations between scales and chords uses a number system of 0 to 11 (12 numbers instead of letters). This is logically the most efficient way to process the data.

The Reality

All that said, you still need to understand the old, convoluted way of doing things because everyone else uses that naming system. To communicate with other musicians, you have to play on their terms. But, however you label them, remember that there are only twelve notes and they have specific frequencies locked to our tuning system.

Here are all twelve notes in music:

A - A#/Bb - B - C - C#/Db - D - D#/Eb - E - F - F#/Gb - G - G#/Ab

It is important to know the 12 notes because we use them as the foundation for building everything else in music.

Half Step (Semitone): This is the shortest distance we use in music theory. It is the distance from one note to the very next note (e.g., A to A#). In formal terms, we also call this a Minor Second interval or semitone.

Whole Step: This is a distance of two half steps. Going from A to B or from B to C# is a whole step. We also call this a Major Second interval.

Naming intervals is based on where they are in relation to the Major Scale (which I will show you in detail later). For now, sticking to "Half Step" and "Whole Step" is fine.

From now on, whenever you see "Half Step," you can just translate it in your brain to "ONE NOTE DISTANCE." You might think a "Whole Step" would mean one note distance, but nope, Whole step is a distance of TWO notes.

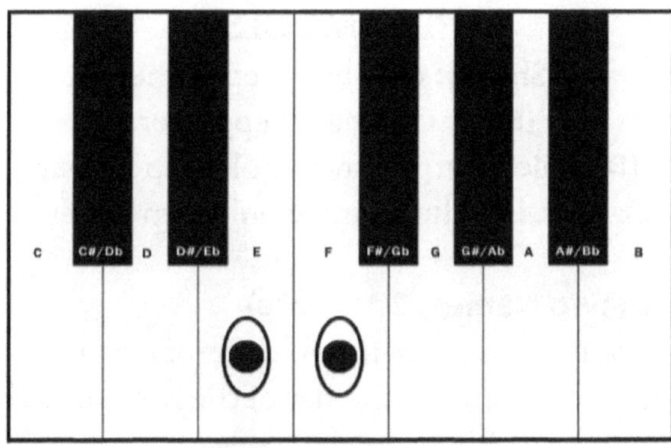

Half step shown above

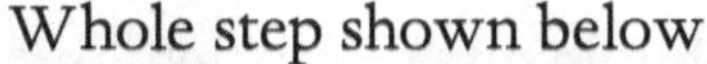
Whole step shown below

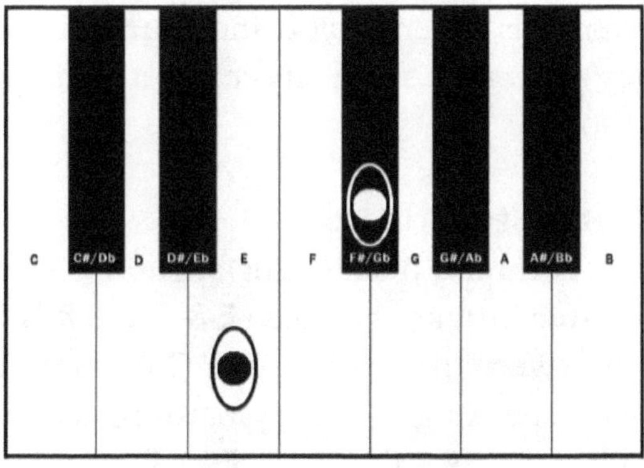

Things to know:

Half Step: Distance of **1 fret** (guitar) or **1 key** (piano). It is the smallest distance we quantify in Western music. Also called a *Minor 2nd or semi-tone.*

Whole Step: Distance of **2 half steps** (2 frets or 2 keys). Also called a Major 2nd.

THE SYMBOLS:

 # (Sharp): One half step higher.
b (Flat): One half step lower.
x (Double Sharp): One whole step higher.
bb (Double Flat): One whole step lower.

Enharmonics (Two Names, One Note)

An enharmonic is simply when two different names refer to the same pitch. Any sharp equals the flat of the note directly above it. **A#** is the same note as **Bb**.

The reason we might call it an "A#" today and a "Bb" tomorrow is based on the specific scale we are building (rules for this coming later). But in a real situation like a jam session, just stick to whatever feels easier for you and your bandmates to communicate. They are on the same physical fret/piano key and produce the same sound.

The "Natural" Half Step Trip Up

This is the most common mistake for beginners. There is **naturally** only a half-step distance between **E & F** and **B & C.** There are no "real" notes between them (like E# or Cb) on our instruments. However, strictly speaking in theory naming conventions, they can exist: **Cb = B** **B# = C** **E# = F** **Fb=E**

(Note: You will also occasionally see **Double Accidentals** like **x** or **bb**. We tend to avoid writing music in keys that require these, but they do technically exist.)

Rethinking Scales (The Loop)

I have restructured how we look at scales to better suit reality. A scale is just a collection of notes. We historically identify the Major Scale by writing it down in this specific structural order: **xx-xxx-** (Whole, Whole, Half, Whole, Whole, Whole, Half)

Sound doesn't know what we call it, and how we write things down doesn't change the reality of the music.

A scale is actually an **Infinite Loop.** It creates a continuous pattern of intervals: ...xxx-xx-xxx-xx-xxx-xx...

Depending on where you "slice" that loop, you get different variations. For example, the Major Scale can look like any of these snippets depending on your perspective, but the DNA remains the same:

XX-XXX- X-XXX-X -XXX-XX XX-XXX- X-XXX-X
-XXX-XX XXX-XX- XX-XX-X X-XX-XX -XX-XXX

It's really just a loop of **XXX-XX-XXX-XX-XXX-XX-**... etc.

The "Skeleton" of Music

Think of the scale as the skeletal structure. In actual music, notes jump around. You rarely play a linear scale in perfect order. A melody with the notes **D G B A D C F E** is made up of the **C Major Scale**, just not in order. We identify the scale based on the notes we hear most prominently, even if the melody occasionally uses "passing tones" (notes outside the scale) or the chords change rapidly.

Musical Alphabet Exercises

Half Steps

Example: E F F#

Fill in the missing notes low to high (left to right) as half steps:

A _ B   C _ _   Eb _ F
G _ _   _ Bb B   _ F _
_ C _   Bb _ _   _ D _
_ _ G   _ _ A   _ _ F

Whole Steps

Example: E F# G#

Fill in the missing notes low to high (left to right) as whole steps:

A _ C#   C _ _   Eb _ _
G _ _   _ Bb C   _ F _
_ C _   Ab _ _   _ D _
_ _ G   _ _ E   _ _ B

Half and Whole Steps mixed

Example: E - w - F# - h - G

Fill in the missing notes low to high (left to right) as a mix of half and whole steps (h = half and w = whole)

A - w - _ - h - C   D - w - _ - h - F   E - w - _ - h - _
B - w - _ - h - _   _ - w - A - h - _   _ - h - _ - h - C
_ - h - _ - w - G   _ - w - _ - w - G   _ - h - _ - w - A
_ - w - _ - h - B   _ - h - _ - w - D   _ - w - _ - h - F#
_ - w - _ - h - D#   _ - w - _ - h - Db   _ - h - _ - w - F#
_ - h - _ - w - D#   _ - w - _ - h - Bb   _ - w - _ - h - E
_ - w - _ - h - Ab   _ - h - _ - w - A#

Remember to reference the musical alphabet and learn to work in both directions. This is important for further development required. Fill out the fretboards or piano sheet from the discord.

Answers on page 232

THE MAJOR SCALE

Why-you-need-to-know-this:

We reference it to name and understand everything else in music involving pitch, Such as every chord and scale.

The Ruler of Music: The Major Scale is the center-point of all music theory and naming. Think of it as the **ruler** we reference constantly. We use it to measure, label and build everything else. There is a specific formula to build Major Scales, attempting to memorize every single one is inefficient. It is far more useful to be able to build them on the fly. The Major Scale is made up of seven notes.

Degrees: Each of the seven notes is assigned a number (degree).

1ST, 2ND, 3RD, 4TH, 5TH, 6TH and 7TH DEGREES

The **1st Degree** is the **Root.** This is the starting note and the letter name of the scale (e.g., in the **G Major Scale**, the root is **G**).

The Blueprint

Every scale has a blueprint or formula in the form of interval distances from each note to the next or also identified as each of the note's distances from the root.

MAJOR SCALE FORMULA

W - W - H - W - W - W - H

W= Whole Step (2 guitar frets/piano keys) H = Half Step (1 guitar fret/piano key)

Instead of memorizing a string of seven W's and H's, just remember this one variable: Every note is a **Whole Step** apart **EXCEPT** the **3rd** and **4th notes.**

The 3rd and 4th degrees are touching (Half Step). Everything else is spaced apart. (Note: The 7th note back to the Root is also a half step, but by the time you reach the 7th, the scale is already finished.)

Here is a look at it with the degrees added. "R" for "Root".

R -w- 2nd -w- 3rd-h-4th -w- 5th -w- 6th -w- 7th-h-(R)

This loop is infinite. The distance from one Root up to the next Root is called an **Octave.**

Diatonic

This term usually refers to keeping your movements within the scale you are using. If I say "move a diatonic 7th," you simply count up 7 steps within the current scale, regardless of whether that distance is major or minor. For instance, if I said move to the diatonic 7th, in one spot of a scale it might mean a minor 7th away and in another, it might mean a major 7th away. The designation of it being a diatonic interval distance makes things easier because you will just adjust the interval to fit whatever it naturally is in the scale you are using. We will look at specific intervals later on so no worry.

The Two Golden Rules: To build a Major Scale correctly and avoid confusion, you must follow two rules:

1. You MUST use each letter name (A-G) exactly ONCE. You cannot skip a letter, and you cannot repeat a letter. This ensures every degree has its own "slot."

2. You may NOT mix Sharps and Flats. If a scale has a sharp, it will only have sharps. If it has a flat, it will only have flats. You simply use whatever accidental is necessary to maintain the "Whole Step / Half Step" formula. This is the G Major scale on piano. Start on the G note and walk through it.

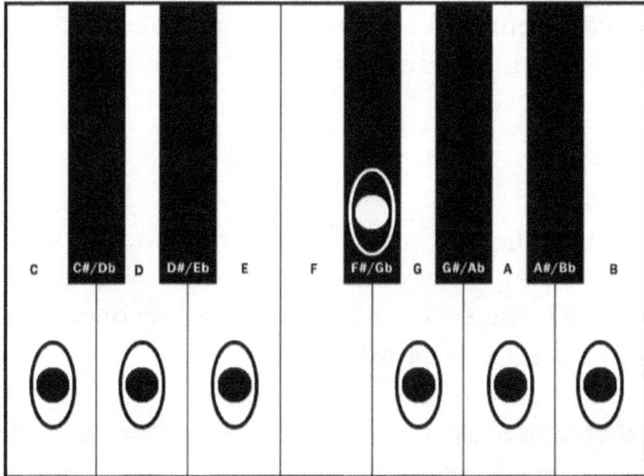

This is the G major scale on piano and the low E string for guitar.

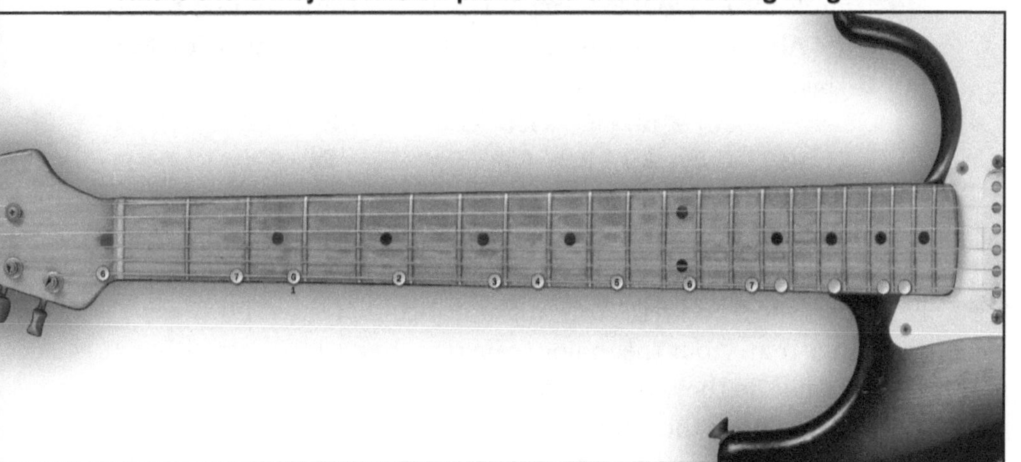

Example 1: The G Major Scale

Start on G. Follow the major scale formula of whole and half steps. You end up with: **G - A - B - C - D - E - F# - G**. (Notice we use F# to maintain the correct distance from E and to avoid repeating the letter G).

Example 2: The F Major Scale

F -(w)- **G** -(w)- **A**-(h)-**Bb** -(w)- **C** -(w)- **D** -(w)- **E**-(h)-(**F**). The 3rd to 4th note A and Bb are a half step along with the 7th back to the 1st, E and F. In the Musical Alphabet section, I said there are rare occasions where you would use B#/Cb and E#/Fb notes. Almost no one will

really ever call them by those names in a real-life band setting but they do arise naturally from some major scales.

For instance:

Cb = B   B# = C   E# = F   Fb = E

You need to be aware of one last beginner issue that occurs when building some of the major scales. When you follow **Golden Rule #1** (use every letter once and only once), you sometimes get forced into awkward names.

Like the **G# Major Scale:** G# - A# - B# - C# - D# - E# - **Fx** - G#

"**Fx**" stands for F "Double Sharp". The easier thing to do is to just call it the **Ab Major Scale** instead. It has the same frequencies (**Fx** is just **G.**) but is much cleaner to read and write:

Ab - Bb - C - Db - Eb - F - **G** - (Ab)
vs G# - A# - B# - C# - D# - E# - **Fx** - (G#)

Extensions (9, 11, 13)

Have you ever heard of a 13 chord? How about a half-diminished b9? Or an add 9 add #11? You might notice that those numbers go higher than 7 but the major scale only has 7. How can this be and what do they mean? This is much easier than it appears. They **ARE** within the 7 notes of the diatonic scale. They are simply another way to name the 2nd, 4th and 6th degrees. Basically, you cycle around the 7-note scale and once you are back to the beginning again, you keep counting higher instead of restarting at 1 or root. (but only for every other note)

1 2 3 4 5 6 7 - 8 **9** 10 **11** 12 **13** 14
is instead 1 2 3 4 5 6 7 - 1 **9** 3 **11** 5 **13** 7

Think of it as a clock that keeps counting past 12.

9th = The **2nd** degree.
11th = The **4th** degree.
13th = The **6th** degree.

It **IS** the exact same as using the 1 through 7 degrees but they are using their second-pass number count for the naming of these. There are only three of them. There is never or rarely a mention of an 8th, 10th, 12th, or 14th scale degrees. We do however have 9th, 11th, and 13th degrees as commonly used names for the 2nd, 4th, and 6th notes of the Major scale. This is actually something annoying to me about music theory.

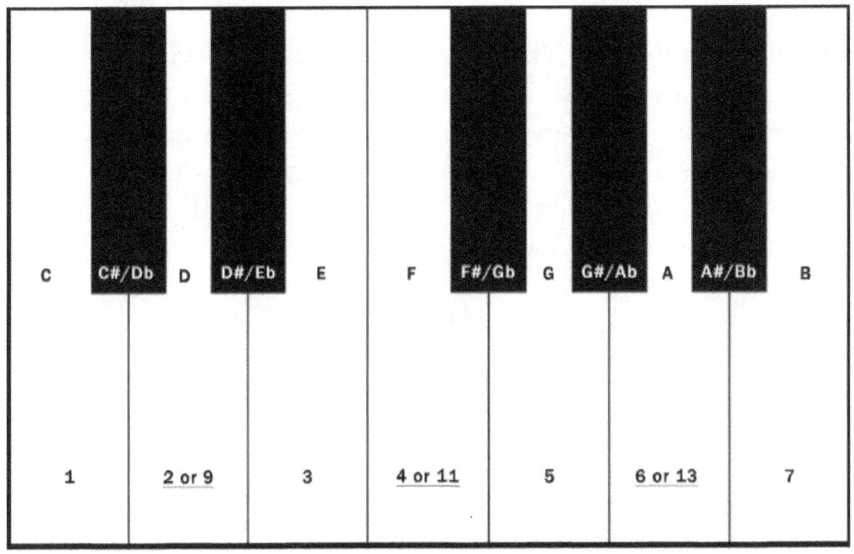

The **9th degree is** just the **2nd degree.**
The **11th is** just the **4th degree.**
The **13th is** just the **6th degree** of the scale.

The specific naming of chords is a lot more complex because of the redundancy between terminology in music theory. They use the same words/names for two different things at times and it can be quite deceiving. I cover all of that in the upcoming theory lessons.

Where does the soup start?

Think of a scale like a bowl of alphabet soup. If you looked down at the bowl while you were eating, you would just see a bunch of letters floating around in the broth. If I asked you, "Which letter does the soup start with?" you couldn't answer. It doesn't start anywhere, it just...is.

Scales are the same way. There is no such thing as a "starting note" in the physics of music because frequencies loop around. In actual songs, scales are rarely played in perfect linear order (A-B-C-D...). They are scattered, skipped and rearranged. However, in the chaotic history of music theory, we decided to lock down one specific frame of reference, calling one note the "Root", just to make it easier to write down.

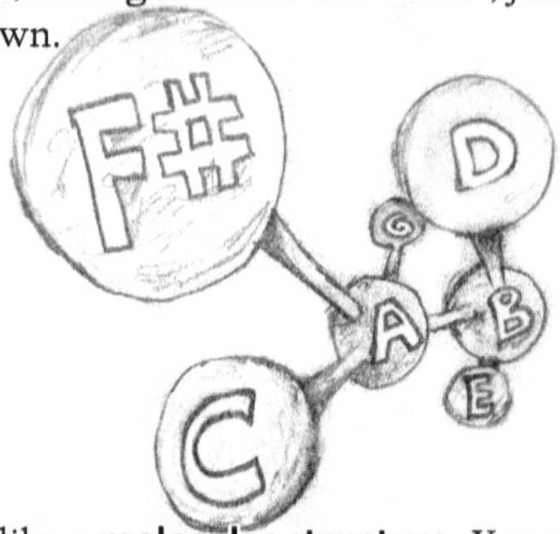

The Molecular View

In reality, a scale is more like a **molecular structure.** You can rotate a molecule in 3D space, looking at it from the top, bottom, or side. It looks different from every angle, but it is still the exact same object. In music, when we rotate the "molecule" of a scale and look at it from a different angle, we have called it a **Mode**. But remember, it is all just the same soup.

Now that we finally have all of the scary oddities out of the way, you will practice building the major scale. Start with the root note and fill in every scale degree from there on. When using the musical alphabet you may notice how much easier this would have been in a system with no sharps or flats, as I mentioned in the previous chapter. Look at the musical alphabet when first doing these. You should strive to eventually do these without an instrument in hand and no musical alphabet cheat sheet. You will also need to build them in both directions while starting from any degree within the scale. You will probably memorize some, if not all of the major scales eventually, but it is important to know how to build them.

Major Scale Exercises

Fill in the blanks

Build these Major Scales

1. A _ _ _ _ _ _	2. B _ _ _ _ _ _
3. _ F# _ _ _ _ _	4. D _ _ _ _ _ _
5. E _ _ _ _ _ _	6. F _ _ _ _ _ _
7. G _ _ _ _ _ _	8. A# _ _ _ _ _ _
9. C# _ _ _ _ _ _	10. D# _ _ _ _ _ _
11. F# _ _ _ _ _ _	12. G# _ _ _ _ _ _
13. Ab _ _ _ _ _ _	14. Bb _ _ _ _ _ _
15. Db _ _ _ _ _ _	16. Eb _ _ _ _ _ _
17. Gb _ _ _ _ _ _	18. _ _ _ _ _ _ G#
19. _ _ _ E _ _ _	20. _ Bb _ _ _ _ _
21. _ _ _ _ D _ _	22. _ D# _ _ _ _ _
23. _ _ _ B _ _ _	24. _ E _ _ _ _ _
25. _ A _ _ _ _ _	26. _ _ _ _ _ G _
27. _ _ _ _ _ C _	28. _ _ E _ _ _ _

Each of the underlined spaces are one of the seven notes of a major scale. For some, you have to start figuring them out from the middle of the scale or even backwards. Fill in the Major scales on blank fretboard diagrams for guitar and piano diagrams for piano. The more angles your brain can use to associate things, the more accurate its representation will be for using it in music.

Answers on page 233

TRIADS

Why·you·need·to·know·this:

> They are the fundamental chords. We use triads as the foundation for larger chords and to identify which chord is which. We also use triads to outline options for lead melody.

The Three-Note Engine

Triads consist of three notes. These are the most common chords used in all of music. We build triads by skipping every other note from the major scale. Pick a note (Root), skip the next, pick the next (3rd), skip the next, pick the next (5th). You then have a stack of 1, 3 and 5.

Three types of triads occur in the major scale. They are all made up of the **root** note, some kind of **3rd**, and some kind of **5th.** They are:

- **Major** triad R - 3rd - 5th
- **Minor** triad R - ***b3rd*** - 5th (The 3rd is flattened)
- **Diminished** triad R - ***b3rd*** - ***b5th*** (3rd and 5th are flattened)

(There is also an **Augmented** triad which is R - 3rd - ***#5th.*** This does not occur naturally in the Major Scale but it is useful to know. "Augmented" just means the 5th is raised by one half step.)

The triad built from the first note of a major scale is always a major triad.

Identifying Chords

How do you know if a random group of notes is Major or Minor? You use the **Comparison Method.** Remember when I told you we name things by comparing them to the major scale like a ruler? This is a very good example of doing exactly that.

Always compare the mystery chord to the **Major Triad of its same Root note.**

Example: Imagine you have the notes **G - Bb - D.** You need to name this chord.

1. **Identify** the root as **G.**

2. **Build the Control Group** of a standard G major triad (G major scale: G A B C D...) Take the 1, 3 and 5. And you get the G Major Triad. G - B - D

3. **Compare the two chords**
   Control chord: G - **B** - D (The G major triad)
   Your chord: G - **Bb** - D

The 3rd (**B**) has been lowered to a **Bb**. So, it is a **G Minor Triad.**

Just look at the triad structures. If it is unchanged, it is a major triad. If the 3rd is lowered compared to the major, its a minor triad. If it has a b3 and b5 compared to the major triad, it is a diminished triad. You are basically looking to see what type of 3rd and 5th are involved.

The DNA of the Major Scale

When we build a triad on every single degree of the Major Scale, a specific pattern emerges. This pattern is universal. It happens in C Major, G Major and every other Major scale in existence.

Let's look at the **G Major Scale** (G A B C D E F#) and build a triad on every note:

1st (G): G-B-D (Matches G Major Triad) → ***Major***
2nd (A): A-C-E (Compare to A Major A-C#-E). The 3rd is flat. → ***Minor***
3rd (B): B-D-F# (Compare to B Major B-D#-F#). The 3rd is flat. → ***Minor***
4th (C): C-E-G (Matches C Major Triad) → ***Major***
5th (D): D-F#-A (Matches D Major Triad) → ***Major***
6th (E): E-G-B (Compare to E Major E-G#-B). The 3rd is flat. → ***Minor***
7th (F#): F#-A-C (Compare to F# Major F#-A#-C#). b3 and b5th. → ***Diminished***

This gives us the Roman Numeral system. We use **Uppercase** for Major chords and **lowercase** for Minor chords. The ° symbol means Diminished.

1 Major triad	**I**
2 Minor triad	**ii**
3 Minor triad	**iii**
4 Major triad	**IV**
5 Major triad	**V**
6 Minor triad	**vi**
7 Diminished triad	**vii°**

REMEMBER THIS: In the worksheet after this chapter you will be using this info to figure out what scale a chord progression belongs to. This is really important due to how useful it is.

Now would be a great time to grab your instrument and start playing all of these note combinations to hear what they sound like. You should also try to move the notes around in different orders and with a large gap between the sounds. You can also arpeggiate the notes. Meaning, play them one at a time in order. They are still the chord but you are activating them in linear order instead of at the same time. On guitar, you can also tap the notes on one string. Eddie

Van Halen did lots of this. It might be useful to notice how they look on the fretboard so you can play them at will when improvising for lead guitar if that is something you are interested in doing.

The chords rooted on the 1st 4th and 5th degrees in the major scale are major triads. The 2nd, 3rd, and 6th rooted chords in the major scale are minor triads. The chord rooted on the 7th note of the major scale is a diminished triad. This will always be the same for any major scale.

Practical Application

Knowing this code allows you to predict the future. If I tell you a song is in the Key of **D Major**, you should instantly know the "safe" chords:

1. **I:** D Major
2. **ii:** E minor
3. **iii:** F# minor
4. **IV:** G Major
5. **V:** A Major
6. **vi:** B minor
7. **vii°**: C# diminished

In real songs, we often use chords that don't fit the scale. We label these based on their relation to the "I" chord. For example, looking at "Creep" by Radiohead in the key of G: **G → B → C → Cm**

G: This is the **I** chord.

B: This is a B Major triad. In the key of G, the "iii" chord should be minor (Bm). Since this is Major, we call it a **III** (Uppercase).

C: This is the **IV** chord.

Cm: This is a C Minor triad. In the key of G, the "IV" chord should be Major. Since this is minor, we call it a **iv** (lowercase).

So the progression is analyzed as: **I - III - IV - iv**

This would assist you in knowing what chords are going to fit in the song to stay in the same key. This also lets you know what chords aren't in the key so you can make some more interesting sounds happen.

If I said we are in the key of **C** and the chord progression was a "**I-ii-IV-V**", you would then know that the chord progression is "**C - Dm - F - G**". The chords are rooted on the 1st, then the 2nd, then the 4th and finally the 5th note of the C major scale.

When people name chord progressions they usually take whatever the **Tonal Center** is (the note that sounds like it's the most important and feels like home) and they consider that the (**major 1**) "**I**" or (**minor 1**) "**i**" chord and adjust the other chords around it. I don't do that because it is an extra step and ends up being much more complex for no good reason.

Here is an example to compare: If the chords were **Em - D - C - D.**
They would list it as: **i - bVII - bVI - bVII**
I would indicate it as: **vi - V - IV - V**

They change normally major chords to minor and normally minor chords to major and also introduce flats into it. This defeats the purpose of a universal system of chord progression naming. My way keeps it to the basics but just puts them on the actual position they are in the actual scale being used. This is another reason why the Minor scale should never have existed (more on that later).

The **Nashville numbering** system does this same thing I am suggesting we should do. They have many session musicians who are hired to record their parts and turn out hit songs in record time. They also happened to notice what the most efficient system is.

I understand that the tonal center and mode will happen regardless of what I call them so I always name everything in relation to the **I** of the **scale** we are using (usually the major scale).

Fill in the blanks

Build these triads

A Major _ _ _
B minor _ _ _
C minor _ _ _
D Major _ _ _
E minor _ _ _
F dim_ _ _
G Major _ _ _
A# minor _ _ _
C# dim _ _ _
D# minor _ _ _
F# minor _ _ _
G# dim _ _ _
Ab minor _ _ _
Bb minor _ _ _
Db dim _ _ _
Eb dim _ _ _
Gb dim _ _ _

Name these triads

E G# B = _______ triad
F A C = _______ triad
G# B D= _______ triad
A C# E = _______ triad
B D F = _______ triad
G Bb Db = _______ triad
A C Eb = _______ triad
Bb Db Fb= _______ triad
D# F# A# = _______ triad
C Eb Gb = _______ triad
F# A C# = _______ triad

Name the Major Scale (also known as the Key) using the chord progression

Dm - G - C = __ Major
E° - C - Gm = __ Major
Am - G - C = __ Major
Dm - Am - Em = __ Major
Am - Em - Bm = __ Major
A - B = __ Major
C - Bb = __ Major
Dm - Am - F - G = __ Major
C - Bm - Am = __ Major
Em - Am - G = __ Major
Dm - Em - F = __ Major
G - A - F#m = __ Major

Remember to check your musical alphabet and learn to work in both directions. This is important for further development required. Fill in various triads on empty piano and/or guitar diagrams.

Answers on page 234

INTERVALS

Why you need to know this:

We name distances between notes using intervals. You use this on the instrument to help remember how the notes in a song move from one to the next.

The Distances of Music

We have been using half steps and whole steps to measure small distances, but now we need a more powerful system. Any two notes have a specific distance between them called an **Interval.**

We name an interval by treating the lower note as the Root and measuring how far away the higher note is. Instead of counting a bunch of half steps (e.g., "that is 8 half steps away"), we simply use the **Major Scale** as our ruler.

The Two Families

In the major scale, we name intervals using the degree number (2nd, 3rd, 4th etc.) and a **Modifier.** The 7 notes of the scale are split into two types. You must memorize which team each note belongs to because they follow different rules.

Type 1: The "Major/Minor" Group

It consists of the 2nd, 3rd, 6th and 7th degrees. When these notes match the Major Scale, they are called **Major.** If you lower them by a half step, they become **Minor.** If you lower a Minor interval another half step, it becomes **Diminished** (rare, but is used to depict movement/intent). The words they traditionally use to describe how much we lower the note is what matters here.

Type 2: The "Perfect" Group

It consists of the rest of the notes not in type 1. So, the 4th, 5th, 1st (Unison) and 8th (Octave). When these match the Major Scale, they are **Perfect.** (There's no such thing as a "Major or Minor 5th.") Perfect intervals lowered by a half step become **Diminished.** Perfect intervals raised by a half step become **Augmented.**

A way to remember these is to store the memory of it in the same location where you keep the info that the 1st, 4th and 5th of a major scale always have major chords on those roots naturally. (Type 2) / The rest aren't major chords (Type 1).

In real life situations of communication, when in doubt about calling something Minor vs Diminished, (or if you simply reject systems that have pointrless complexity like I do) you can just call it **flat.** Again, we compare the Major scale to figure out if the degrees are natural or somehow altered.

The Comparison Algorithm

To identify any interval, run this simple mental program to compare it to its own major scale:

1. **Identify the Lower Note.**
2. **Build that note's Major Scale.**
3. **Compare the Upper Note to the scale.**

Some Examples:

To find E to F Build the E Major Scale (E - F# - G#...). The Major 2nd is F#. **Notice** that we have an F natural. That is one half step lower than the Major 2nd. So we see that, E to F is a **Minor 2nd.**

To find A to Eb build the A Major Scale (A - B - C# - D - E...) The Perfect 5th is E. We have an Eb. That is one half step lower than the Perfect 5th. Therefore, A to Eb is a **Diminished 5th/Augmented 4th.**

To find D to F build the D Major Scale (D - E - F#...) The Major 3rd is F#. We have an F natural. That is one half step lower than the Major 3rd. So, D to F is a **Minor 3rd.**

Building Triads with Intervals

We use these intervals by stacking them to build and name chords.

The D Major Triad (D - F# - A)

- D to F# is a **Major 3rd.**
- D to A is a **Perfect 5th.**
- Formula: Root + Major 3rd + Perfect 5th = **Major Triad.**

The D Minor Triad (D - F - A)

- D to F is a **Minor 3rd** (lowered half step).
- D to A is a **Perfect 5th.**
- Formula: Root + Minor 3rd + Perfect 5th = **Minor Triad.**

The D Diminished Triad (D - F - Ab)

- D to F is a **Minor 3rd.**
- D to Ab is a **Diminished 5th** (half step down from Perfect).
- Formula: Root + Min 3rd + Dim 5th = **Diminished Triad.**

We can figure out what chords the major scale contains and use that information to learn songs faster, write songs with more control and also improvise better.

Interval Inversions (The Mirror)

There is a fascinating symmetry in music math. If you take an interval and flip it (move the bottom note up an octave so it becomes the top note), the interval changes into its exact opposite.

The Rule of 9

The two interval numbers will always add up to **9.**
2nds become 7ths. (2+7=9).
3rds become 6ths. (3+6=9).
4ths become 5ths. (4+5=9).
So 7ths also become 2nds, 6ths are 3rds and 5ths are 4ths.

The Opposite Quality

Major flips to Minor, Minor flips to Major, Perfect stays Perfect and Diminished flips to Augmented.

The Master List:

Minor 2nd ↔ Major 7th
Major 2nd ↔ Minor 7th
Minor 3rd ↔ Major 6th
Major 3rd ↔ Minor 6th
Perfect 4th ↔ Perfect 5th
Tritone (Aug 4) = Tritone (Dim 5)

[Tritone stays the same. This is the centerpoint of an octave. I think of it as a mirror]

Practical Application

This isn't just some weird pointless theory. You need to see these shapes on your instrument. For guitar, memorize the physical shape of these intervals relative to the root note.

- **E-Shape Root** (Low E string on index)
- **A-Shape Root** (A string on index)
- **C-Shape Root** (A string on pinky)

On piano, memorize the physical shape of these intervals relative to the root note by flipping your lower note up an octave or the reverse by taking the higher note down an octave. Notice the complementary distance. When you can look and see that "this note is a major 3rd away from my root," you stop guessing and start actually improvising.

If on some other instrument, play the notes of these and if there is any repeating visual pattern or matrix of shapes you can identify, memorize them and use it to help you work faster.

Interval Exercises

Name these intervals

1. E - C
2. F# - Db
3. G - A
4. A - Gb
5. B - E
6. C# - D
7. D - A
8. F - Bb
9. G# - C
10. A - E
11. C - F
12. D - Bb
13. E - C#
14. G - E
15. B - E

Name the note at the interval shown

1. Minor 3rd above E
2. Minor 6th above B
3. Major 3rd above D
4. Minor 7th above C
5. Perfect 4th above F
6. Perfect 5th above D
7. Major 2nd below G
8. Minor 3rd below A
9. Minor 2nd below F
10. Perfect 4th below A
11. Perfect 5th below D
12. Minor 6th below C
13. Minor 7th below G
14. Major 7th above F#
15. Diminished 5th above Bb

Answers on page 235

7th CHORDS

Why-you-need-to-know-this:

You will likely end up playing or encountering 7th chords so it is a good idea to know the difference between them or understand how they are constructed.

Adding the Flavor

Seventh chords are just triads with one more note added. This is easy yet many guitarists struggle with it because of weird naming systems and confusing teaching methods. To build a 7th chord, we simply take our existing triad (Root, 3rd, 5th) and skip one more scale degree to grab the **7th.**

Here are the four variations of diatonic 7th chords you get when you stay within the Major Scale:

1. Major 7th (Major triad with a major 7th interval)
Formula: Root + 3rd + 5th + **7**
It's found on the 1st and 4th degrees (I and IV)
It sounds Dreamy, jazz-like, floating.

2. Minor 7th (Minor triad with a minor 7th interval)
Formula: Root + b3rd + 5th + **b7**
It's found on the 2nd, 3rd and 6th degrees (ii, iii and vi)
It sounds Mellow, cool, relaxed.

3. Dominant 7th (Major triad with a minor 7th interval)
Formula: Root + 3rd + 5th + **b7**
It's found on the 5th degree (V) only.
It sounds Tense, bluesy, wants to move.
This is the most confusing name. It has a major triad but a **flat 7.** We just call it "7" (e.g., G7).

4. Minor 7b5 (Diminished triad with a minor 7th interval)
Formula: Root + b3rd + b5th + **b7**
It's found on the 7th degree (vii) only.
It sounds Unstable, dark, tense.
Also called Half-Diminished.

(Note: There is also a "**Full Diminished 7th**" chord [R-b3-b5-**bb7**] but that does not occur naturally in the Major scale so we will save it for later.)

The Physics of Resolution (The "Pull")
Why do certain chords feel like they "pull" us toward home? It isn't magic. It is simple proximity.

Let's look at the **G7** chord and the **Bm7b5** chord. They both create a strong pull toward **C major.**

G7 Notes: G - **B** - D - **F**
Bm7b5 Notes: **B** - D - **F** - A
Target (C Major): **C** - **E** - G

Notice that both tension chords contain the notes **B** and **F.** This interval (B to F) is called a tritone and it is very unstable. It creates a gravitational pull to resolve.

The Mechanics of Movement Our brains love efficient movement. We like notes to move by the smallest distance possible (half steps).

B is one half step below **C.** It wants to slide **up** to C.

F is one half step above **E.** It wants to slide **down** to relieve tension.

When you play a G7 followed by a C, you are satisfying the brain's desire for those two notes to snap into their nearest neighbors.

The "Vanishing" Act

You notice the note **D** in those chords. The D is a whole step away from both C and E. It doesn't have that same "magnetic pull." In voice leading, we often just let the D vanish or move to whatever note fits the melody.

If the melody goes D → Db → C, we hear a chromatic slide down.

If the melody goes D → D# → E, we hear an upward lift.

This suggests that "gravity" in music is really just the science of moving notes to their closest available slot without creating a sonic collision or cluster by touching with adjacent notes where it lands.

The Movie Analogy

The reality is that "motion" in music doesn't actually exist. It is an illusion. When you watch a movie, you aren't seeing movement. You are seeing 24 still photographs (snapshots) flashed before your eyes every second. Your brain stitches them together to create the illusion of continuity.

Music is the same. We hear static snapshots of sound (chords) one after another. Our brain stitches them together and imagines a "line" moving from B to C or F to E.

The magic of being a musician is understanding how to craft these snapshots of sound so that the listener hallucinates a story. It is also to get attention. I never wanted attention, I just wanted to make that feeling happen inside me when I heard music and was moved emotionally and it helped me escape my angry mother telling me to leave my room and be like all those normal kids at my school. "He should be out getting laid...not in this room with the endless clicking sound all day... every day. I know what he is, he's a fat faggot."... The woman who told me Monsignor Essif could levitate and someday if I go to this fucked church enough where they stand, sit and kneel 48 times an hour I'd get

to see it. My dad would tell her, "Honey, he wants to be the best guitarist ever, let him practice. He is getting really good. It takes time and practice." Then I met a girl and my life fell apart. My mom said I would never be allowed back in to live with them if I went to move in with this girl. My dad told her to stop and that I am always welcome back. Not long after, I jumped out of my window instead of giving a guitar lesson to some local kid that was about to come over for their weekly lesson. I walked to the girl many miles away. Years passed, I was asked to audition for Guns N' Roses as lead guitar, she told me I wouldn't follow through so why even waste my time with it. She ended up divorcing me years later.

7th Chords Exercises

Build these 7th chords

1. E Major 7
2. F# Minor 7
3. G Dominant 7
4. A Major 7
5. B Minor 7
6. C# Minor 7b5
7. D Dominant 7
8. F Major 7
9. G Minor 7
10. A Dominant 7
11. C Major 7
12. D Minor 7
13. E Dominant 7
14. G Major 7
15. B Diminished 7

Reverse work - Name these chords

1. A, C#, E, G#
2. C#, E, G#, B
3. D, F#, A, C
4. F, A, C, E
5. E, G, B, D
6. G, B, D, F
7. B, D, F, A
8. A#, C##, E#, G##
9. D#, F##, A#, C#
10. E, G#, B, D
11. C, E, G, B
12. F#, A, C#, E
13. G#, B#, D#, F#
14. A, C, Eb, Gb
15. B, D#, F#, A#
16. D, F, A, C
17. G, B, D, F

Name the key(s) that the chords all belong to

1. Dm7 - G7 - C = __ Major scale
2. Em7b5 - C - Gm7 = __ Major scale
3. Am7 - G - C = __ Major scale
4. Dm - Am7 - Em = __ Major scale
5. Am - Em - Bm7 = __ Major scale
6. AMaj7 - B7 = __ Major scale
7. C7 - Bb = __ Major scale
8. Dm - Am7 - F - G = __ Major scale
9. CMaj7 - Bm7 - Am = __ Major scale
10. Em7 - Am - G = __ Major scale
11. Dm7 - Em - F = __ Major scale
12. G - A - F#m = __ Major scale

Answers on page 236 + 237

DIMINISHED THINGS

Why you need to know this:

The word diminished is used for too many different instances within music theory so it is common for people to get it confused.

The "Diminished" Confusion
They have used the word "Diminished" in various ways to name different things in music theory. This is (of course) confusing to people. Here are the different parts of the "Diminished" family:

1. Diminished Triad

Formula: Root - b3 - **b5** (A - C - Eb for instance). The name refers to the **Diminished 5th** interval the chord contains.

2. Half-Diminished 7th (m7b5)

Formula: Root - b3 - b5 - **b7** (A - C - Eb - G). It is half-diminished because the triad is diminished but the 7th is just a standard minor 7th.

3. Full Diminished 7th (dim7)

Formula: Root - b3 - **b5** - **bb7** (bb7 is really just the 6) (A - C - Eb - Gb). It is called "Fully" diminished because both the 5th and the 7th are each lowered to their diminished state. The **bb7** (Double Flat 7) sounds exactly the same as a Major 6th, but we spell it as a bb7 to keep the theory consistent.

Substitution
The Diminished Triad is rarely used on its own in modern chord progressions. It usually sounds weak or incomplete. I view the Diminished Triad simply as a **Dominant 7th chord without the root.**

See here:

G7 is G - **B - D - F**
B Dim is **B - D - F**

Because they share these identical notes, they can serve the same function. They both create tension that wants to pull to the **I** chord (C Major).

The V vs vii Substitute
I prefer to play the **V chord** (G7) instead of the **vii chord** (Bm7b5). The V chord creates the same pull but has a stronger foundation (the root G) which anchors the harmony.

The Geometric Magic (Symmetry)
The **Full Diminished 7th** (dim7) is unique because it is **Symmetrical.** Every note in the chord is exactly **1.5 steps (3 semitones)** apart from the next.

A to C = 1.5 steps
C to Eb = 1.5 steps
Eb to Gb = 1.5 steps
Gb back to A = 1.5 steps

Why does this matter?
Since the distance is identical between all notes, **any of the four notes can be considered the Root.** This means an **A dim7** is the exact same shape and sound as a **C dim7, Eb dim7** or **Gb dim7.**

This makes it a "Master Key" for modulation. You can use this one chord to resolve up a half step from any of it's notes.

The "Diminished Scale"
People often teach a "Diminished Scale" (Whole-Half or Half-Whole). I don't consider this a true scale. It is really just two Diminished 7th chords stacked a half step apart. You can't extract enough useful chords from it to use in musical sounding chord progressions.

Diminished Intervals

Remember that "Diminished" can also describe an interval that has been flattened from "Perfect" or "Minor."

Diminished 5th: b5
Diminished 3rd: bb3 (The same sound as a Major 2nd)

That second one, the Dim3 seems like a break in a logical system to me. I never think that way. I would call it a 2nd because it also is and that seems less confusing.

Chord Progression Examples

Here is how you might actually use these in the wild.

1. The Blues Function A - Fdim - E7 - A
Here, the F dim acts as a chromatic passing chord pushing us toward the E7 (the V chord).

2. The Tension Builder A - A#dim7 - Bm - E
This is a classic "passing chord" technique. The A#dim7 bridges the gap between the I (A) and the ii chord (Bm).

The "Visual" Jazz Method

A famous jazz guitarist (if that's a thing) promoted a method using the Diminished 7th chord and the Augmented triad as the "parents" of all other chord shapes. While visually interesting on the fretboard, comparing everything to a Diminished 7th instead of the Major Scale is needlessly complex for understanding the actual harmony options of music.

I wish they would have at some point diminished their bullshit and, I don't know... named these things using more than one word.

9th CHORDS

Why you need to know this:

You don't have to memorize every chord voicing on your instrument but it would be a good idea to understand what the chords are and how they are constructed.

The "Color" Layer

Ninth chords are simply 7th chords with yet another note added on top. We are continuing to follow the "skip a note" pattern. We took the Root, skipped to the 3rd, skipped to the 5th and skipped to the 7th. Now we skip one more scale degree and pick up and include the **9th.** Remember that the **"9" is just a "2".** The **9th degree** is really just the **2nd degree** of the scale.

Confusing Naming

Even though a chord might be called a **Minor 9** (e.g., Cm9), the "9th" interval itself is actually **Major** (a whole step above the root). The "Minor" in the name refers to the **3rd** and **7th.** The **9th** is natural.

We get five variations of 9th chords in the major scale:

1. Major 9th (Root 3 5 7 **9**) It's rooted on the 1st and 4th degrees (I and IV).

2. Minor 9th (Root b3 5 b7 **9**) It's rooted on the 2nd and 6th degrees (ii and vi).

3. Dominant 9th (Root 3 5 b7 **9**) It's rooted on the 5th degree (V)

4. Minor 7 (Root b3 5 b7 **b9**) It's rooted on the 3rd degree (iii). This creates a specific, dissonant "Phrygian" sound.

5. Half-Diminished b9 (Root b3 b5 b7 b9) It's rooted on the 7th

degree (vii). The Half diminished b9 chord can also be seen as a guitar version of a dominant 13 chord but the root note of it would be the b3 of the half diminished b9. It is missing two of the notes to consider it an actual 13 chord, but on guitar we only have six strings and four fingers so we play an approximated version.

The "Add 9" vs. "Sus 2"

This is a common source of confusion. The naming convention depends entirely on what other notes are present. **The "Add 9" Chord** is when you add the 9th degree but **remove the 7th**, it is no longer a "9th chord." It is an **Add 9.**

Major Add 9: R 3 5 **9** (no 7, just the 9)

Minor Add 9: R b3 5 **9** (no 7, just the 9)

These have a cleaner, less "jazzy" sound. Progressive metal and modern rock use these constantly.

The "Sus 2" Chord

If you add the 9th (2nd) but **remove the 3rd**, it becomes a **Suspended 2nd** chord. (R 2 5). **Remember** that the 3rd determines if a chord is major or minor. Without it, the chord is "suspended" and ambiguous.

I personally prefer to visualize these chords in numerical order rather than "stacked" order. Instead of thinking R - b3 - 5 - **9**,
I see it as R - **2** - b3 - 5. This linear view often makes more sense on the fretboard or keyboard.

A Double Agent

The Suspended 2 chord is the same as a **suspended 4 chord** but a different note is considered to be the root. An example would be the **C sus 2 chord.** It's notes are C D G and a **G sus 4 chord's** notes are G C D. People will argue this because they say the context of the music will change which name they use. So, it's still the same chord, you just used one of three inversions of it.

The Skyscraper Chords (11ths & 13ths)

If we keep stacking thirds, we eventually get **11th** and **13th** chords. Remember that the 11th is Just the 4th degree and the 13th is Just the 6th degree.

Reality Check

A full 13th chord contains 7 notes (Root, 3, 5, 7, 9, 11 and 13). **A 7-note chord is just a scale.** At that point, you aren't playing a chord, you are smashing the entire Major Scale at once. Since we only have four fingers (and six strings on a guitar), we can't play these full voicings. We play approximated versions by leaving out the less important notes (usually the 5th or the 9th). On piano it is easier to play. Just know that they follow the exact same logic we have built so far.

The major scale's diatonic 9th chords are:

1 Major 7th chord + Major 9	**Major 9th chord**
2 Minor 7th chord + Major 9	**Minor 9th chord**
3 Minor 7th chord + Minor 9	**Minor b9th chord**
4 Major 7th chord + Major 9	**Major 9th chord**
5 Dom 7th chord + Major 9	**Dominant 9th chord**
6 Minor 7th chord + Major 9	**Minor 9th chord**
7 Minor 7b5 chord + Minor 9	**Half diminished b9 chord**

9th Chord Exercises

Build these 9th chords

1. B Major 9 _ _ _ _ _
2. C minorMajor 9 _ _ _ _ _
3. B minor 9 _ _ _ _ _
4. E add 9 _ _ _ _ _
5. E dom 9 _ _ _ _ _
6. Fm9 _ _ _ _ _
7. AΔ9 _ _ _ _ _ _
8. G# minor 9 _ _ _ _ _
9. C# half dim b9 _ _ _ _ _
10. D# minor add 9 _ _ _ _ _
11. A#m9 _ _ _ _ _
12. D# add 9 _ _ _ _ _
13. Gb major add 9_ _ _ _ _
14. Bb dom 9 _ _ _ _ _
15. Ab min9 _ _ _ _ _
16. Fb half dim b9 _ _ _ _ _
17. Eb9 _ _ _ _ _

Reverse work - Name these chords

1. C E G B D
2. D F A C Eb
3. E G# B D F#
4. F A C E Gb
5. G B D F A#
6. A C Eb G B
7. Bb D F Ab Cb
8. C Eb G Bb D
9. D F# A C Eb Bb
10. E G# B D F
11. F# A C# E G#
12. G B D F# A#
13. A C# Eb G Bb
14. Bb D F A C
15. C# E G A# D#

Name the key(s) that the chords all belong to for each line

1. Bbmaj9 - C9
2. D#7 - Fx(F##) halfdim9
3. Dm9 - G7 - Bm7(b5 b9)
4. Dm9 - Gm7
5. F#7 - Bmaj9
6. Fm9 - Gm7
7. G#m9 - C#m9 - D#m7
8. Am9 - D7 - F#m7(b5)
9. A7 - Bm9
10. C#min9 - F#7
11. Ebmaj9 - F9 - Gm9
12. Fm9 - Gm7b9
13. D#m9 - G#7
14. E7 - F#m9 - G#m7(b5)
15. Abm9 - Db7 - Fm7b5b9

Answers on page 237 + 238

NAMING CHORDS

Why you need to know this:

It is important to understand how to associate chords and use proper identification.

Precision Naming

Chords should have exact names that detail exactly what frequencies are present. Without precision, we cannot easily categorize or identify what we are hearing.

The Problem with traditional naming

In current music theory, people often play a chord like **G - B - F - E** and call it a **G13! The Reality is** that they are playing a Root, 3rd, b7 and 13. They are missing the 5th, 9th and 11th. Traditionalists say "it doesn't matter" or "the ear implies the missing notes." **I disagree.** If we are treating music as a science, we cannot just guess what notes are "implied." There must be a name that identifies the chord based on the **physics of what is actually being played.**

Some argue that guitarists physically cannot play 7 unique notes at once... **I don't care.** The limitation of your fingers does not change the definition of the harmony. If you leave notes out, the name must change to reflect that. In my own logical system, I name chords based strictly on the notes present. We do not leave anything to the imagination.

One might say we are... "diminishing" the chord down to a smaller version of it. Just joking. Could you imagine, using the word diminished yet another time in another form for music theory. Sorry, that was last chapter. It is funny how they have taken so many different things and call them one thing though. It is as if they were gatekeeping it or intentionally making it more difficult for others. Or, they were just not very logically minded. Maybe both. Imagine working in a kitchen somewhere and they tell you that a cheeseburger is also a burrito because the wrap, beans, rice and whatever else stuff ends up in a burrito is IMPLIED and it's up to the person eating it to decide what it is. Yeah, thats crazy.

The Hierarchy of Extensions: 7 → 9 → 11 → 13

The Rule: You must have **all** lower extensions present to earn the higher name. If there is a "gap" in the ladder, everything above the gap becomes an **ADD.**

How to Apply It:

1. Start with the base (Triad).
2. Look for the next logical extension (7). Is it there?
    - **If it is there:** It is now called a 7th chord. Now move on and look for the next extension up (the 9).
    - **It there isn't:** The chain is broken. Any higher extension now gets an "ADD" before it to indicate that we skipped a note(s).

The Naming Algorithm
Let's test this logic against standard chords.

The "Unbroken" Chain:
1 - 3 - 5 = Major Triad
1 - 3 - 5 - 7 = Major 7
1 - 3 - 5 - 7 - 9 = Major 9
1 - 3 - 5 - 7 - 9 - 11 = Major 11
1 - 3 - 5 - 7 - 9 - 11 - 13 = Major 13 (The entire Major Scale)

The "Broken" Chain (The ADDs):
1 - 3 - 5 - 9 (Skipped 7) → **Major Add 9**
1 - 3 - 5 - 7 - 11 (Skipped 9) → **Major 7, Add 11**
1 - 3 - 5 - 9 - 11 (Skipped 7) → **Major Add 9, Add 11**
1 - 3 - 5 - 7 - 13 (Skipped 9 & 11) → **Major 7 Add 13**
1 - 3 - 5 - b7 - 13 (Skipped 9 & 11) → **Dominant 7 Add 13**
1 - 3 - 5 - b7 - 9 - 13 (Skipped 11) → **Dominant 9 Add 13**

A Note on "Implied" Notes
From a compositional view, you might consider all instruments together. If the bass plays the Root, the piano plays the 3rd/7th, and the trumpet plays the 13th, the **total sum** is the chord. But if no one is playing the 9th or 11th, we should not name the chord as if they are there.

The Numerical Preference (1 vs 13)
Again, I personally prefer to list intervals in **numerical order** (1, 2, 3...) rather than "stacking" order (1, 3, 5, 7, 9...). It is more logical for a human brain to process the data linearly.

For Example, Instead of listing the intervals of a **Dominant 9 Add 13** (R, 3, 5, b7, 9, 13), I prefer to see the raw data: **1 - 2 - 3 - 5 - 6 - b7** **9 shows up as a 2** and **13 shows up as a 6.**

This also applies to the **Diminished 7th** chord. Standard theory calls the last note a "Double Flat 7" (bb7). I call that last note what it physically is: a **Major 6th.**

Standard: 1 - b3 - b5 - **bb7**
Logical: 1 - b3 - b5 - **6**

Why make it complicated when the frequency is just a 6th? They argue context so you can imply motion and intention. When you hear sound you will experience that stuff. Notating it with chords in code names isn't necessary.

As an exercise, play some random notes as a chord and see what names you can call the chord. You can check for accuracy against the names in this book. **Another exercise idea** is to take songs you like and start to identify the chords of it by listing their notes and checking which intervals they occupy and how that affects the chord name. I also have students build chords on their instrument, a computer DAW piano roll or staff and then trying to alter the notes to cause another chord to happen. This will help you visually understand options faster. This is a great exercise for many reasons.

CHORD SHORTHAND

Why·you·need·to·know·this:

There are different ways people indicate the same chords with short hand and symbols. You don't want to be confused when they show up.

The Rosetta Stone

Musicians need to read charts fast. Instead of writing out "C Dominant Seventh Flat Nine," we use shorthand symbols. In different circles (Jazz, Rock, Classical) you may find variations in the shorthand. Here is a exactly what to watch for so you never get lost. Remember some musicians are also doctors with bad handwriting and they often own many PRS guitars, here is what to look for within their faint scribbles:

1. The Triads

- **Major:** Usually implied. If you see just a letter like **C**, it means **C Major Triad.**
- **Minor:** Shown as min, a small m or a minus sign -. Sometimes an underscore _. For example: **Cmin, Cm, C-, C_**

2. Dominant Chords

If you see a number without any "Maj" or "min" label, it is Dominant. Marked as **C7**. It can also be listed as **C Dom7, Cdom 9** etc.
Extensions (9, 11, 13): If you see **C9** or **C13**, it implies the entire chain of lower extensions is present.

C9 = 1, 3, 5, b7, 9

C dom 13 = 1, 3, 5, b7, 9, 11, 13

3. Major 7th Chords

- Shown as **Maj7** or a triangle **Δ** or **Δ7**.
- Example: **C Maj7**, **CΔ7**

4. Minor 7th Chords

- Shown as **m7**, **min7**, **-7** or **_7**.
- Example: **Cm7**, **Cmin7**, **C-7**, **C_7**

5. The "Spy" Chord (Minor/Major 7)

- This is a Minor triad with a Major 7th on top. Often used in a mystery or spy movies.
- Shown as **m (maj7)** or **minMaj7** or **_Δ7** or **-Δ7**.

6. Augmented & Diminished

- **Augmented:** Shown as **aug** or a plus sign **+**.
  Example: **Caug**, **C+**
- **Diminished Triad:** Shown as **dim** or a small open circle **°**.
  Example: **Cdim**, **C°**
- **Diminished 7th:** Shown as **dim7** or **°7**.
  Example: **Cdim7, C°7**
- **Half-Diminished (m7b5):** Shown as a circle with a slash through it **ø** or **ø7**.
  Example: **Cø7**, **Cm7b5**

7. Suspended & Add Chords

- **Suspended:** Shown as **sus**.
  - **Csus** or **Csus4** = Replace the 3rd with the 4th.
  - **Csus2** = Replace the 3rd with the 2nd.
  - **Note:** If it just says "sus" it always means **sus4**.
- **Add Chords:** Explicitly tells you to add a note without including the **7th.** You might see them with a **+** sign.

Example: **Cadd9, Cm7add11, C+9+11.**
(notice how this is an issue due to it also appearing for augmented chord shorthand historically)

8. Slash Chords (Inversions)

- **How it is indicated:** [Chord] / [Bass Note]
- **Example: C/E** means play a **C** Major chord, but use **E** (the 3rd) as the lowest note. People use the root after the slash for extending the chord without naming it like C/Bb. I put the full chord name that includes the bass note before the slash personally. Like C7/Bb.

OTHER SCALES

(modified versions of the Major Scale)

Why you need to know this:

These appear in music more than you might expect. It is a good idea to be able to notice them when they happen and be able to use them to add depth to your scale options.

The "Other" Scales

You will find massive lists of scales on the internet and in books. I found that almost every scale is really just the **Major Scale** with a slight modification.

My Philosophy:

- **Avoided Notes:** If you just skip notes (like in Pentatonic), it's not a new scale. You are just deciding to avoid two notes of the base scale.

- **Passing Tones:** If you add a chromatic note for flavor (like in the Blues or Bebop "scale"), it is just melody happening on weak beats. Unless you are landing on strong beats with chords derived from those notes, it's not a separate scale.

- **The "Minor Scale" Myth:** There is no such thing as the "Minor Scale." It is simply the Major Scale but the 6th note of the scale structure is heard as the tonal center (Aeolian Mode). We shouldn't have ever named the identical entity twice. It is also worth noting, they didn't do this with any other mode. Why didn't the Dorian mode get an extra scale name and new chord progression naming systems based on it? Because it was used less often during the time they tried building music theory. They based it off of current stylistic trends instead of science.

Here are the primary variations of the Major scale worth learning

1. AUGMENTED MAJOR SCALE (HARMONIC MINOR SCALE)

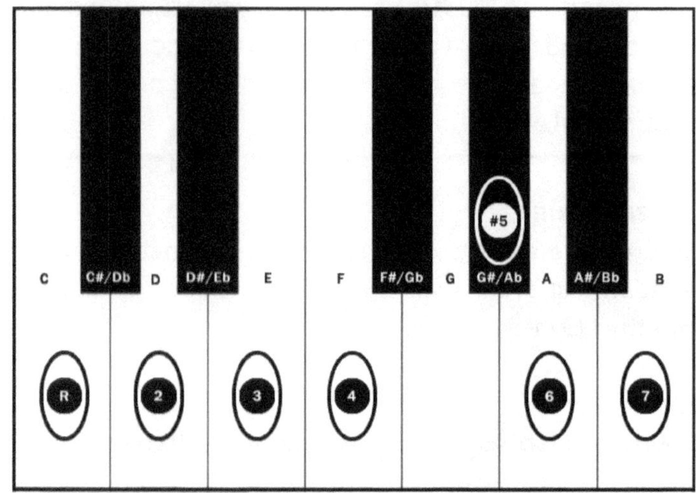

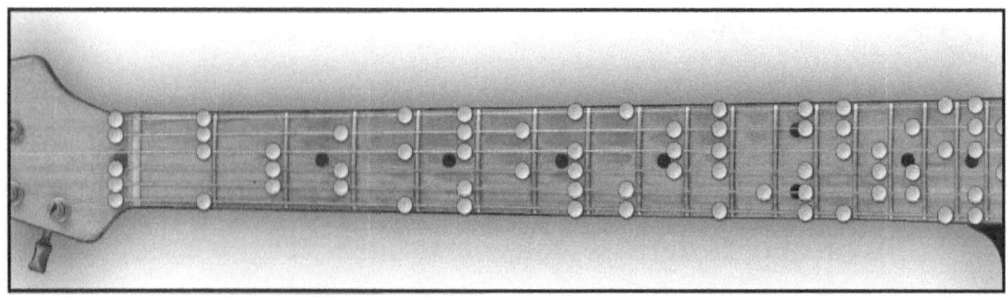

C Augmented Major scale above (A Harmonic Minor)

In traditional theory, they take the "imaginary" Minor Scale and raise the 7th. In my system, we view it from the **Major Root.**

The Formula: Major Scale but **raise the 5th (#5)**
Take the **C Major Scale:** C - D - E - F - G - A - B
Raise the 5th: (**G→G#**). **You get:** C - D - E - F - **G#** - A - B
This set of notes is traditionally called the A Harmonic Minor scale (starting on the 6th note, A).

- **Traditional method:** Start on A (Their imaginary scale they called the Minor scale), raise the 7th of that.
- **My method:** Start on C (Major), raise the 5th. (No imag inary scale tied to a trend of a time period needed).

Augmented Major/Harmonic Minor is one of the most popular scales used in pop and dance music for the last twenty years. The 3rd mode of this scale (Phrygian Dominant) is especially common.

2. MELODIC MINOR SCALE

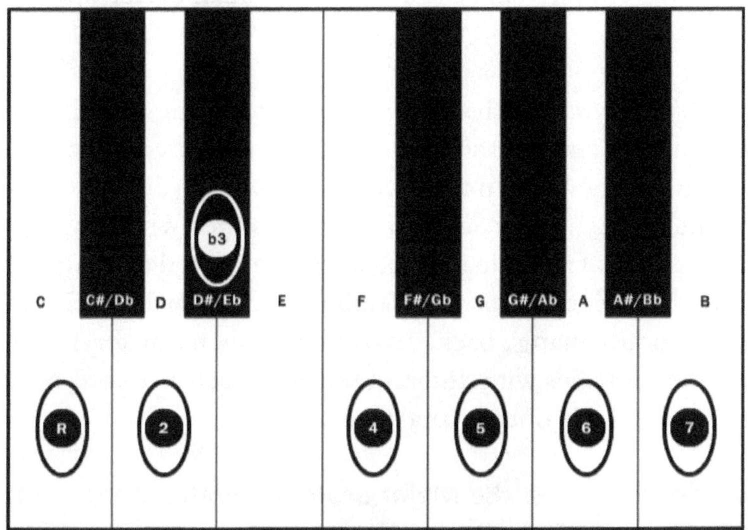

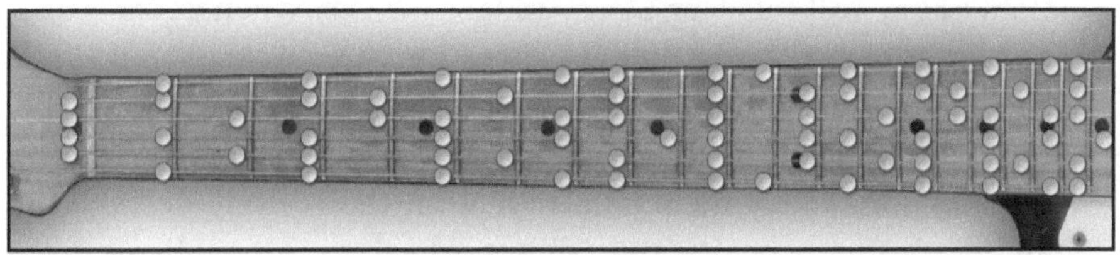

C Melodic Minor scale above

Traditional textbooks teach this as a complex ritual: "Take the major scale but write it down starting from the 6th note, raise the 6th and 7th notes above that 6th note you consider the new first note when ascending, but revert to natural minor when descending. Except don't call it natural minor anymore, call it melodic minor descending, even though it's still the Natural Minor scale, which is the 6th note of the Major scale as a pretend scale." **This is ridiculous!**

Melody exists and melody decisions that were based on trends in one specific time shouldn't change how we name and consider scales. This is a total break in logic and common sense. Why would we name two totally different sets of notes as the same scale? This is a one-off outlier compared to how they name scales normally. It also has too many conditions and steps compared to the simple reality I present as a much better option below.

Even if you like that as a way to look at things, it still doesn't make sense to change the name of the scale based on what the melody has done once in the song. Why would you even change the name on the Minor Scale to Melodic minor when its still the exact same set of notes just because you happened to change two notes in the melody while the melody went upwards ONCE, even when the notes change back. To use the same name for TWO totally different scales with different notes just because you changed to the second scale once is total insanity.

How I do it: It is just the **Major Scale** but with a **minor 3rd instead of a major 3rd.** That's it! It is the same regardless of direction. (They call this Jazz Minor in Jazz already when its the same one scale regardless of melodic direction). In jazz they still see it as a minor scale with two notes raised though. I am describing the same one scale but with less complexity or steps involved. Tons of popular songs play melodic minor with the melody descending and don't lower the 6th and 7th notes back to the Aeolian mode. It was once a specific trend. **I think that any naming conventions based or built on temporary trends are a bad idea for any serious system.** I like using a more universally applicable scientific system instead. I think that is why my way is easier and involves exceedingly less bullshit to understand, define and apply. You don't have to pretend there is an "extra" scale called minor, and you don't have to alter two notes. You just take the Major Scale and change one note. We raise and lower melody away from scale notes into chromatic passing tones often with other scales in all sorts of music, do we change the names of those into some extravagant scale name and keep that new name even when we go right back to the first unchanged scale? Of course not, because that would be exactly as illogical and simply put, bad.

Their way of doing this (5 STEPS):

1. Take the C Major Scale: C - D - E - F - G - A - B
2. Start on the A: A - B - C - D - E - F - G
3. Change the 6th up one: A - B - C - D - E - **F#** - G
4. Change the 7th up one: A - B - C - D - E - F# - **G#**
5. Revert it back to A B C D E F G when the melody goes down

My way (1 STEP):

1. Major Scale but flat the 3rd (b3).

The A Major Scale: A - B - C# - D - E - F# - G#
Flat the 3rd (**C# → C**).
You still get: A - B - **C** - D - E - F# - G#

You just take the Major Scale and change one note. **I would have actually called THIS the "Minor Scale"** because it is the major scale with the minor 3rd, but at this point it would be very confusing due to them already naming it a different (but redundant) Scale they made when accidentally renaming the Aeolian mode into its own scale.

3. HARMONIC MAJOR SCALE

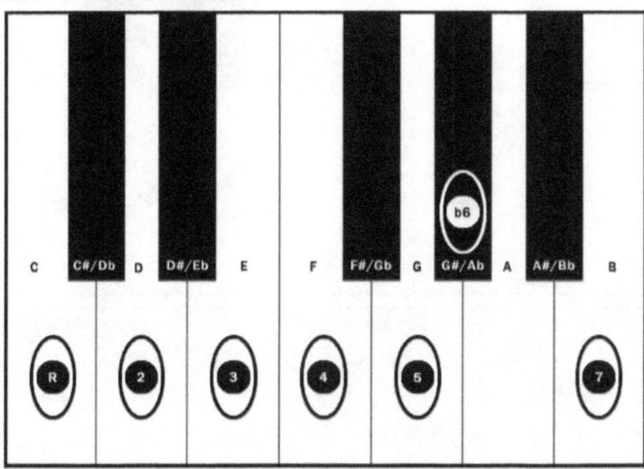

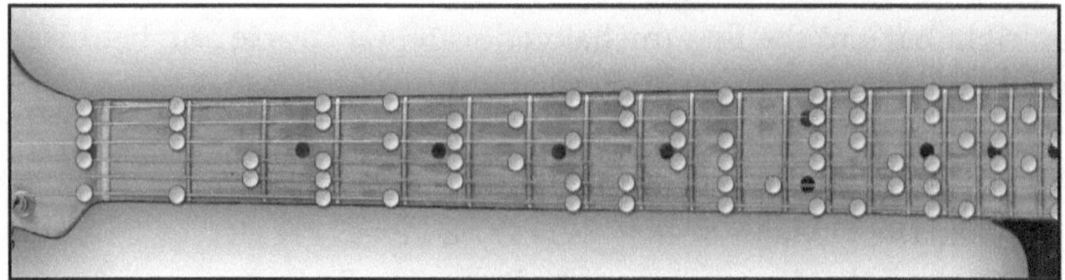

The Formula: Major Scale but **flat the 6th (b6)**
The Logic: Take the C Major Scale: C - D - E - F - G - A - B
Flat the 6th: (**A → Ab**). **This gives you:** C - D - E - F - G - **Ab** - B

The "Creep" Effect: When you hear that emotional shift in songs like Creep (Radiohead) or In My Life (Beatles), Buddy Holly solo (Weezer), Layla (Clapton) etc., Where the **IV chord turns minor (iv)**, this is the scale that fits with the least notes changed. (Note: Often bands will play the Melodic Minor on the root of the iv chord instead, which alters two notes from the first scale, but Harmonic Major is the more direct "one-note" change even though it is used less frequently).

4. HUNGARIAN MINOR SCALE / (HARMONIC MINOR WITH A PASSING TONE BASICALLY)

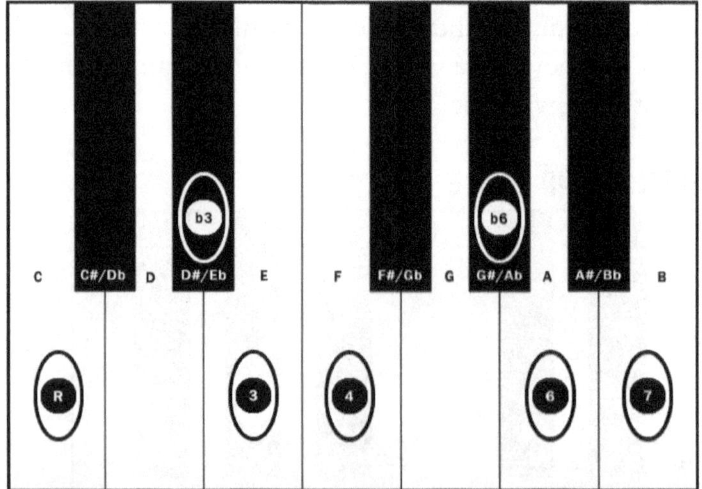

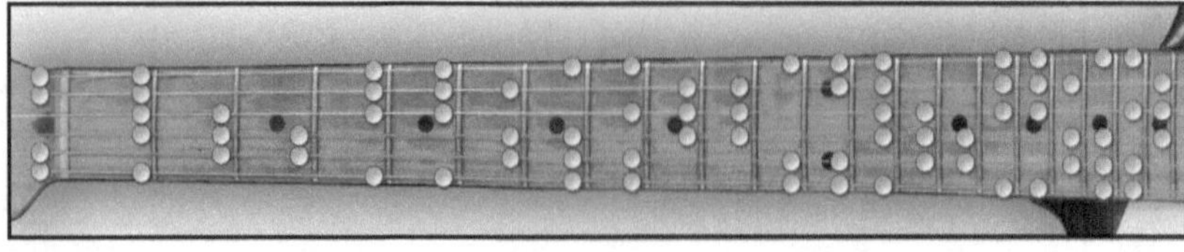

A Hungarian Minor scale above

This is more simply seen as the Harmonic Minor scale with a raised 4th. Notes: A - B - C - **D#** - E - F - **G#**

Since we have been using the Augmented Major scale instead of Harmonic Minor, for that you can see it as **Augmented Major with a raised 2nd.** So, 1, **#2**, 3, 4, **#5**, 6, 7 (C - **D#** - E - F - **G#** - A - B). The unique feature is the cluster of chromatic notes **(D#, E, F)** that give it a distinct "exotic" or "metal" sound.

My take: I am on the fence about calling this a standalone scale. I often view this not as a standalone scale, but as the Augmented Major scale with a specific chromatic passing tone added for melody.

5. PENTATONIC "SCALE" / MUSICAL EVENT

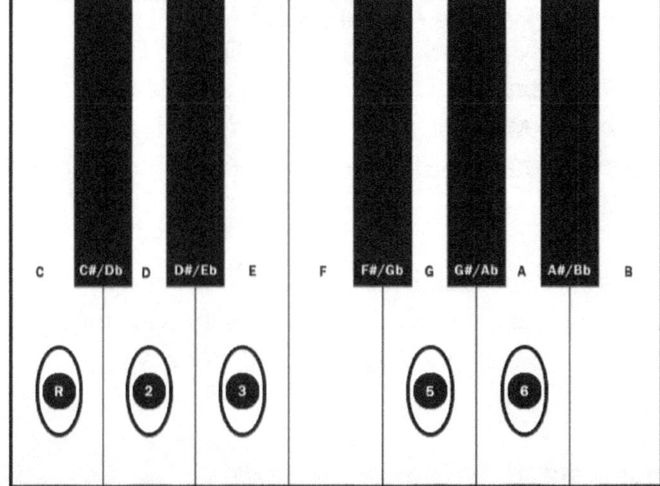

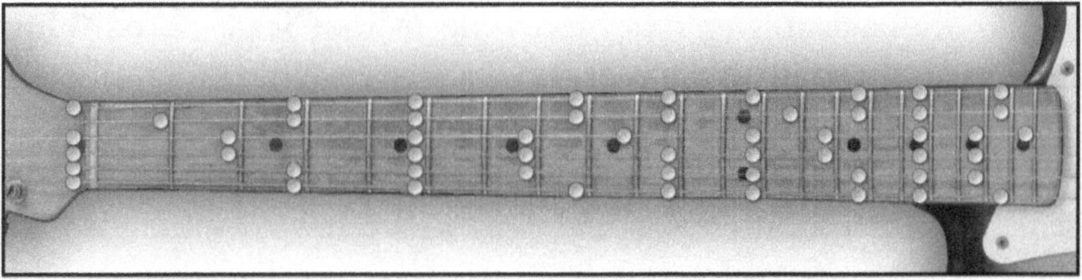

C Major Pentatonic "scale" above

I call this a **Musical Event**, not a scale. It is just a Major Scale with **two notes avoided.** I don't consider it a scale of its own because the five notes don't give us enough chord material that would be useful for making many interesting chord progressions.

Major Scale but avoid two notes. Take the major scale: 1 - 2 - 3 - 4 - 5 - 6 - 7 but remove either the **(4 and 7),** or **(1 and 4),** or the **(3 and 7).**

C major pentatonic is: C D E G A <- notice these notes below

The Secret is that the "C Major Pentatonic" is **three** different major scales at the same time. (I put the C major penta in bold below for each option.) We can see it as:

- **C Major scale** but avoiding **F (4) and B (7).**
    - C Major scale is **C D E** F **G A** B
- **F Major scale** but avoiding **F (1) and Bb (4).**
    - F Major scale is F **G A** Bb **C D E**
- **G Major scale** but avoiding **B (3) and F# (7).**
    - G Major scale is **G A** B **C D E** F#

Depending on which two notes you avoid you get a different Major scale.

I have noticed and been upset that many teachers confuse students by implying there is only one parent scale for a pentatonic. In reality, the pentatonic fits over multiple keys.

The minor scale should never have existed.

You might have noticed that there is no "Minor Scale" listed. This is because **there is no such scale.** Or, there shouldn't have been. In the history of music theory textbooks, you will often see the minor scale, however, it is simply the exact same as the Major scale but with a different tonal center. We have a different and more accurate term for this in music theory called the Aeolian Mode (details later).

- ABCDEFG is the same collection of notes as CDEFGAB.
- The order of notes written down doesn't matter because music doesn't know what you wrote down or what you call it, nor does that change what we hear.

The reality is that the **COLLECTION** of notes we find mostly on strong beats is what we call the scale. Since we already name everything in music by comparing it to the Major Scale. We know that the Major Scale written down in any order is still just the Major Scale regardless of the mode being experienced. We can see why calling the Major Scale the Minor Scale whenever the Aeolian mode is experienced was **the biggest mistake in the history of music theory.**

Modes Came First!
Musical modes existed long before the modern concept of scales. The ancient Babylonians and Greeks were using systems of modes and diatonic pitch collections thousands of years before the Western major/minor scale system became standard.

Ancient Greece originated the concept. In the **Middle Ages** it was adopted into Church Modes. In the **16th Century** the standardization of "Major/Minor" overtook the modal system. The weird thing is, they sort of kept both because modes came back in a limited scope in the 1900s in jazz. Some people seemed to actually understand them and how to use them. But many still thought of them as their own scales.

I will tell you my findings about what modes actually are later in this book. For now, just know that the minor scale should never have existed because it is already called the Major Scale.

Other Scales Exercises

Build these scales

1. C Harmonic Major:
2. D Harmonic Minor (F Augmented Major):
3. C# Melodic Minor:
4. E Hungarian Minor:
5. F# Augmented Major:
6. C Major Pentatonic:
7. C# Minor Pentatonic:
8. A Melodic Minor:
9. B Augmented Major:
10. D Augmented Major:

Reverse work - Name these scales (They may not be in order)

Start on different notes and see if it spells out a scale. Or, use half step distances as a clue.

1. Eb F G A B C D
2. B C D# E F# G A
3. D E F G A B C#
4. F G Ab B C D E
5. C D# E F G# A B
6. G A Bb C D E F#
7. A B C D Eb F# G
8. G A B C# D# E F#
9. B C## D# E F## G# A#
10. C D# E F# G A B

Answers on page 239

Harmonizing Other Scales

Why-you-need-to-know-this:

> You will need to understand what changes happen to the chords within the modified major scales

Now that we have defined the scales, we need to build the chords that live inside them. This is called **Harmonizing.** Just like we did with the Major Scale, we simply run the algorithm: Pick a note, skip a note.

The logic is simple

If a chord contains the "altered" note of the scale, that chord changes. If a chord avoids the "altered" note, it stays exactly the same as it would be if in the Major Scale. I will be comparing each chord to the major scale's chord of the same length and position.

HARMONIZING HARMONIC MINOR (AUGMENTED MAJOR SCALE)

To connect with traditional theory, we will list these chords starting from the 6th Degree (A), because that is where the "A Harmonic Minor" scale traditionally begins. Just remember: A Harmonic Minor is just C Augmented Major.

A Harmonic Minor Scale's Chords (from A B C D E F G#)

6	A C E	Normal 6th of the C Major scale no change
7	B D F	Normal 7th of the C Major scale no change
1	C E G#	**Augmented triad** instead of Major
2	D F A	Normal 2nd of the C Major scale no change
3	E G# B	**Major triad** instead of the regular minor
4	F A C	Normal 4th of the C Major scale no change
5	G# B D	**Diminished triad** instead of the major

You could expand these to add the 4th note to discover the diatonic 7th chords of the Harmonic Minor Scale. The easy logic

to follow is that any chord that includes the changed note (in this case the G# as the raised 5th of the C Major scale) will be a different chord than it was in the regular Major Scale.

A Harmonic Minor Scale's 4 note chords

6	A C E G#	**MinorMajor7** chord instead of min7 (R b3 5 7)
7	B D F A	Normal 7th of the C Major scale no change
1	C E G# B	**Augmented Major 7th** instead of major 7
2	D F A C	Normal 2nd of the C Major scale no change
3	E G# B D	**Dom 7th** instead of minor 7
4	F A C E	Normal 4th chord of the C Major scale
5	G# B D F	**Fully Diminished 7th** instead of the Dom7

A harmonic Minor Scale's 5 note chords.

6	A C E G# B	**Minor Major 9** chord on the 6 instead of Minor9
7	B D F A C	Normal 7th of the C Major scale no change
1	C E G# B D	**Augmented Major 9th** instead of Major9
2	D F A C E	Normal 2nd of the C Major scale no change
3	E G# B D F	**Dom 7th b9** instead of minor7
4	F A C E G#	Major #9 chord instead of Major9
5	G# B D F A	**Fully Diminished 7th b9** instead of m9b5

HARMONIZING MELODIC MINOR

This will be the C Melodic Minor scale which is just the C Major scale with the 3rd flatted one half step. We have C D Eb F G A B for the C Melodic Minor Scale. If I could go back in time and change the names of music theory elements I would call **THIS** the MINOR SCALE instead of what they call the Minor scale currently.

C Melodic Minor Scale's Chords (from C D Eb F G A B)

1	C Eb G	**Minor triad** on the 1 chord instead of Major
2	D F A	Normal 2nd of the C Major scale no change
3	Eb G B	**Augmented triad** instead of the E minor triad
4	F A C	Normal 4th chord of the C Major scale
5	G B D	Normal 5th chord of the C Major scale
6	A C Eb	**Dim triad** on 6th instead of the Minor triad
7	B D F	Normal 7th of the C Major scale no change

Diatonic 7ths chords of the Melodic Minor Scale:

1	C Eb G B	**minorMaj7** on the 1 chord instead of Major 7
2	D F A C	Normal 2nd of the C Major scale no change
3	Eb G B D	**Major 7th Augmented** as the 3rd chord

4	F A C Eb	**Dominant 7th** instead of the Major 7th
5	G B D F	Normal 5th chord of the C Major scale
6	A C Eb G	**m7b5** on the 6th instead of the Minor 7
7	B D F A	Normal 7th of the C Major scale no change

Diatonic 9th chords of the Melodic Minor Scale:

1	C Eb G B D	**minorMaj9** on the 1 chord instead of Major 9
2	D F A C Eb	**Minor b9** instead of Minor 9 on the 2 chord
3	Eb G B D F	**Major 9th Augmented** instead of Minor 9
4	F A C Eb G	**Dominant 9th** instead of the Major 9th
5	G B D F A	Normal 5th chord of the C Major scale
6	A C Eb G B	**m9b5** on the 6th instead of the Minor 9
7	B D F A C	Normal 7th of the C Major scale no change

HARMONIZING HARMONIC MAJOR

I would consider calling this the Minor 6th Scale but it is traditionally referred to as the Harmonic Major scale. **C Harmonic Major Scale's Chords** (from C D E F G **Ab** B). Any chord that contains the b6/Ab is going to be different compared to the triad in the same slot for the C Major Scale of course.

1	C E G	Same as the Major Scale
2	D F Ab	**Diminished Triad** instead of Minor
3	E G B	Same as the Major Scale
4	F Ab C	**Minor triad** instead of Major
5	G B D	Same as the Major Scale
6	Ab C E	**Augmented triad** instead of A minor triad
7	B D F	Same as the Major Scale

Diatonic 7th chords of Harmonic Major:

1	C E G B	Same as the Major Scale
2	D F Ab C	**m7b5** instead of Minor7
3	E G B D	Same as the Major Scale
4	F Ab C E	**Minor Major7** instead of Major7
5	G B D F	Same as the Major Scale
6	Ab C E G	**Augmented Major 7** instead of the A minor7
7	B D F Ab	**Diminished 7th** instead of m7b5

Diatonic 9th chords of Harmonic Major:

1	C E G B D	Same as the Major Scale
2	D F Ab C E	**m9b5** instead of Minor9
3	E G B D F	Same as the Major Scale
4	F Ab C E G	**Minor Major9** instead of Major9

5	G B D F Ab	**m7b9** instead of dominant9
6	Ab C E G B	**Ab Augmented Major7#9** instead of A minor9
7	B D F Ab C	**Diminished b9th** instead of m9b5

The Hungarian Minor set of notes can also be harmonized with chords but it contains some options where you have a major OR a minor third available in a chord. Whenever there are three consecutive half steps clustered together I consider it a passing tone for melody and I disregard the note set as a scale. I would consider it Harmonic Minor with a passing tone as mentioned above.

As an exercise, harmonize the Hungarian Minor scale like we did the other scales. You can start it on the Major Scale 1 like Augmented Major and sharp the 2 and the 5 or you can take the Harmonic minor starting note for that same thing by starting it on the 6 and raise the 4 and the 7. Either way the A hungarian minor is A B C **D#** E F **G#** as a head start to help you out. Just do the basic note skip literal diatonic chords for now. You can see how changing one note out can allow other interesting chords.

HARMONIZING THE PENTATONIC SET OF NOTES

People call this the pentatonic minor and or the pentatonic major scale but it isn't really a scale and we don't harmonize it due to it having only a few chord options from it.

Here is an example:
C pentatonic is C D E G A. There are only a few chord options given the short note set. The pentatonic set of notes is just one of three Major Scales with notes missing, it is better to just see it as the major scale and use those chords.

I don't consider it an actual scale but you should still practice it in isolation because it is so heavily used in all sorts of music. Everything involving scales should be thought of as some kind of version of the major scale because it is.

You will find things people call diminished scales or wholetone scales but those are just one chord played in two places and considered symmetrical scales by textbooks of the past. I just consider these musical events or note sets. I don't consider them to be scales because we don't harmonize them into chords we can use for progressions or songs.

For fun, when you see any scale with a fancy name or one claimed to be exotic in some way, write down the notes of it and figure out which major scale or version of the major scale it is with either notes added as passing tones in the melody or with notes removed or some combination. It will always be one of the mentioned scales we went over. Some of them will have three or four names for the exact same modified version of the Major Scale which of course adds to a sense of confusion for people. A common set of notes that people accidentally didn't notice was just the major scale would be this.: (E F A B) (3 4 6 7). They call it some fancy "exotic" name(s) as usual. It is just the C Major scale but we are avoiding some notes, you can also think of it as a chord.

Now that you know there are only a few actual scales in music, things should feel a bit easier to manage and use for making music.

As an exercise, you can take chords from some of these scales and try to make chord progressions with them that sound nice. Then record it and improvise over it using the scale they come from. For extra fun, make a progression that changes the scale by modifying a chord such as using chords from the G Major scale but then play a B Major chord and use the G Augmented Major scale over that B chord.

Harmonizing Other Scales Exercises

What scale is the chord progression using?

1. E - AmMaj7
2. Eb Aug - A Dim - Cm
3. C Dim - Dbm
4. Fm - Ab Aug - B Dim
5. Bb maj7 - A7 - DmMaj7
6. D7 - E7
7. G AugMajor9 - B Maj #9
8. C# Dim - Emb9
9. BminMaj9 - D AugMaj7#9
10. Ebm7b5 - Fm7b5

Reference the chapter to check for chords that stand out as unique per scale and make sure they all fit the same scale.

Answers on page 239

EVERY CHORD IN MUSIC

This is every chord in music when you remove anything that contains three consecutive half steps. I also list every scale and event association for each of them. Just play the scale or event starting on the interval indicated in relation to the root of the chord. You will use these associations when deciding what notes to use when improvising or composing melody, basslines and even adjacent chords. This gives you literally every option in music for any chord.

How to Use This List

1. **Find your chord.**
2. **Look at the associations.** (It will tell you which scales contain this chord).
3. **Apply the Scale.**

~The list tells you the chord's function within that scale.

~Example: If you have a G Major Chord:

~Major Scale (I): Play G Major. (G is the 1st note).

~Major Scale (IV): Play D Major. (G is the 4th note of D).

~Major Scale (V): Play C Major. (G is the 5th note of C).

This gives you literally every melodic option available for any chord you encounter.

A Note on "Missing" Chords (Inversions)

You might look for a chord name and not find it. This is because many chords are actually identical to others on this list, just with a different bass note (inversion). I removed the redundancy to keep things clean. **Example: Dsus2 (D-E-A) is the exact same set of notes as Asus4 (A-D-E).**

If you can't find a specific chord name, look for the other potential names for those notes (start on a different root), and you will find it here. I went with the more accessible or common naming in most cases. The beginning of this book now has the other roots

listed as options. Check those by looking for the interval makeup of the chord, then check which of these pages it is on.

C is the root note used for every diagram shown. You can of course transpose universally to any root note, I use absolute intervals for the scale options so you can do just that with ease!

To practice these on guitar, break them down into CAGED shapes and focus specifically on the E-shape (Root on E-string) and A-shape (Root on A-string) for maximum mobility. To build your own chord shapes and voicings, make sure you have **at least one of EACH of the chord tone (interval numbers) included.**

3 NOTE CHORDS

Major Triad (R 3 5)

Is in the Major Scales on the 1st, 4th and 5th
Is in the Augmented Major Scales on the 5th and b6th
Is in the Melodic Minor Scales on the 4th and 5th
Is in the Harmonic Major Scales on the 1st, 4th and #5th
Is in the Pentatonic Major Event on the 1st
Is in the Pentatonic Minor Event on the 6th
Is in the Blues Event on the 6th
Is in the Hungarian Minor Event on the b2nd, 3rd and 4th
Is in the Diminished Scale Event on the 1st

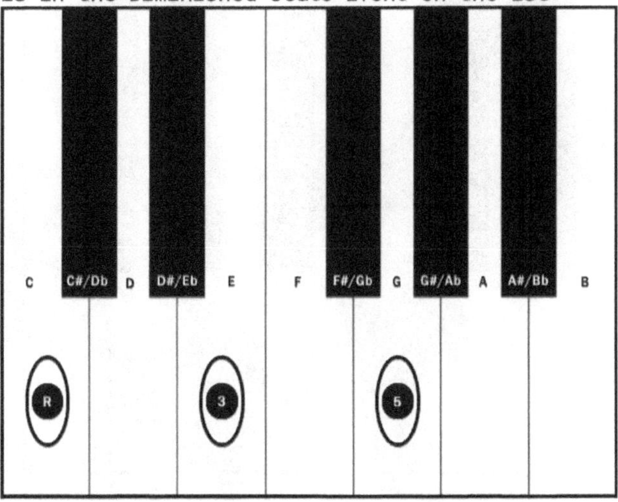

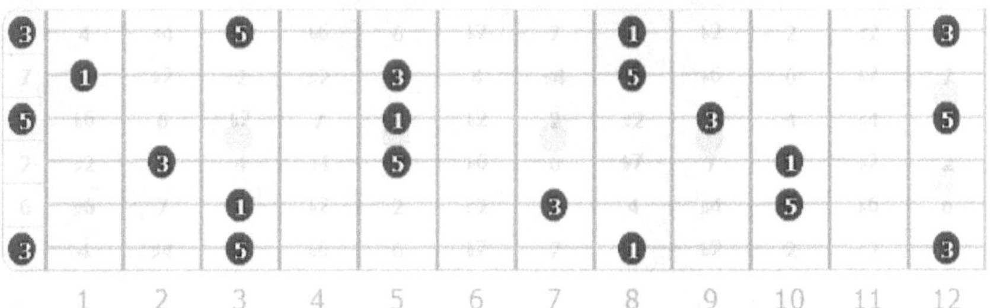

Minor Triad (R b3 5)

Is in the Major Scales on the b3rd, b6th and b7th
Is in the Augmented Major Scales on the b3rd, 5th and b7th
Is in the Melodic Minor Scales on the 1st and b7th
Is in the Harmonic Major Scales on the 5th and #5th
Is in the Pentatonic Major Event on the b3rd
Is in the Pentatonic Minor Event on the 1st
Is in the Blues Event on the 1st and 6th
Is in the Hungarian Minor Event on the 1st, b2nd and 3rd
Is in the Diminished Scale Event on the 1st

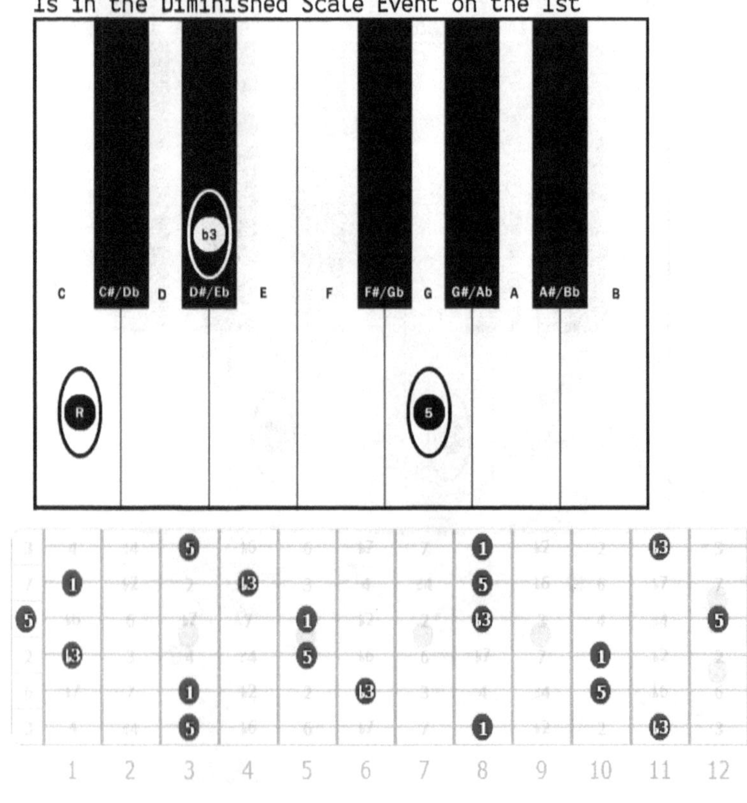

Suspended 2nd (R 2 5)

Is in the Major Scales on the 1st, b3rd, 4th, 5th and b7th
Is in the Augmented Major Scales on the b3rd and b7th
Is in the Melodic Minor Scales on the 1st, 4th and 5th
Is in the Harmonic Major Scales on the 1st and 5th
Is in the Pentatonic Major Event on the 1st, 4th and 5th
Is in the Pentatonic Minor Event on the 2nd, 5th and 6th
Is in the Blues Event on the 2nd, 5th and 6th
Is in the Hungarian Minor Event on the 1st
Is in the Diminished Scale Event on the 1st

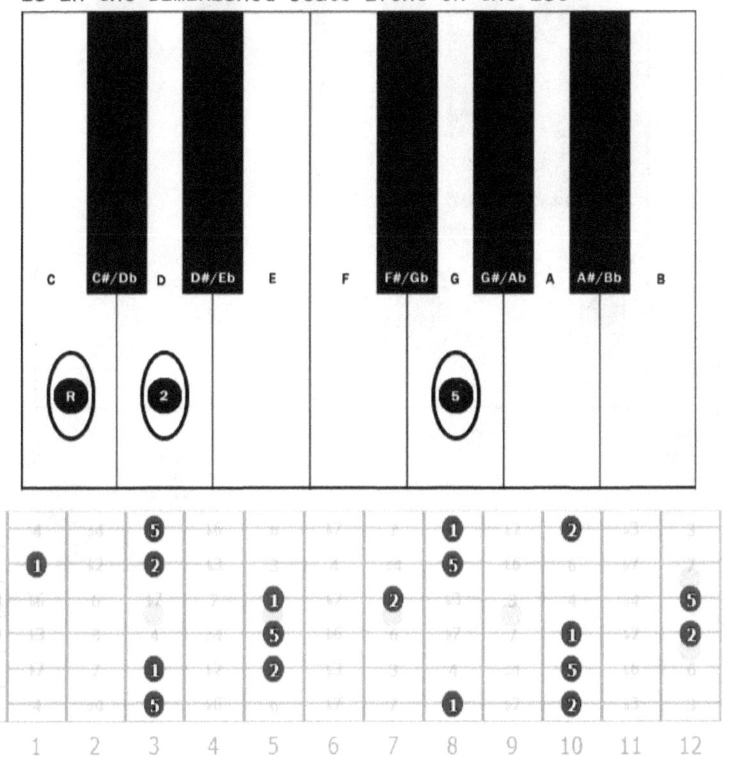

Augmented Triad (R 3 #5)

Is in the Augmented Major Scales on the 1st, 3rd and b6th
Is in the Melodic Minor Scales on the b2nd, 4th and 6th
Is in the Harmonic Major Scales on the 1st, 3rd and #5th
Is in the Hungarian Minor Event on the b2nd, 4th and 6th
Is in the Whole Tone Event on the 1st

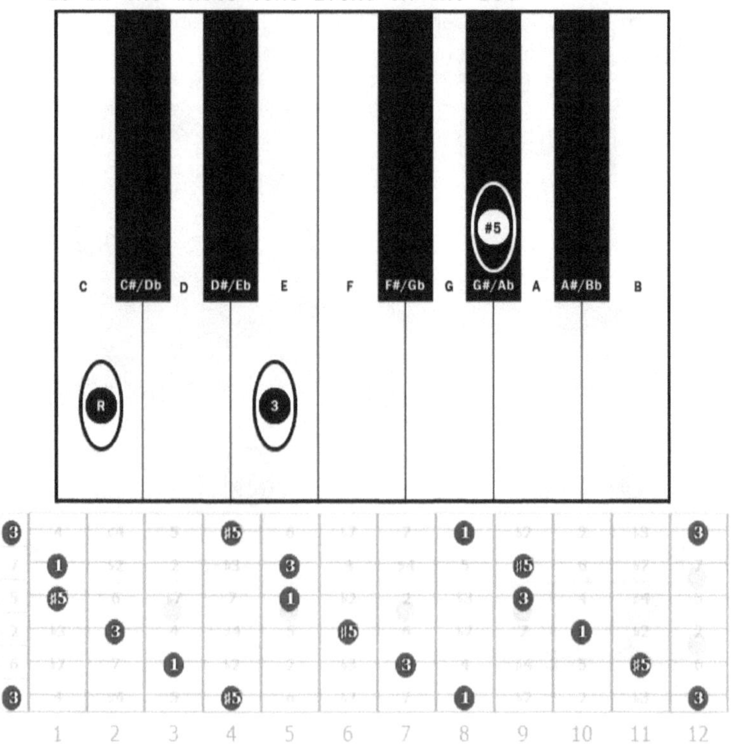

Diminished Triad (R b3 b5)

Is in the Major Scale on the b2nd
Is in the Augmented Major Scales on the b2nd, 3rd, 5th and b7th
Is in the Melodic Minor Scales on the b2nd and b3rd
Is in the Harmonic Major Scales on the b2nd, 3rd, 5th and b7th
Is in the Blues Event on the 1st
Is in the Hungarian Minor Event on the 1st and 3rd
Is in the Diminished Scale Event on the 1st and 7th

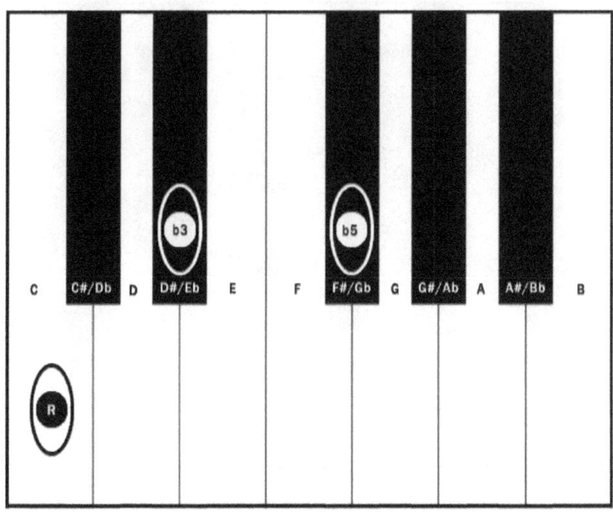

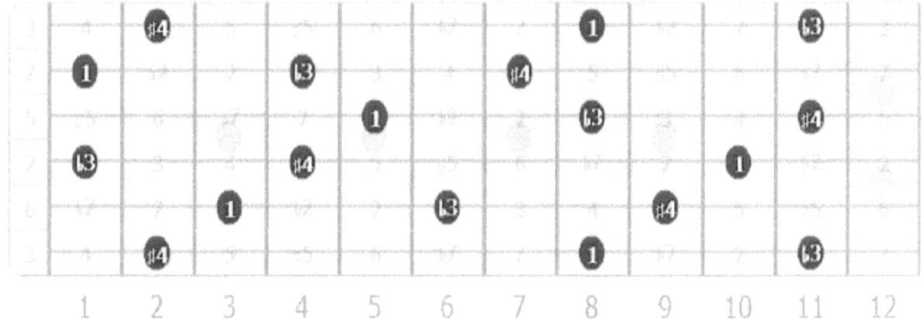

Augmented 4th (R #4 5)

Is in the Major Scale on the 5th
Is in the Augmented Major Scales on the 5th and b7th
Is in the Melodic Minor Scale on the 5th
Is in the Harmonic Major Scale on the 5th
Is in the Blues Event on the 1st
Is in the Hungarian Minor Event on the 1st and 3rd
Is in the Diminished Scale Event on the 1st

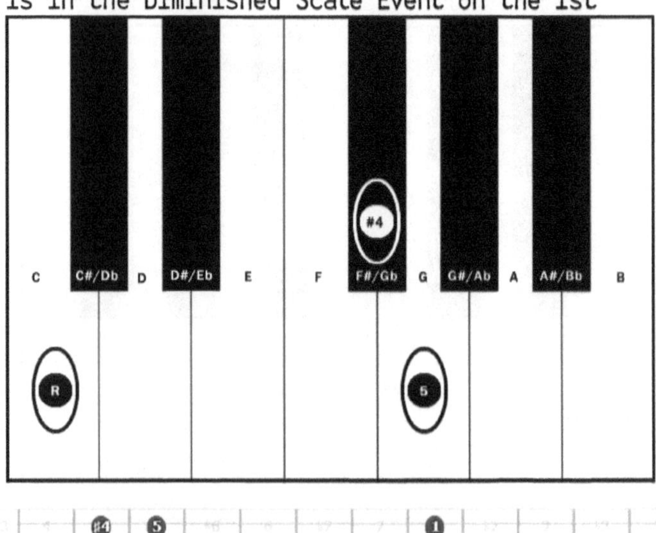

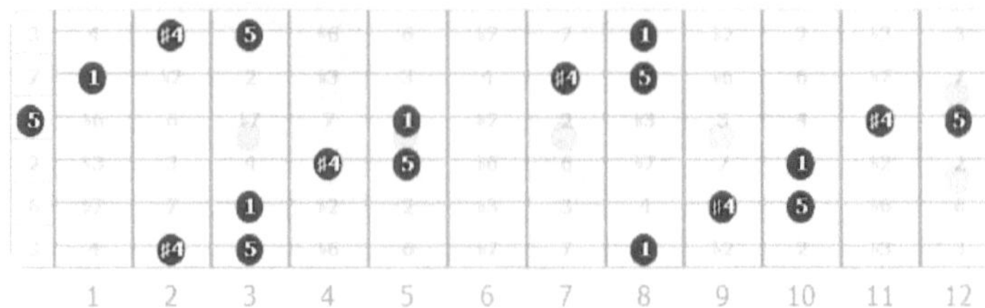

Flat 5th (R 3 b5)

Is in the Major Scale on the 5th
Is in the Augmented Major Scales on the 3rd and 5th
Is in the Melodic Minor Scales on the b2nd, 5th and 6th
Is in the Harmonic Major Scale on the 3rd
Is in the Blues Event on the b5th
Is in the Hungarian Minor Event on the 3rd and b7th
Is in the Whole Tone Scale Event on the 1st
Is in the Diminished Scale Event on the 1st

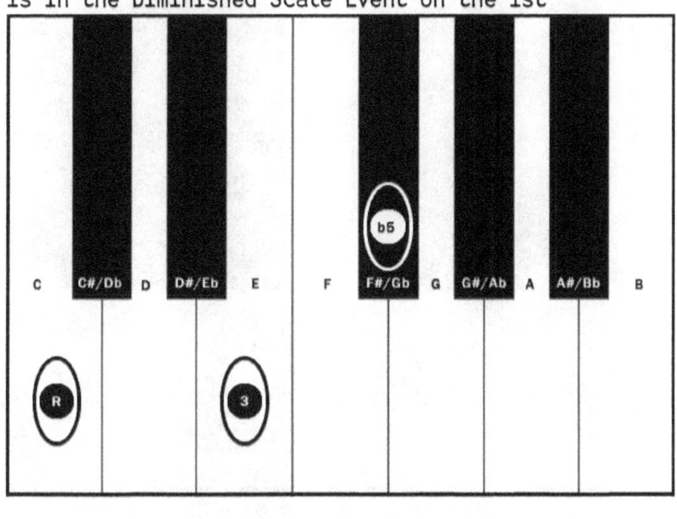

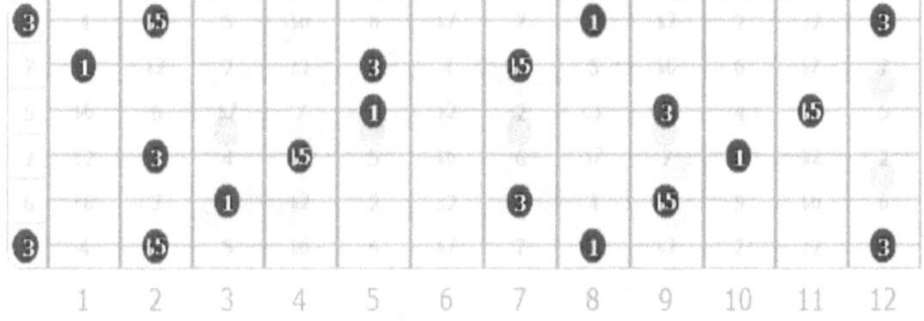

4 NOTE CHORDS

Major 7th (R 3 5 7)

Is in the Major Scales on the 1st and 5th
Is in the Augmented Major Scale on the 5th
Is in the Harmonic Major Scale on the 1st
Is in the Hungarian Minor Event on the 3rd and 4th

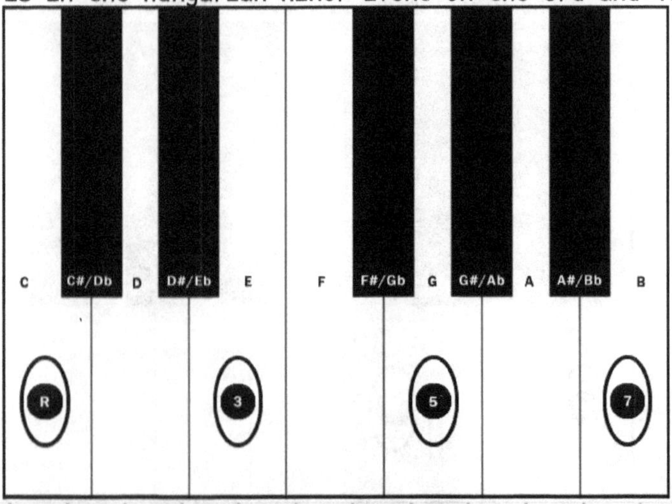

C C#/Db D D#/Eb E F F#/Gb G G#/Ab A A#/Bb B

R 3 5 7

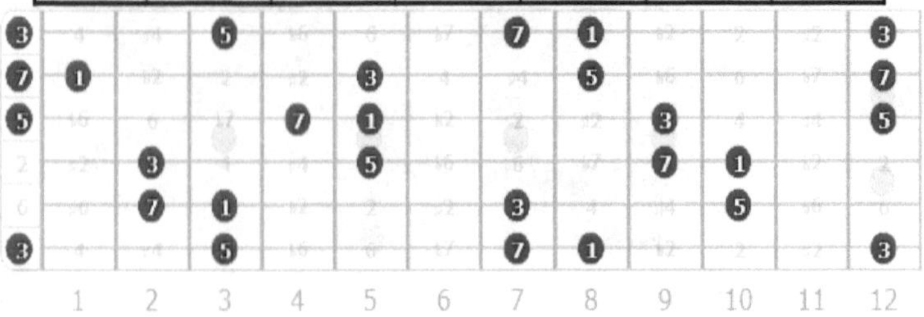

1 2 3 4 5 6 7 8 9 10 11 12

Major 7 Sus 4 (R 4 5 7)

Is in the Major Scale on the 1st
Is in the Augmented Major Scale on the b3rd
Is in the Melodic Minor Scale on the 1st
Is in the Harmonic Major Scale on the 1st
Is in the Hungarian Minor Event on the 4th

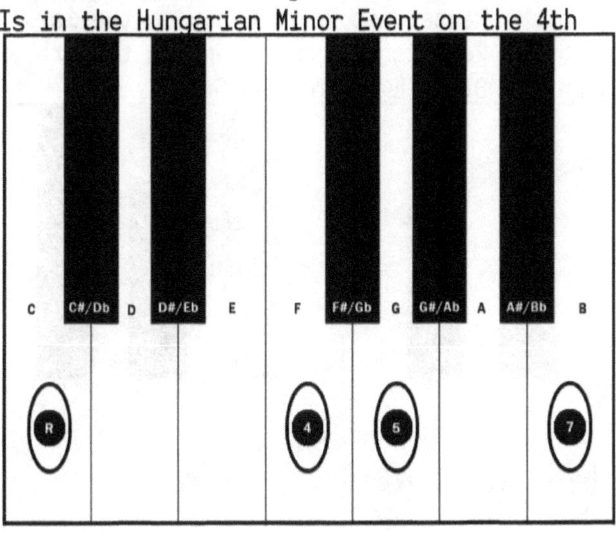

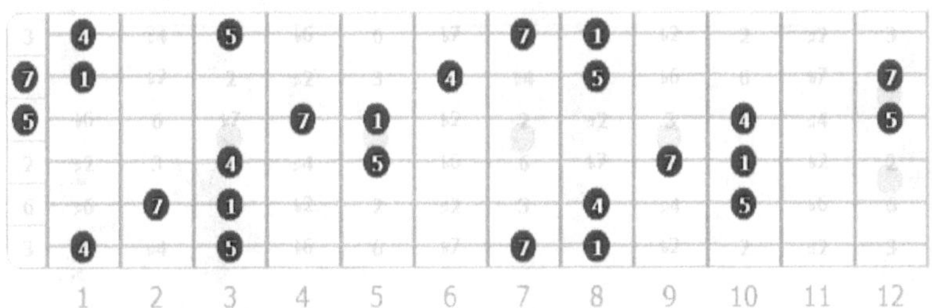

Major Add 9 (R 2 3 5)

Is in the Major Scales on the 1st, 4th and 5th
Is in the Melodic Minor Scales on the 4th and 5th
Is in the Harmonic Major Scale on the 1st
Is in the Pentatonic Major Event on the 1st
Is in the Pentatonic Minor Event on the 6th
Is in the Blues Event on the 6th

C C#/Db D D#/Eb E F F#/Gb G G#/Ab A A#/Bb B

1 2 3 4 5 6 7 8 9 10 11 12

Major Add #9 (R #2 3 5)

Is in the Augmented Major Scale on the 5th
Is in the Harmonic Major Scale on the b6th
Is in the Blues Event on the 6th
Is in the Hungarian Minor Event on the b2nd and 3rd
Is in the Diminished Scale Event on the 1st

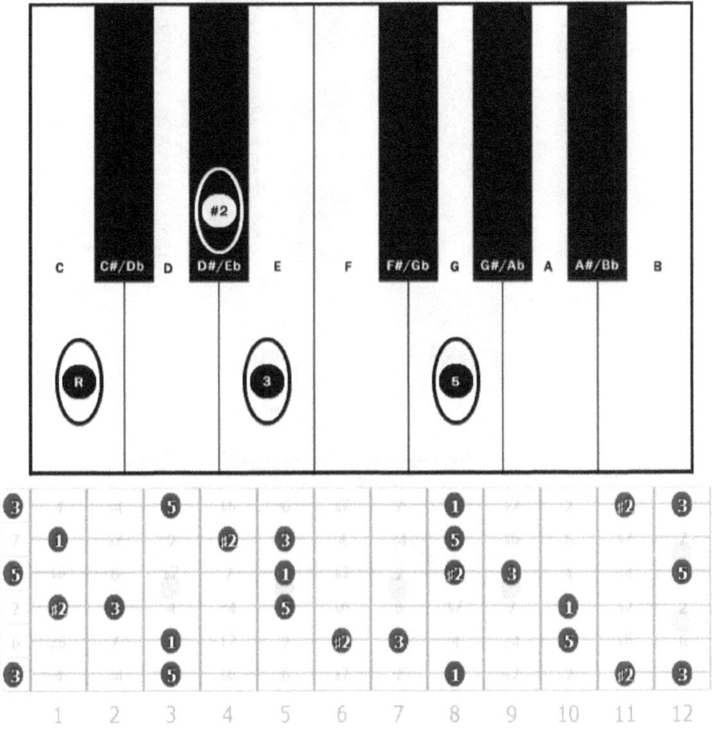

Major Add b9 (R b2 3 5)

Is in the Augmented Major Scale on the b6th
Is in the Harmonic Major Scales on the 4th and #5th
Is in the Hungarian Minor Event on the b2nd and 4th
Is in the Diminished Scale Event on the 1st

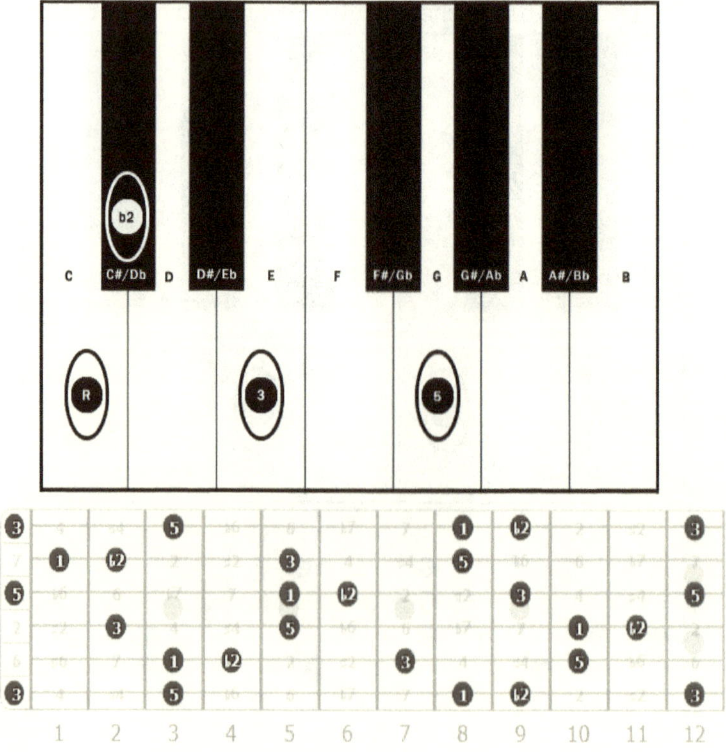

Major Add 11 (R 3 4 5)

Is in the Major Scales on the 1st and 4th
Is in the Augmented Major Scale on the b6th
Is in the Melodic Minor Scale on the 4th
Is in the Harmonic Major Scales on the 1st and 4th
Is in the Hungarian Minor Event on the 4th

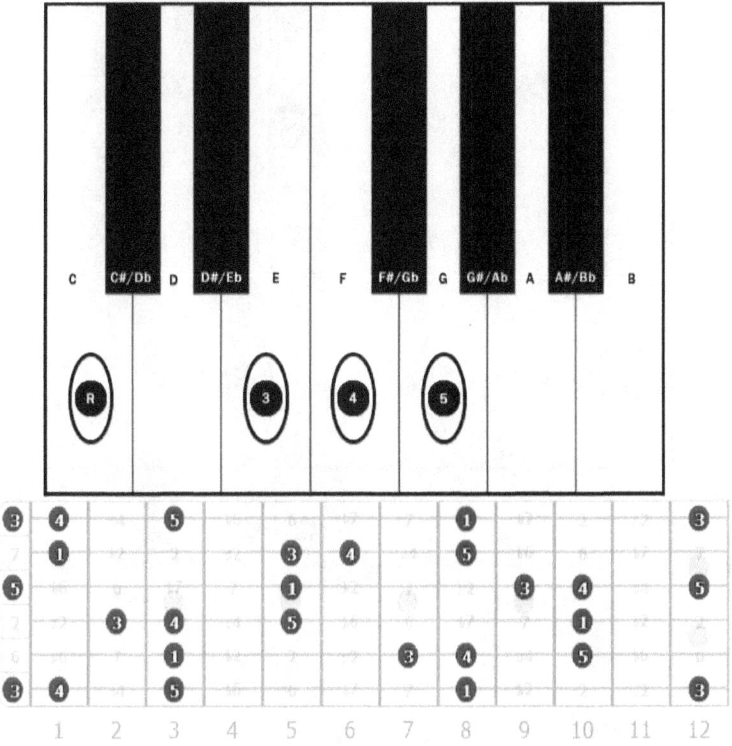

Major Add #11 (R 3 #4 5)

Is in the Major Scale on the 5th
Is in the Augmented Major Scale on the 5th
Is in the Melodic Minor Scale on the 5th
Is in the Hungarian Minor Event on the 3rd
Is in the Diminished Scale Event on the 1st

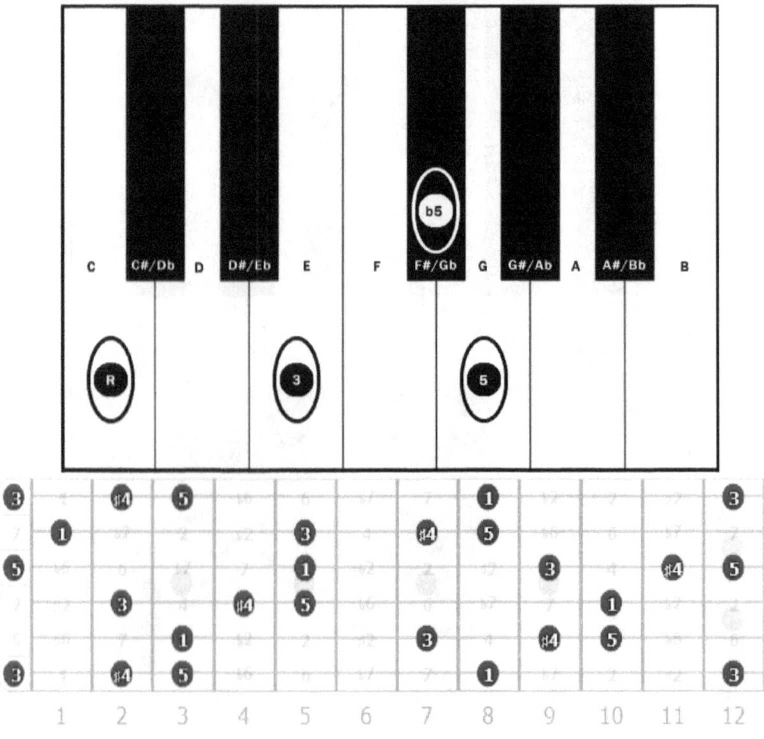

Dominant 7th (R 3 5 b7)

Is in the Major Scale on the 4th
Is in the Augmented Major Scales on the b6th
Is in the Melodic Minor Scales on the 4th and 5th
Is in the Harmonic Major Scales on the 4th and #5th
Is in the Hungarian Minor Event on the 3rd
Is in the Diminished Scale Event on the 1st

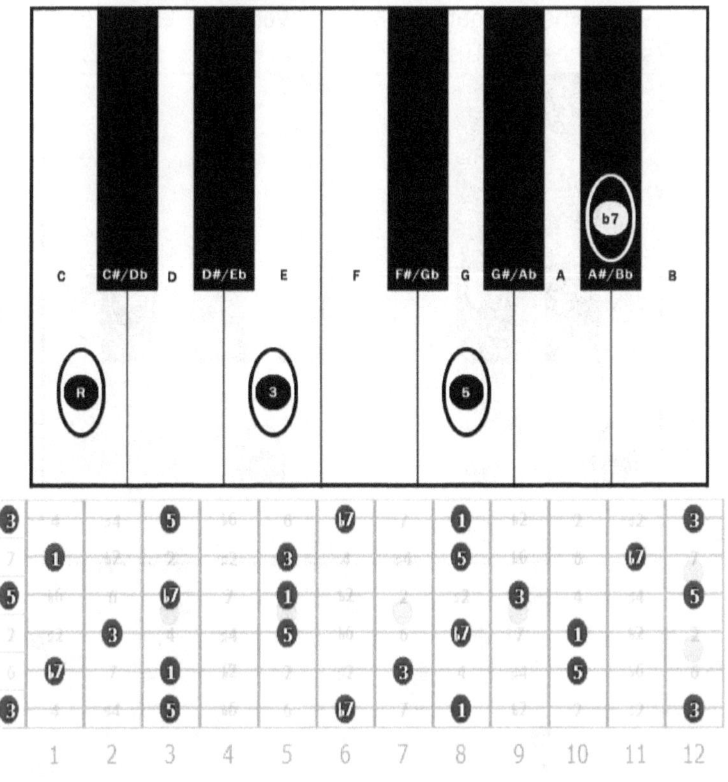

Minor 7th (R b3 5 b7)

Is in the Major Scales on the b3rd, b6th and b7th
Is in the Augmented Major Scale on the b7th
Is in the Melodic Minor Scale on the b7th
Is in the Harmonic Major Scale on the b6th
Is in the Pentatonic Major Event on the b3rd
Is in the Pentatonic Minor Event on the 1st
Is in the Blues Event on the 1st
Is in the Hungarian Minor Event on the 3rd
Is in the Diminished Scale Event on the 1st

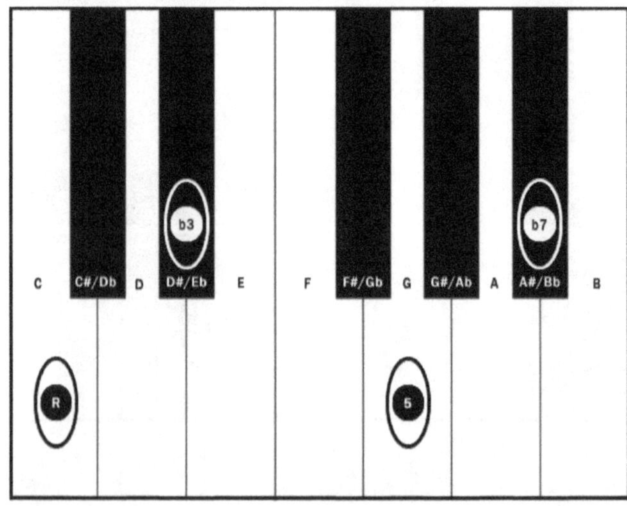

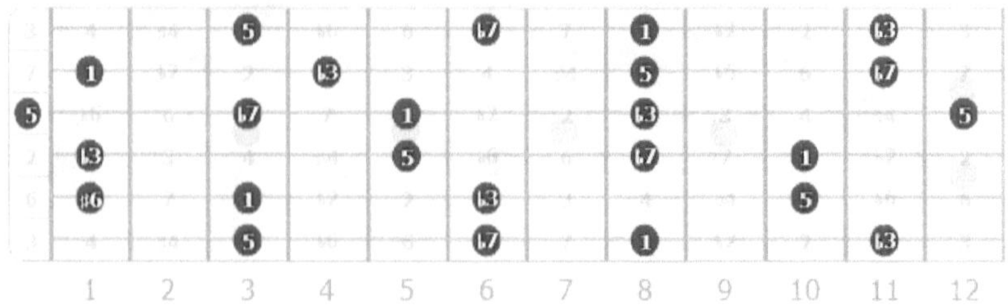

Minor 7 Sus 4 (R 4 5 b7)

Is in the Major Scales on the b3rd, 4th, b6th and b7th
Is in the Augmented Major Scale on the b6th
Is in the Melodic Minor Scales on the 4th and b7th
Is in the Harmonic Major Scale on the 4th
Is in the Pentatonic Major Event on the b3rd and b7th
Is in the Pentatonic Minor Event on the 1st and 5th
Is in the Blues Event on the 1st and 5th

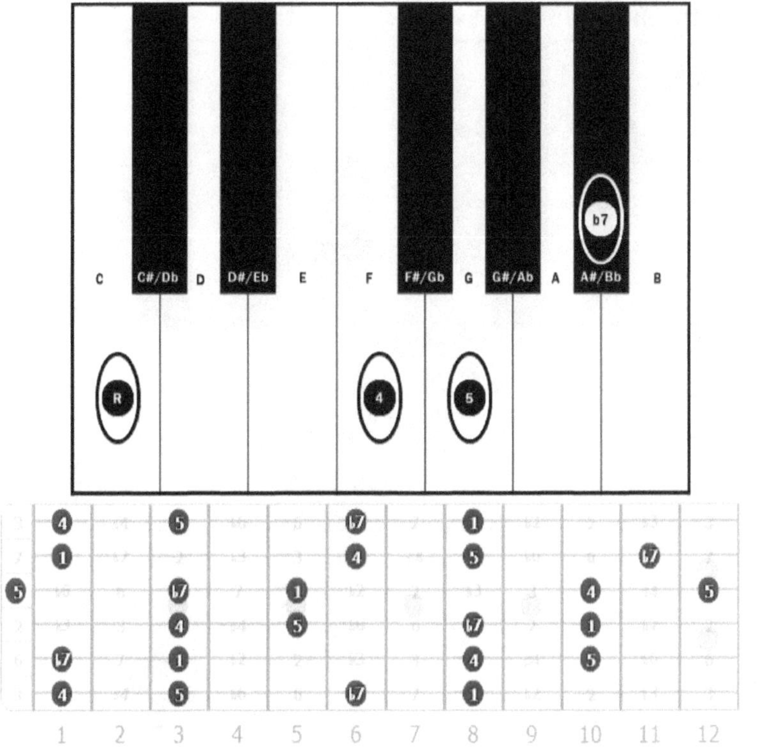

Minor Add 9 (R 2 b3 5)

Is in the Major Scales on the b3rd and b7th
Is in the Augmented Major Scales on the b3rd and b7th
Is in the Melodic Minor Scales on the 1st
Is in the Harmonic Major Scale on the 5th
Is in the Hungarian Minor Scale on the 1st
Is in the Blues Event on the 1st

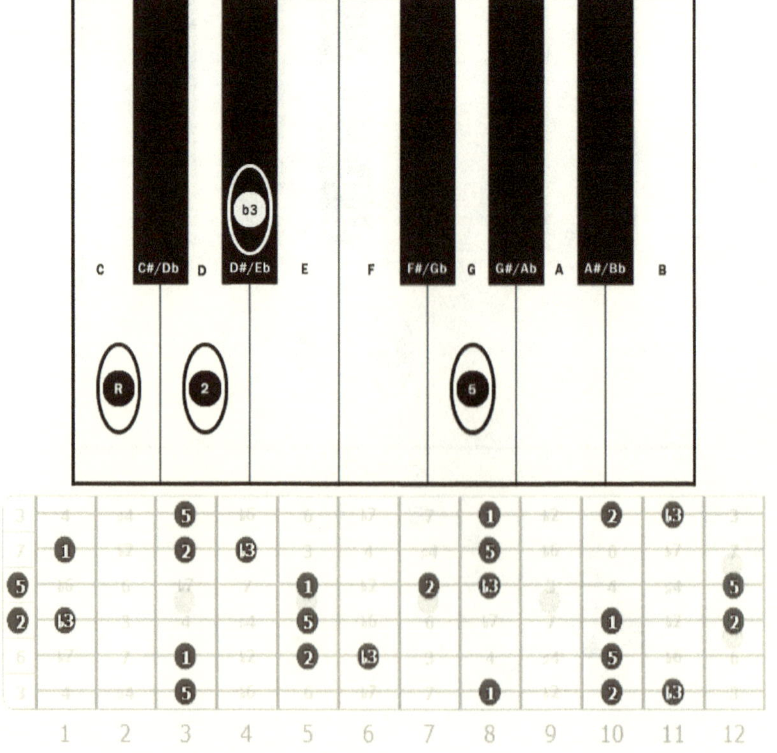

Minor Add 11 (R b3 4 5)

Is in the Major Scales on the b3rd, b6th and b7th
Is in the Augmented Major Scale on the b3rd
Is in the Melodic Minor Scales on the 1st and b7th
Is in the Pentatonic Major Event on the b3rd
Is in the Pentatonic Minor Event on the 1st
Is in the Blues Event on the 1st

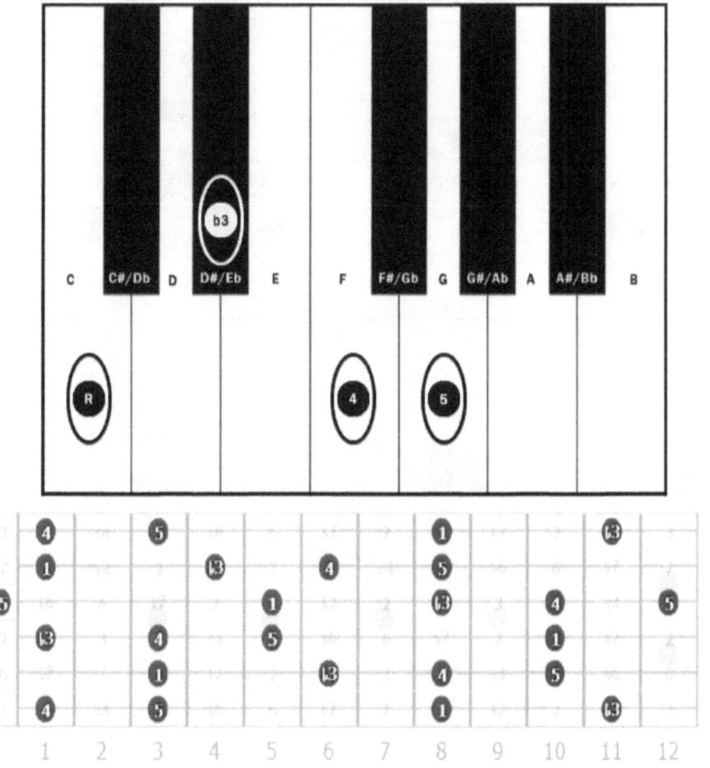

Minor-Major 7th (R b3 5 7)

Is in the Augmented Major Scales on the b3rd and 5th
Is in the Melodic Minor Scale on the 1st
Is in the Harmonic Major Scale on the 5th
Is in the Hungarian Minor Event on the 1st and 3rd

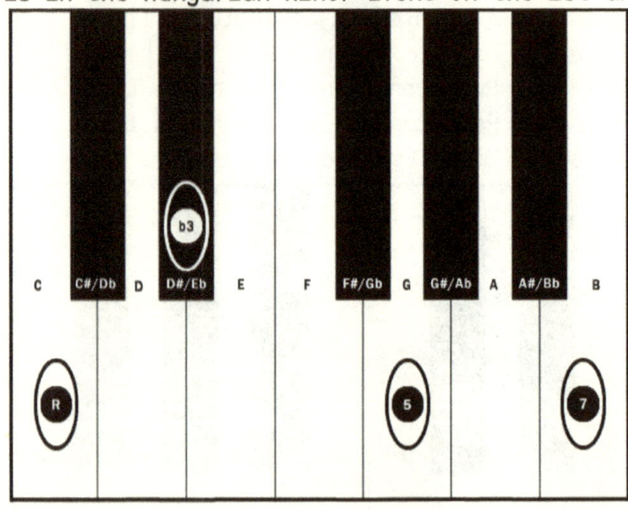

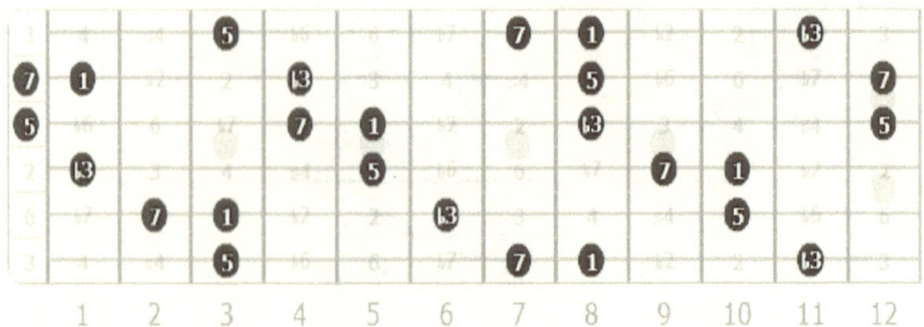

Sus2 Add b13 (R 2 5 b6)

Is in the Major Scale on the b3rd
Is in the Augmented Major Scale on the b3rd
Is in the Melodic Minor Scale on the 4th
Is in the Harmonic Major Scale on the 1st
Is in the Blues Event on the 2nd
Is in the Hungarian Minor Event on the 1st

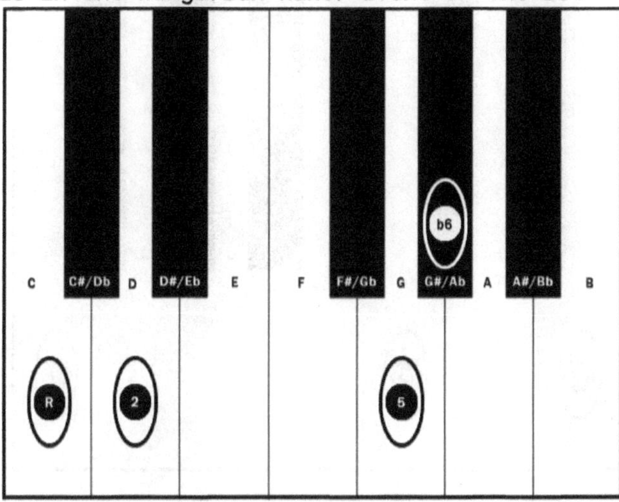

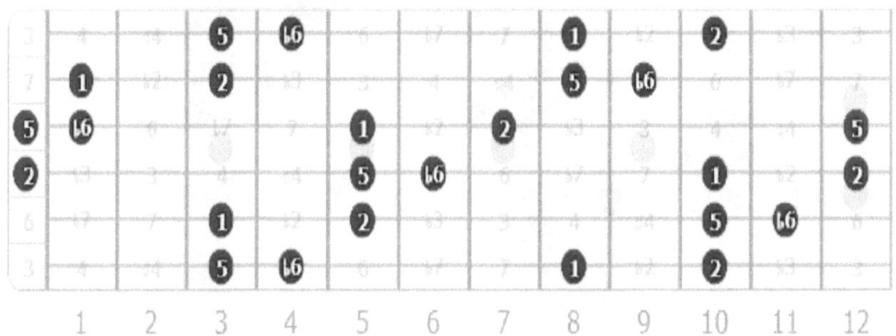

Augmented Major 7th (R 3 #5 7)

Is in the Augmented Major Scale on the 1st
Is in the Melodic Minor Scale on the 6th
Is in the Harmonic Major Scales on the 1st and 3rd
Is in the Hungarian Minor Event on the 4th and 6th

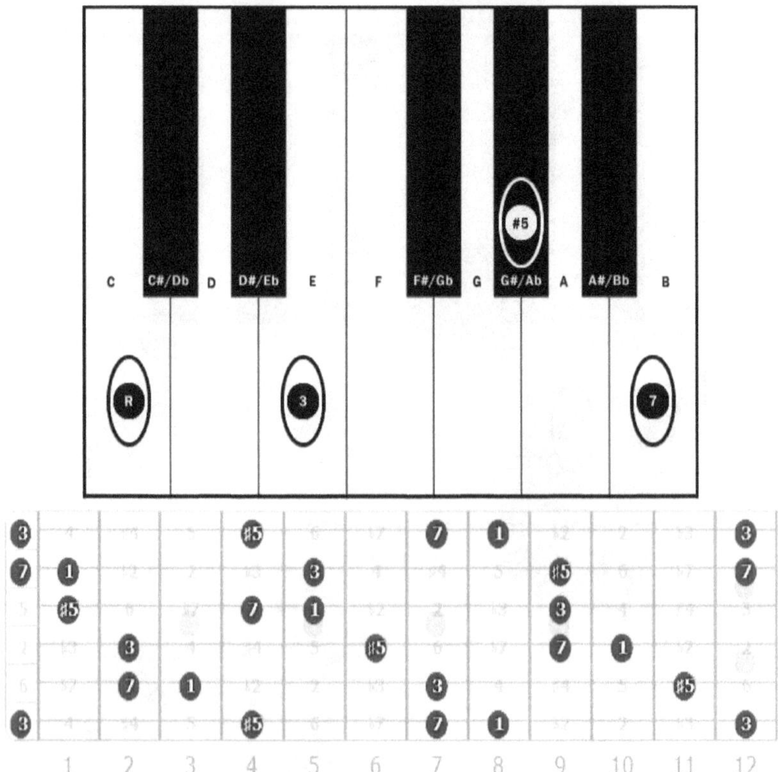

Augmented 7th (R 3 #5 b7)

Is in the Augmented Major Scale on the b6th
Is in the Melodic Minor Scales on the b2nd and 4th
Is in the Harmonic Major Scale on the b6th
Is in the Whole Tone Scale Event on the 1st

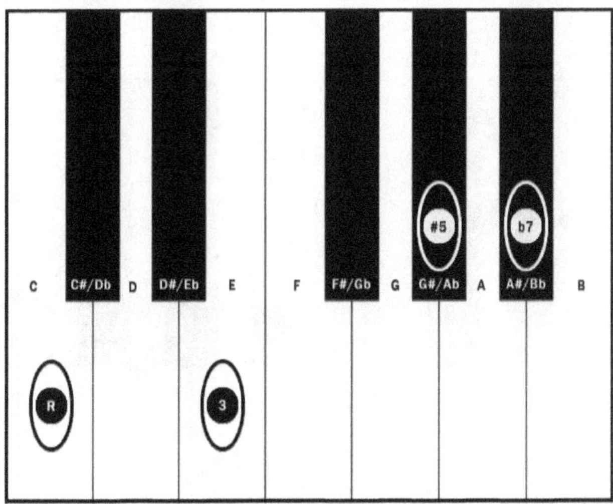

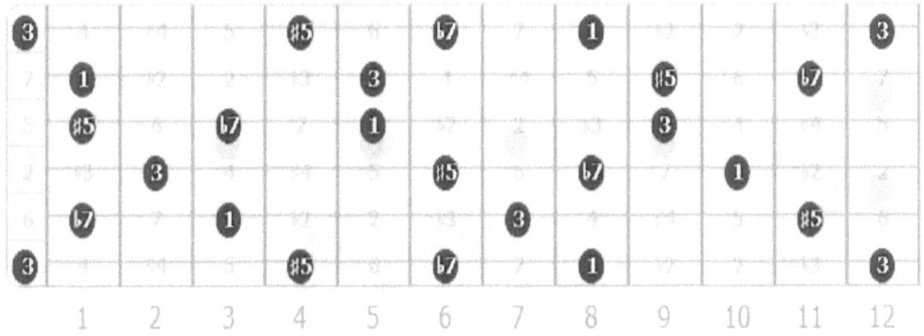

Half Diminished (R b3 b5 b7)

Is in the Major Scale on the b2nd
Is in the Augmented Major Scales on the b7th and b2nd
Is in the Melodic Minor Scales on the b2nd and b3rd
Is in the Harmonic Major Scale on the b7th
Is in the Blues Event on the 1st
Is in the Hungarian Minor Event on the 3rd
Is in the Diminished Scale Event on the 1st

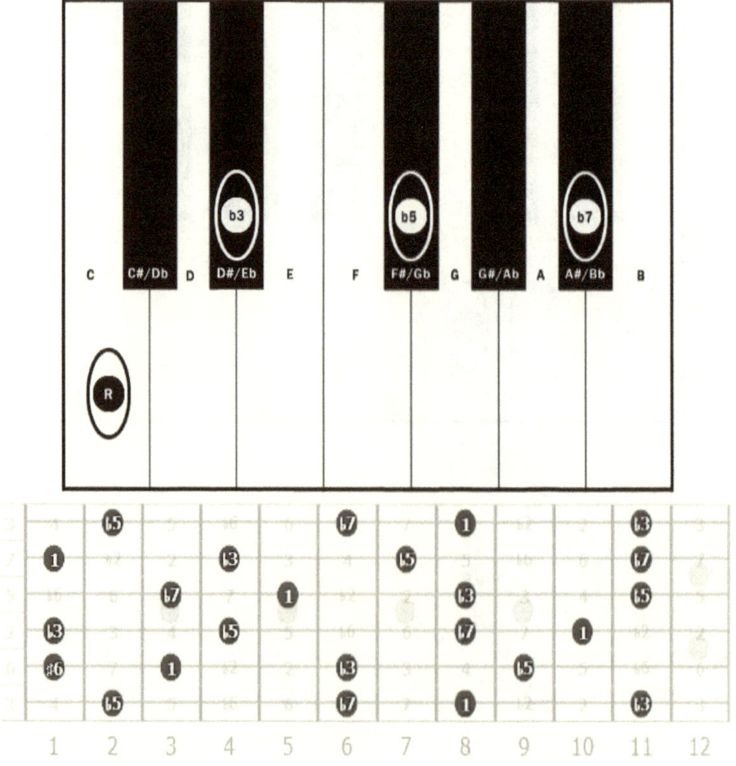

Diminished 7th (R b3 b5 6)

Is in the Augmented Major Scale on the b2nd, 3rd, 5th and b7th
Is in the Harmonic Major Scale on the b2nd, 3rd, 5th and b7th
Is in the Diminished Scale Event on the 1st and 7th

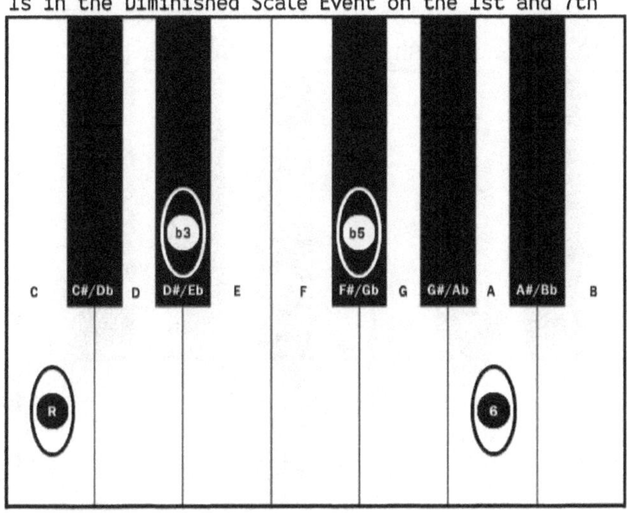

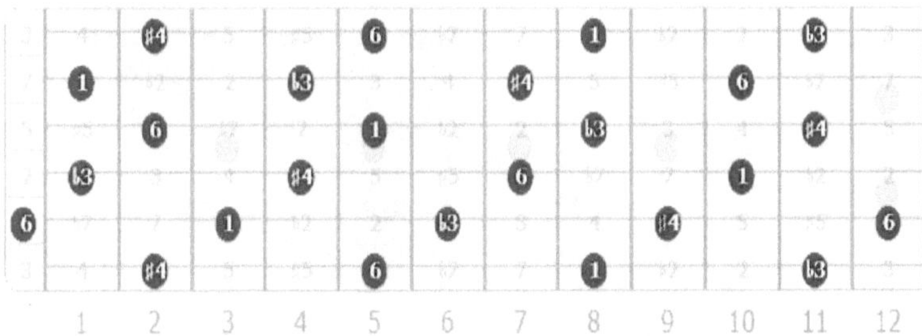

Diminished Add 9 (R 2 b3 b5)

Is in the Augmented Major Scale on the b7th
Is in the Melodic Minor Scale on the b3rd
Is in the Harmonic Major Scales on the 5th and b7th
Is in the Hungarian Minor Event on the 1st
Is in the Diminished Scale Event on the 7th

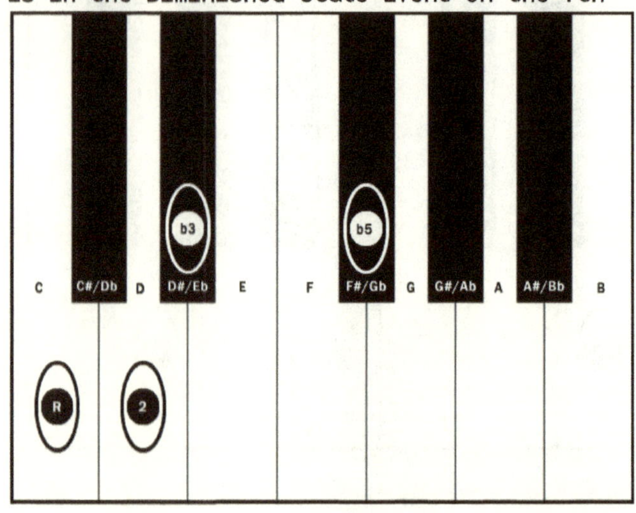

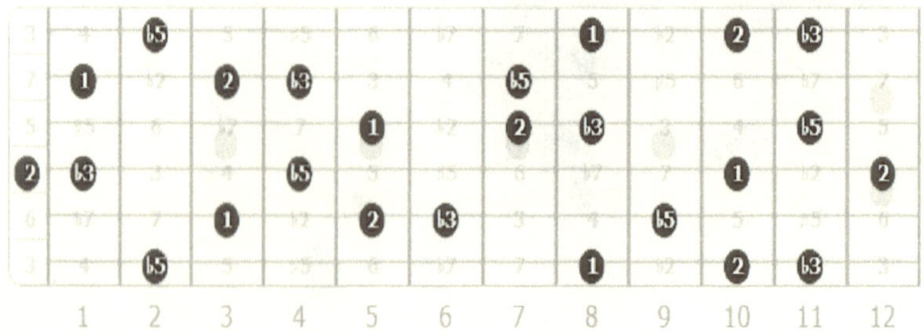

Diminished Add b9 (R b2 b3 b5)

Is in the Major Scale on the b2nd
Is in the Augmented Major Scales on the b2nd and 3rd
Is in the Melodic Minor Scale on the b2nd
Is in the Harmonic Major Scale on the b2nd
Is in the Diminished Scale Event on the 1st

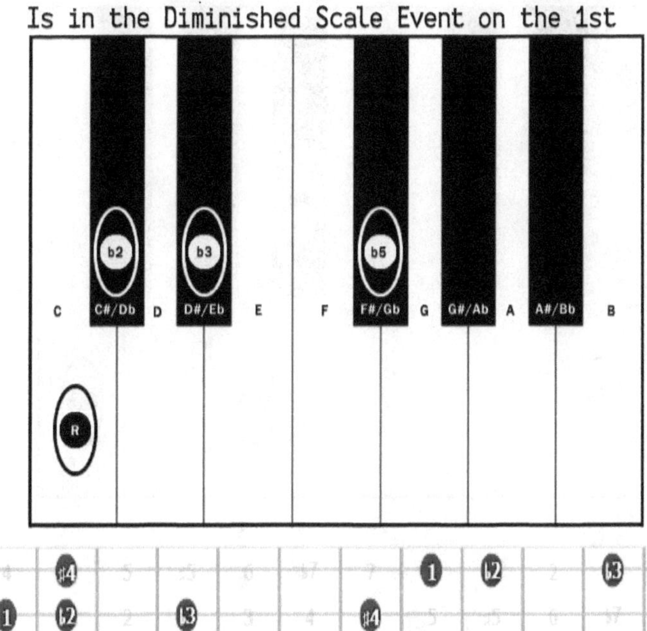

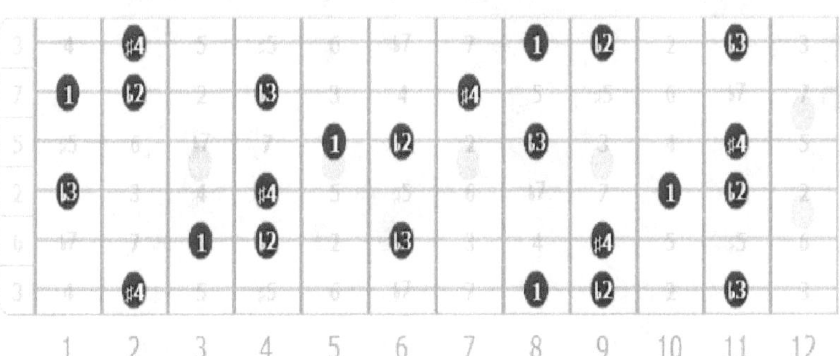

Augmented 4th Add 7th (R #4 5 7)

Is in the Major Scale on the 5th
Is in the Augmented Major Scales on the 5th
Is in the Harmonic Major Scale on the 5th
Is in the Hungarian Minor Event on the 1st and 3rd

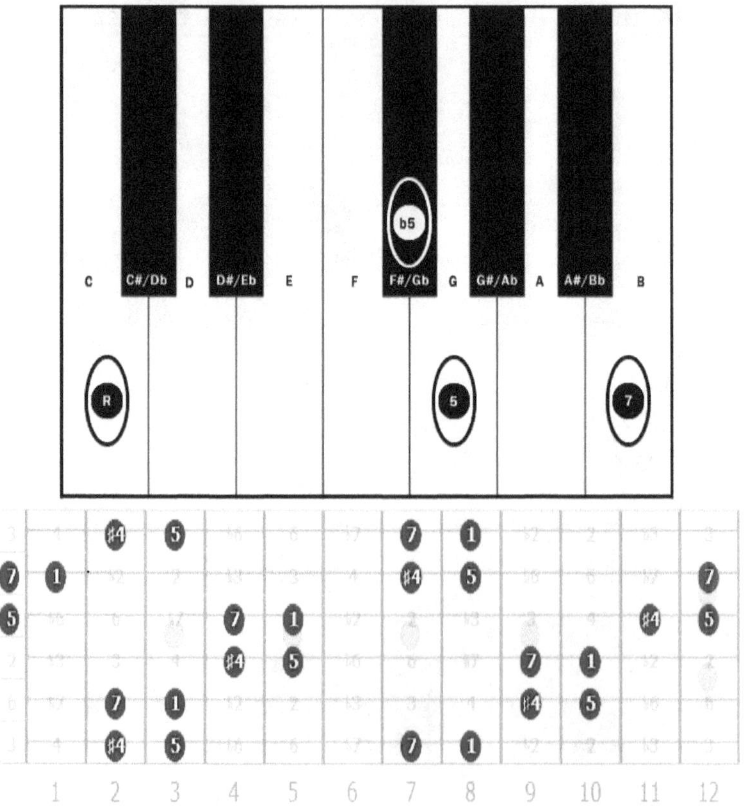

Augmented 4th Add b7th (R #4 5 b7)

Is in the Augmented Major Scale on the b7th
Is in the Melodic Minor Scale on the 5th
Is in the Blues Event on the 1st
Is in the Hungarian Minor Event on the 3rd
Is in the Diminished Scale Event on the 1st

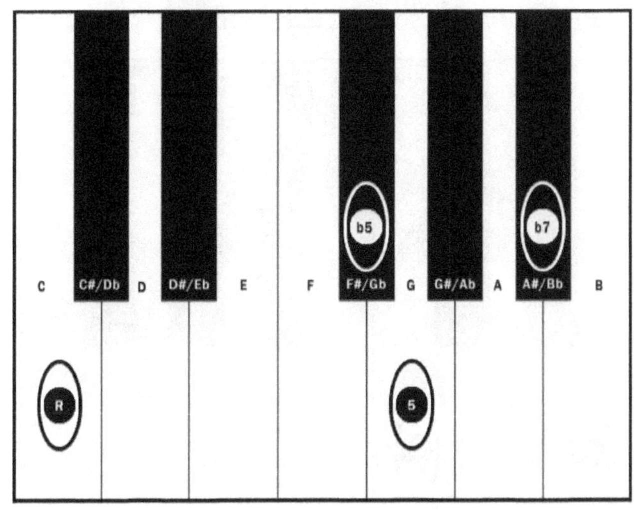

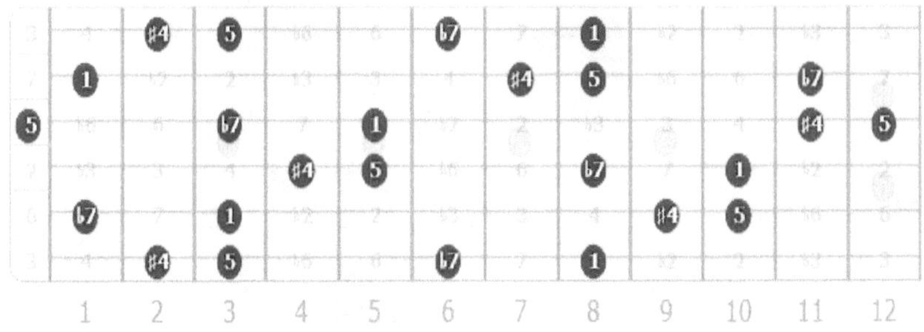

Dominant 7th b5 (R 3 b5 b7)

Is in the Melodic Minor Scales on the b2nd and 5th
Is in the Hungarian Minor Event on the 3rd and b7th
Is in the Whole Tone Scale Event on the 1st
Is in the Diminished Scale Event on the 1st

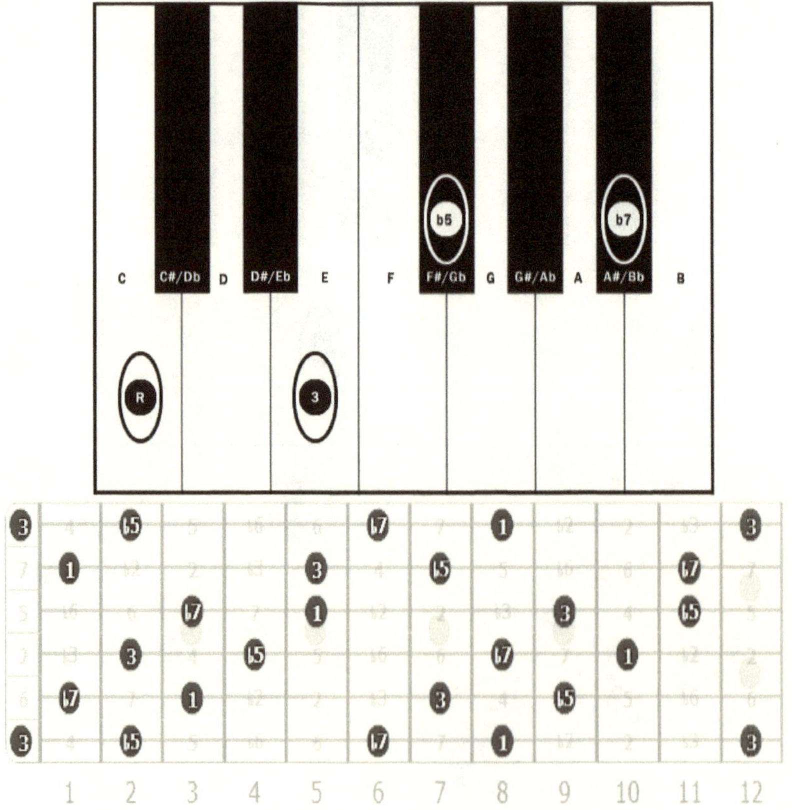

Flat5 Add 9 (R 2 3 b5)

Is in the Major Scale on the 5th
Is in the Melodic Minor Scales on the 5th and 6th
Is in the Whole Tone Scale Event on the 1st

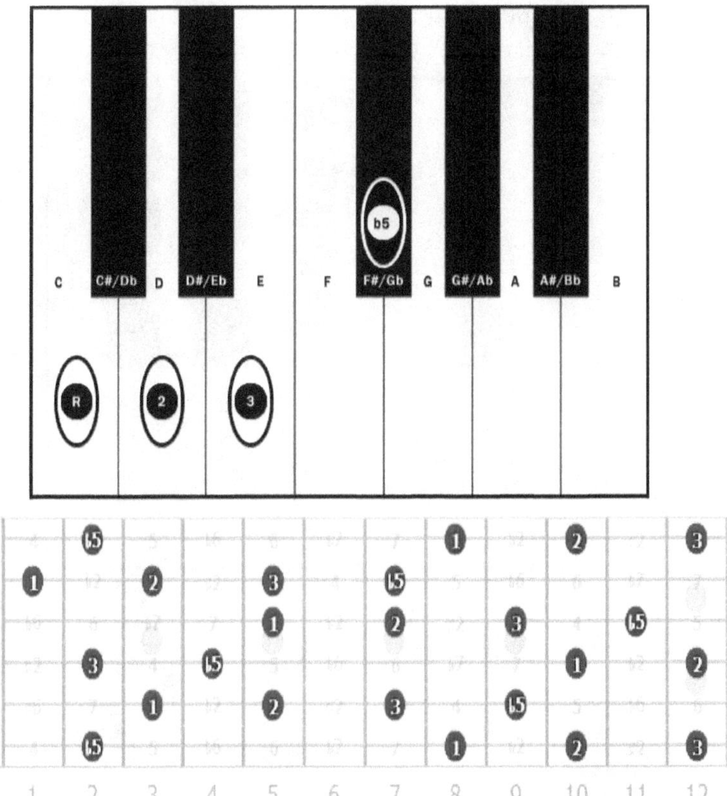

Flat 5 Add #9 (R #2 3 b5)

Is in the Augmented Major Scales on the 3rd and 5th
Is in the Melodic Minor Scale on the b2nd
Is in the Harmonic Major Scale on the 3rd
Is in the Hungarian Minor Event on the 3rd
Is in the Diminished Scale Event on the 1st

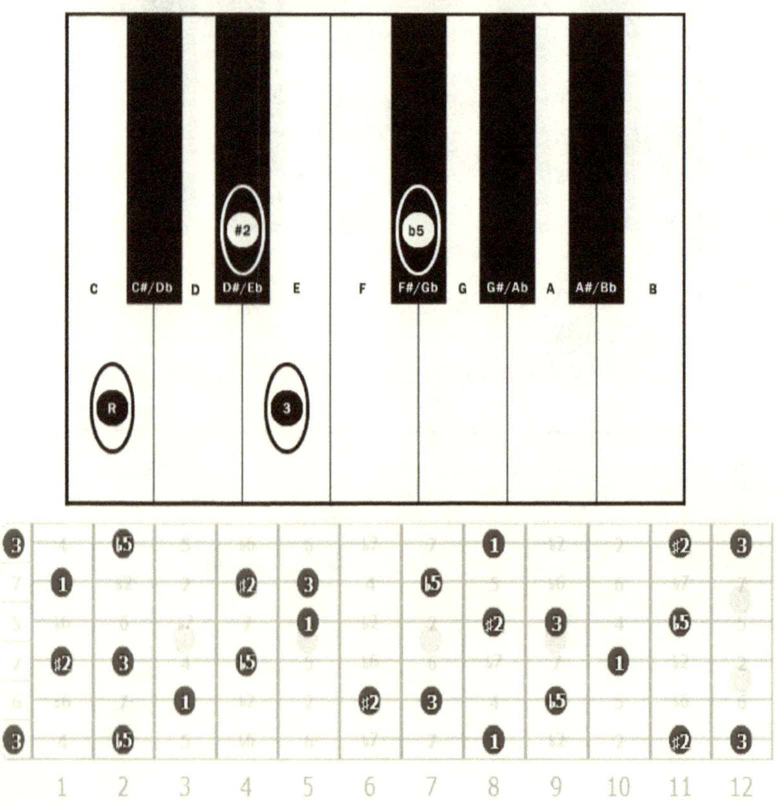

5 NOTE CHORDS

Major 9 (R 2 3 5 7)

Is in the Major Scales on the 1st and 5th
Is in the Harmonic Major Scale on the 1st

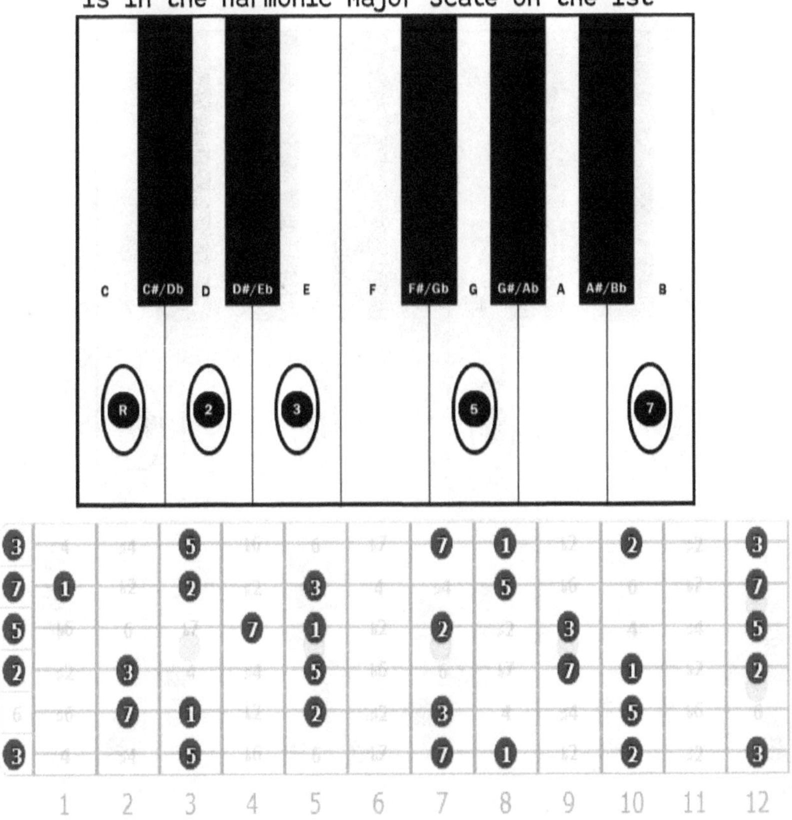

Major #9 (R #2 3 5 7)

Is in the Augmented Major Scale on the 5th
Is in the Hungarian Minor Event on the 3rd

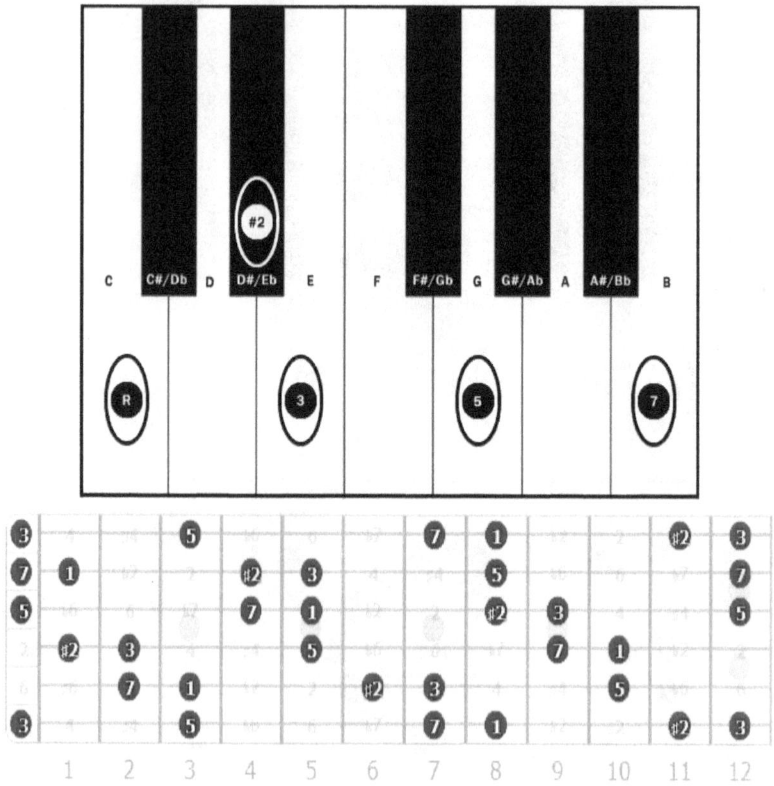

Major 7 Add 11 (R 3 4 5 7)

Is in the Major Scale on the 1st
Is in the Harmonic Major Scale on the 1st
Is in the Hungarian Minor Event on the 4th

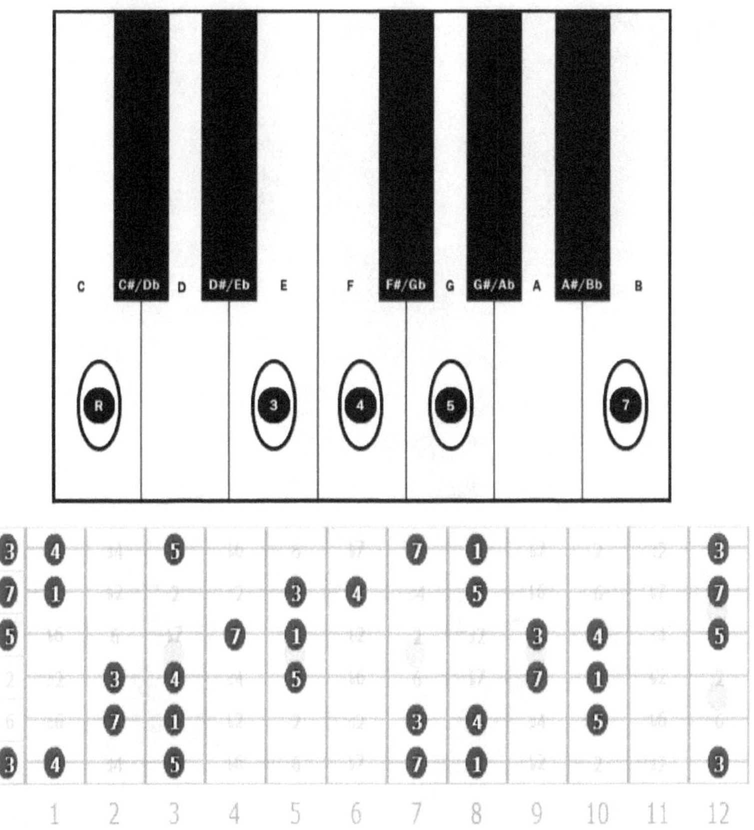

Major 7 Add #11 (R 3 #4 5 7)

Is in the Major Scale on the 5th
Is in the Augmented Major Scale on the 5th
Is in the Hungarian Minor Event on the 3rd

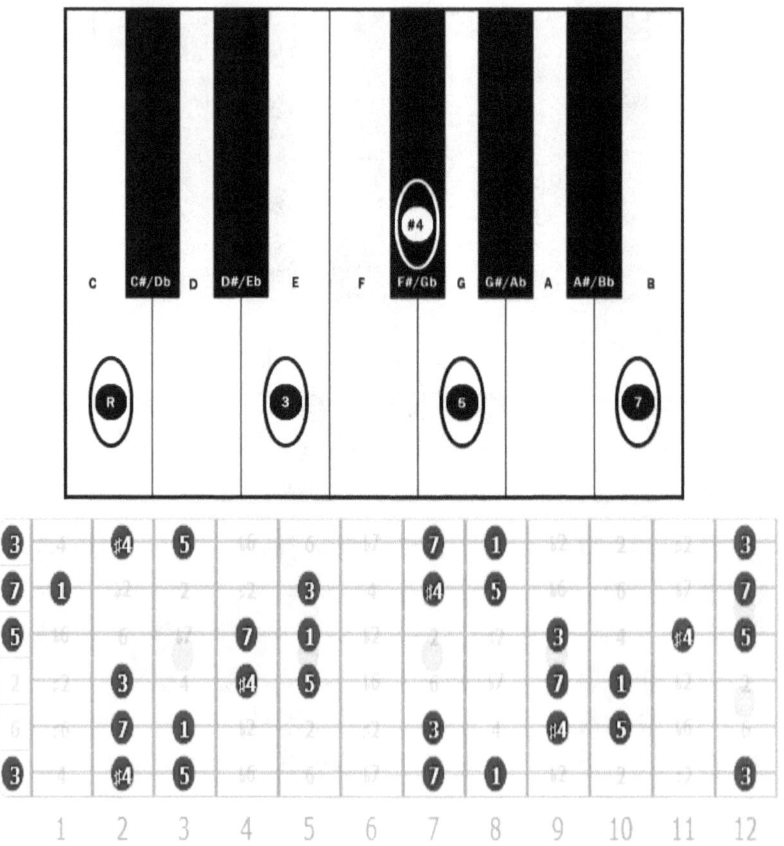

Major 7 Add b13 (R 3 5 b6 7)

Is in the Harmonic Major Scale on the 1st
Is in the Hungarian Minor Event on the 4th

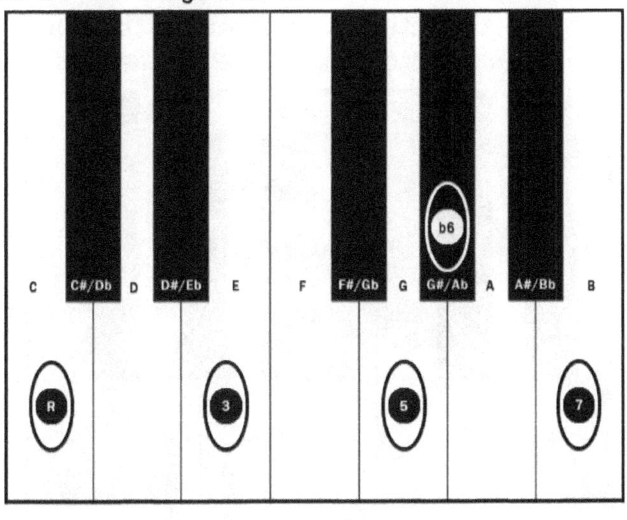

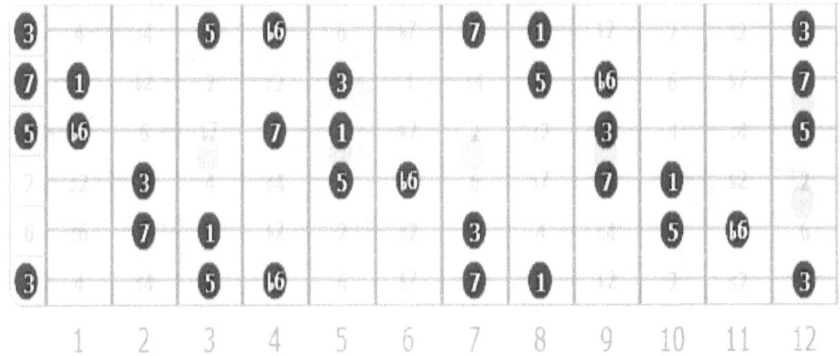

Major 7 Augmented 4th Add 13 (R #4 5 6 7)

Is in the Major Scale on the 5th
Is in the Augmented Major Scale on the 5th
Is in the Harmonic Major Scale on the 5th

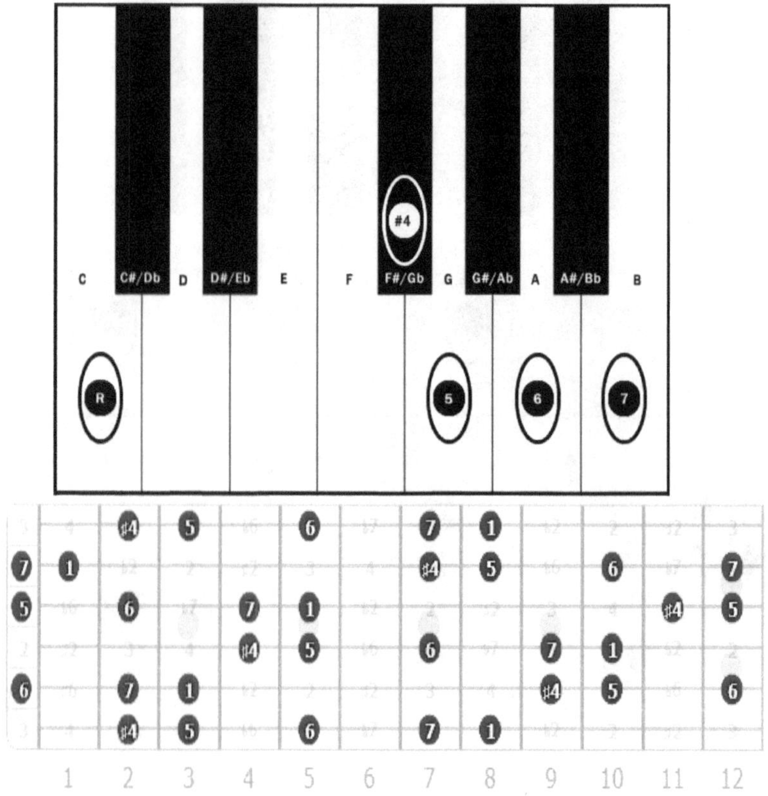

Major Add 9 Add 11 (R 2 3 4 5)

Is in the Major Scales on the 1st and 4th
Is in the Melodic Minor Scale on the 4th
Is in the Harmonic Major Scale on the 1st

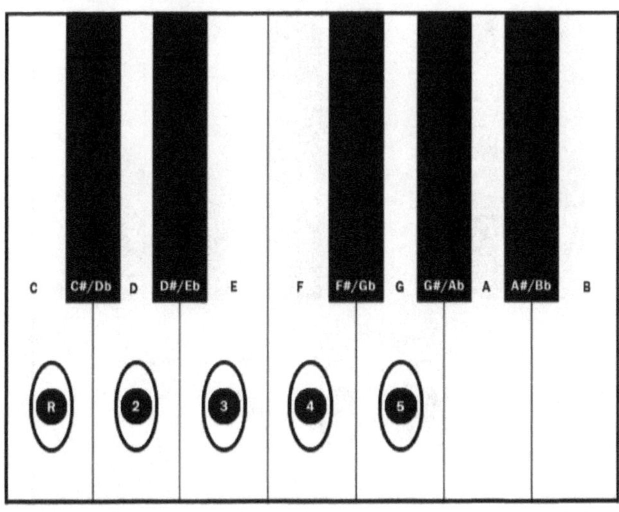

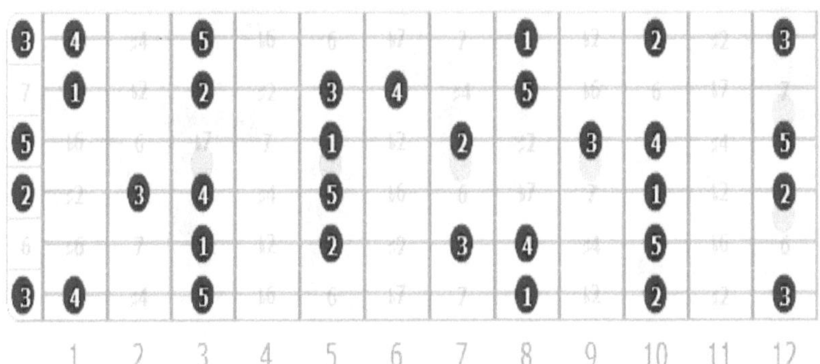

Major Add b9 Add 11 (R b2 3 4 5)

Is in the Augmented Major Scale on the b6th
Is in the Harmonic Major Scale on the 4th
Is in the Hungarian Minor Event on the 4th

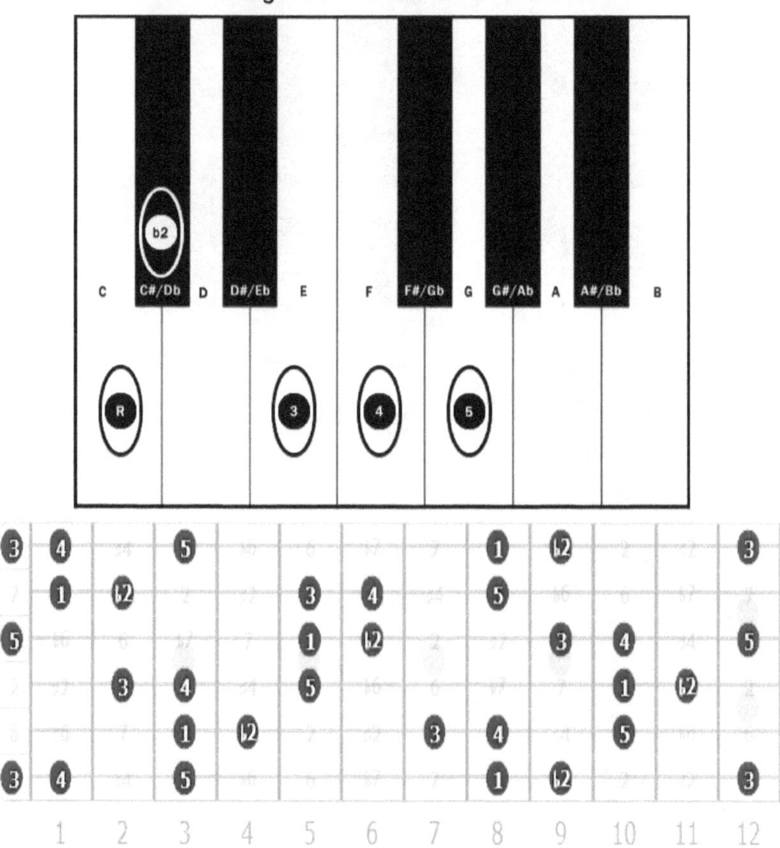

Major Add 9 Add #11 (R 2 3 #4 5)

Is in the Major Scale on the 5th

Is in the Melodic Minor Scale on the 5th

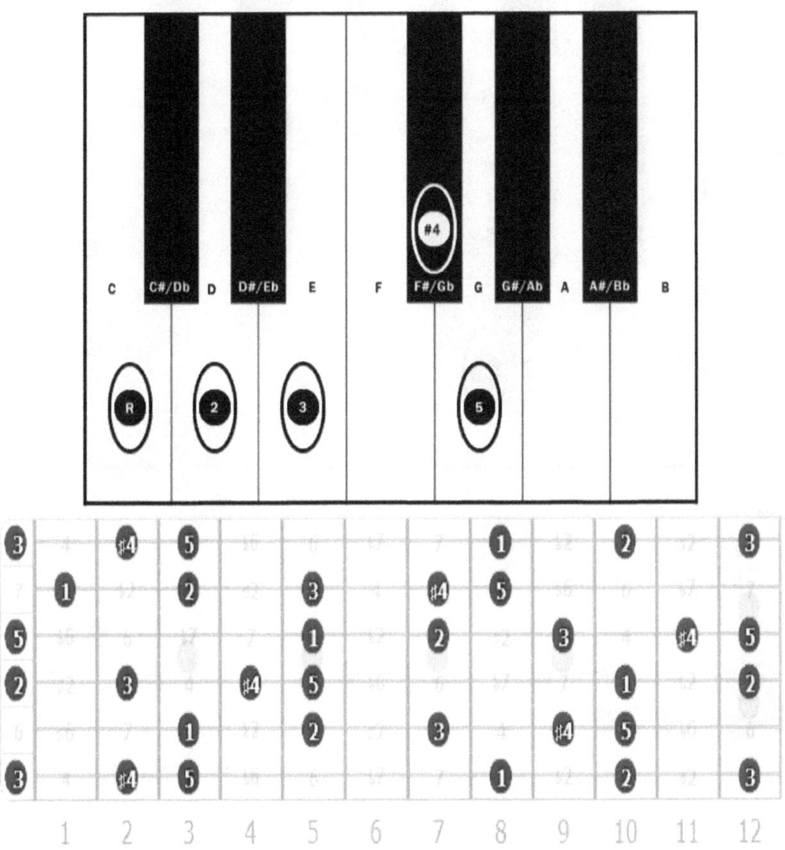

Major Add b9 Add #11 (R b2 3 #4 5)

Is in the Diminished Scale Event on the 1st

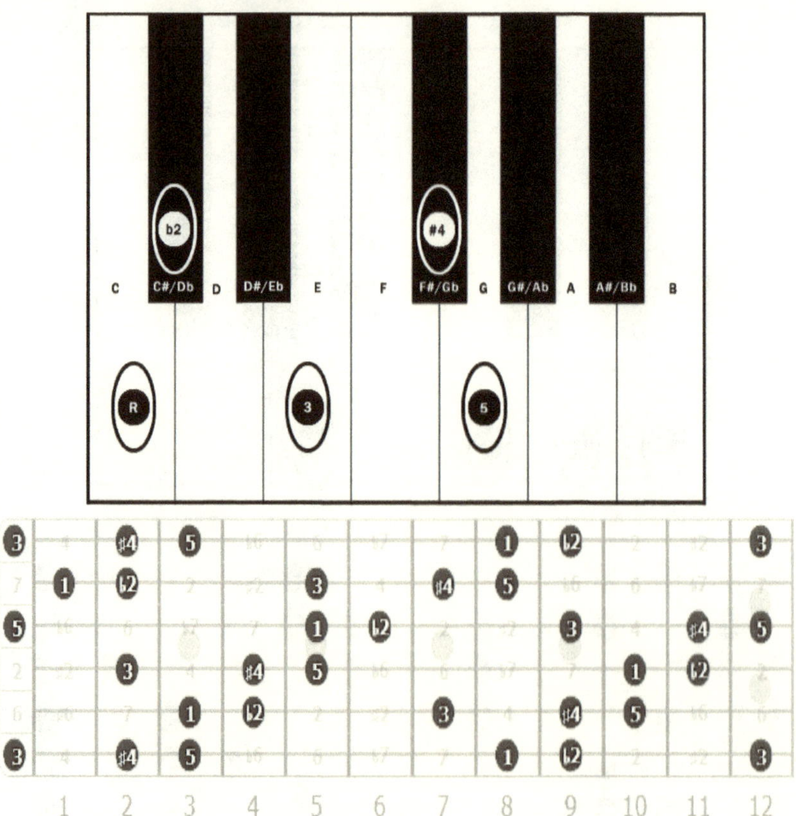

Major Add #9 Add #11 (R #2 3 #4 5)

Is in the Augmented Major Scale on the 5th
Is in the Hungarian Minor Event on the 3rd
Is in the Diminished Scale Event on the 1st

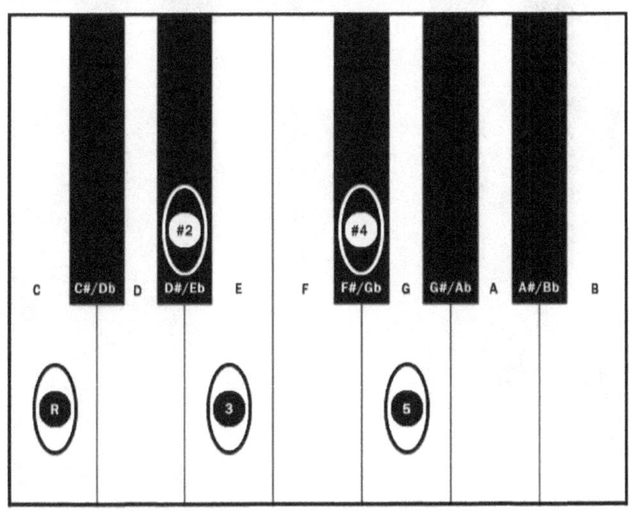

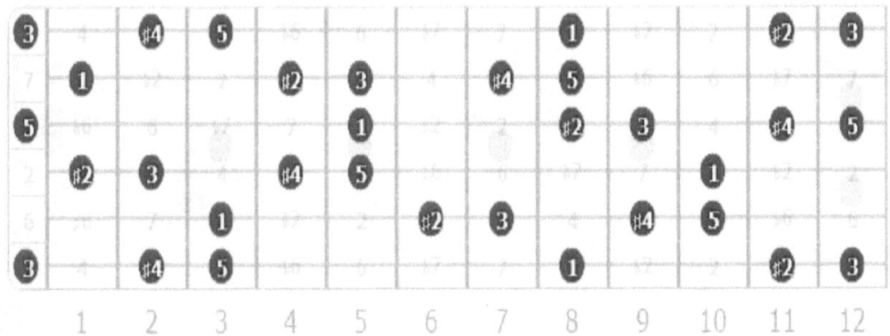

Major Add 9 Add b13 (R 2 3 5 b6)

Is in the Melodic Minor Scale on the 4th
Is in the Harmonic Major Scale on the 1st

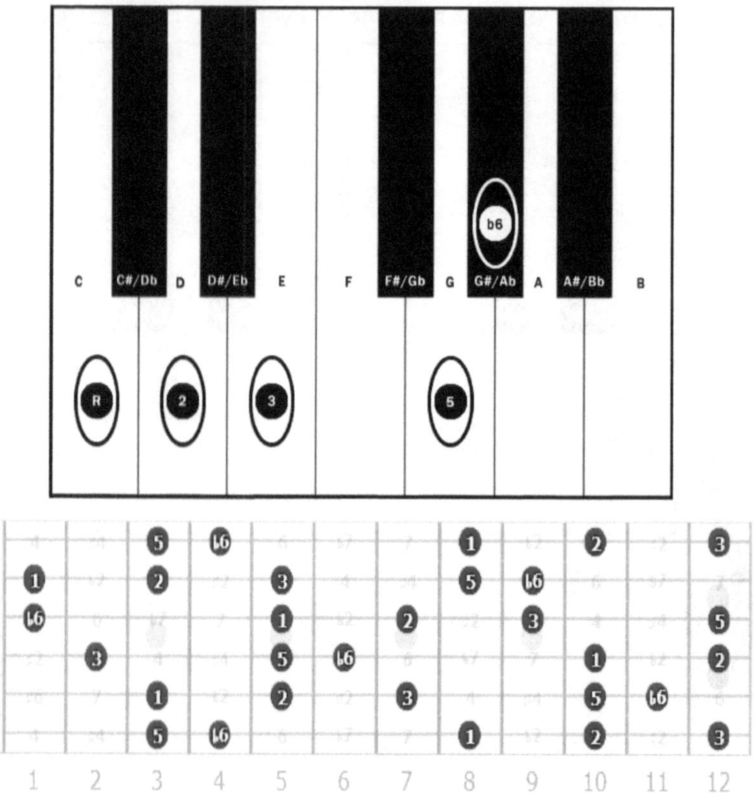

Dominant 9 (R 2 3 5 b7)

Is in the Major Scale on the 4th

Is in the Melodic Minor Scales on the 4th and 5th

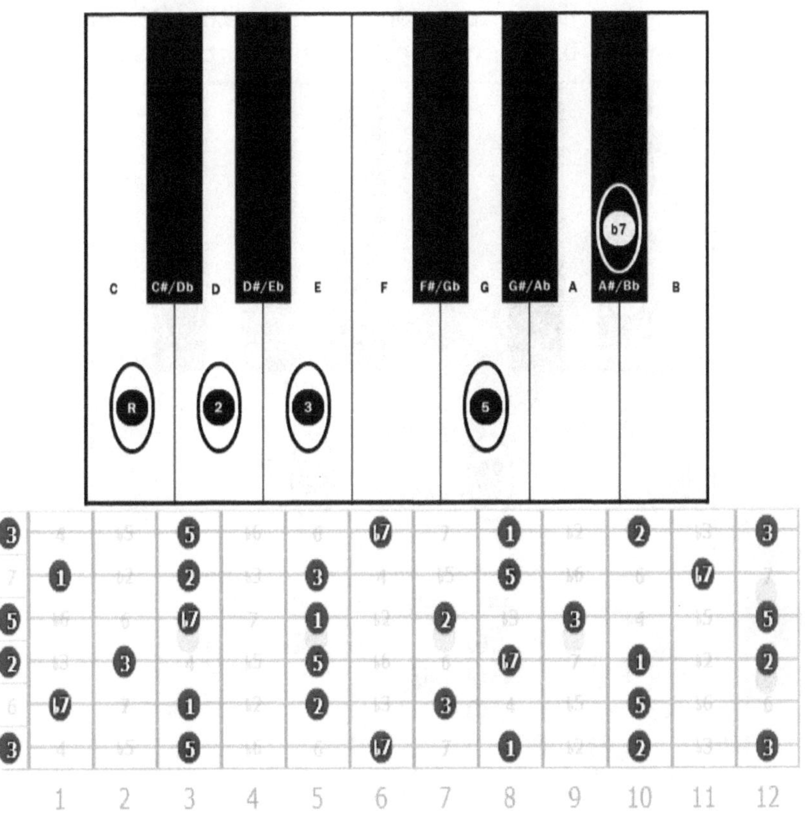

Dominant b9 (R b2 3 5 b7)

Is in the Augmented Major Scale on the b6th
Is in the Melodic Minor Scale on the 4th
Is in the Harmonic Major Scales on the 4th and b6th
Is in the Diminished Scale Event on the 1st

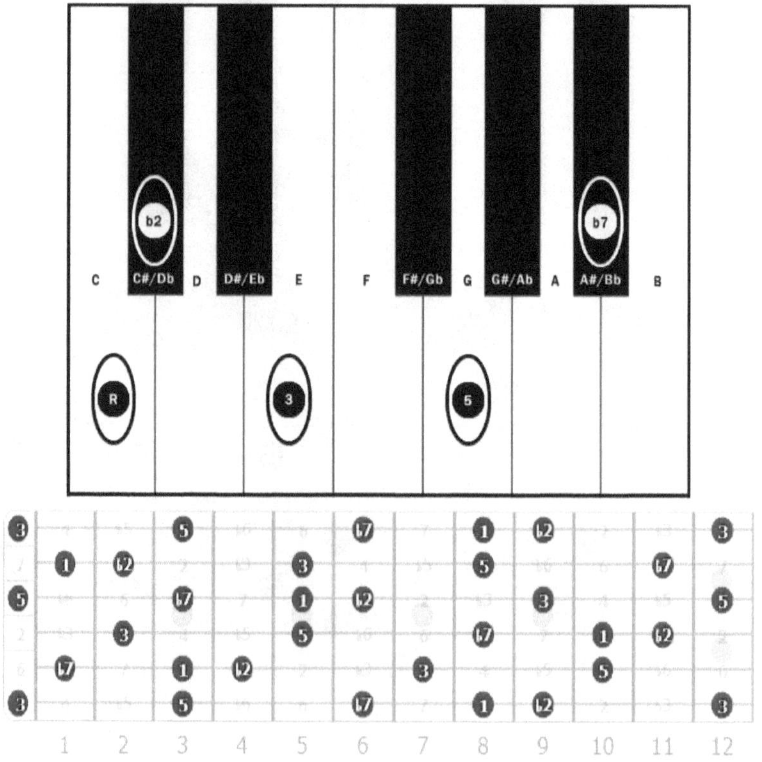

Dominant #9 (R #2 3 5 b7)

Is in the Harmonic Major Scale on the b6th
Is in the Hungarian Minor Event on the 3rd
Is in the Diminished Scale Event on the 1st

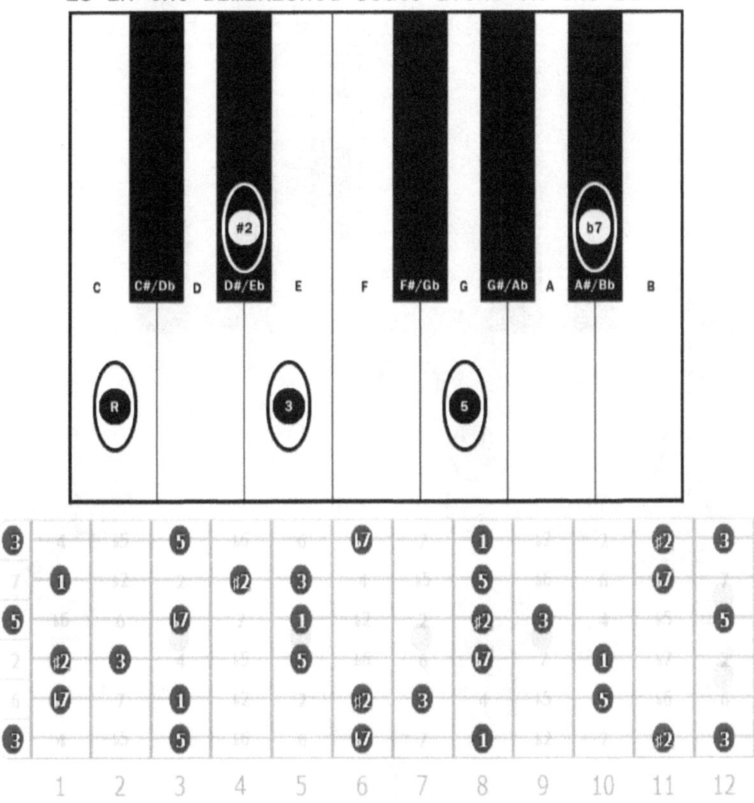

Dominant #9 b5 (R #2 3 b5 b7)

Is in the Melodic Minor Scale on the b2nd
Is in the Hungarian Minor Event on the 3rd
Is in the Diminished Scale Event on the 1st

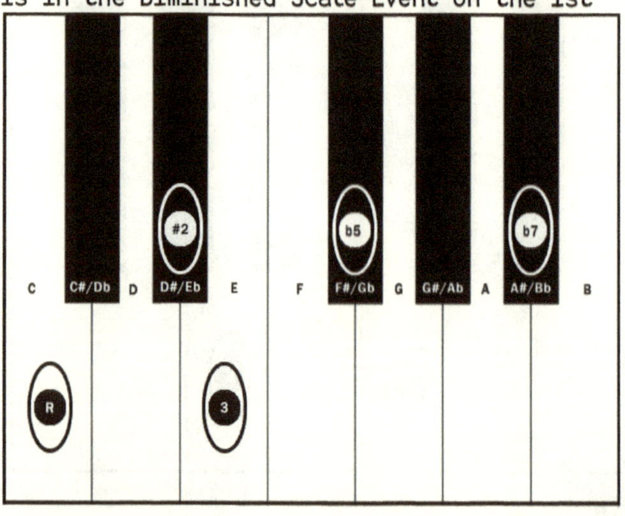

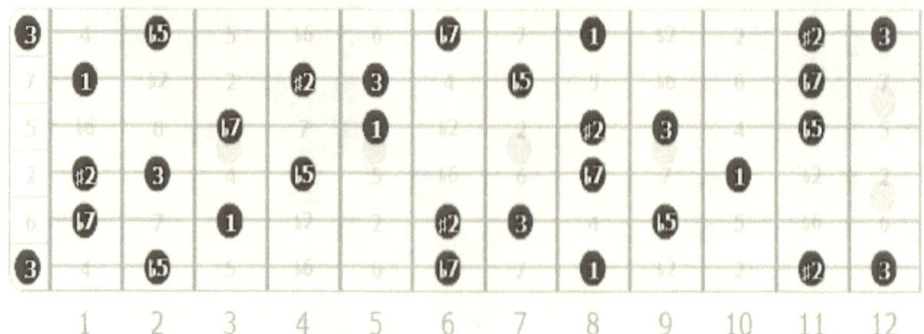

Dominant 7 Add #11 (R 3 #4 5 b7)

Is in the Melodic Minor Scale on the 5th
Is in the Hungarian Minor Event on the 3rd
Is in the Diminished Scale Event on the 1st

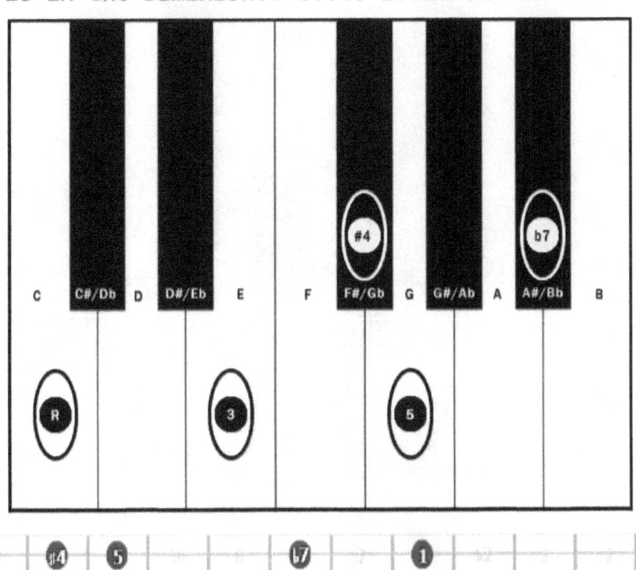

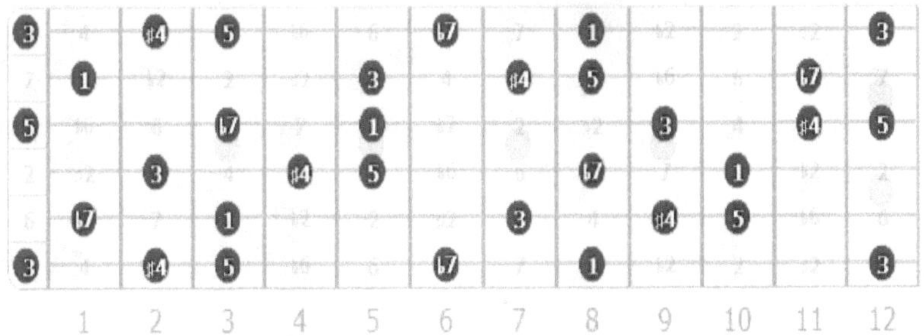

Dominant 7 Add 13 (R 3 5 6 b7)

Is in the Major Scale on the 4th
Is in the Melodic Minor Scale on the 5th
Is in the Harmonic Major Scale on the 4th
Is in the Diminished Scale Event on the 1st

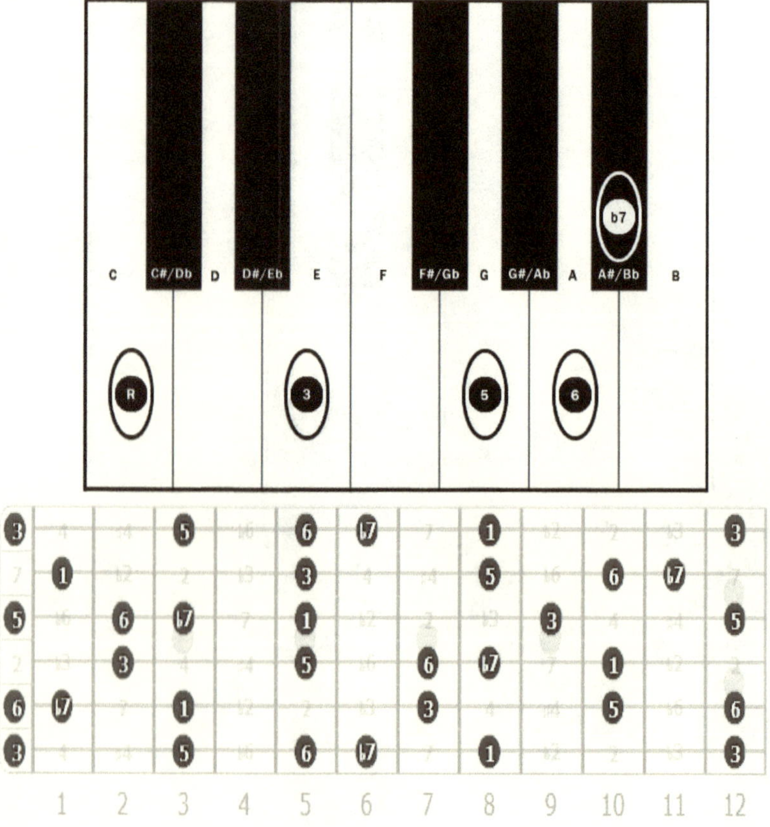

Dominant 7 Add b13 (R 3 5 b6 b7)

Is in the Augmented Major Scales on the b6th
Is in the Melodic Minor Scale on the 4th
Is in the Harmonic Major Scale on the b6th

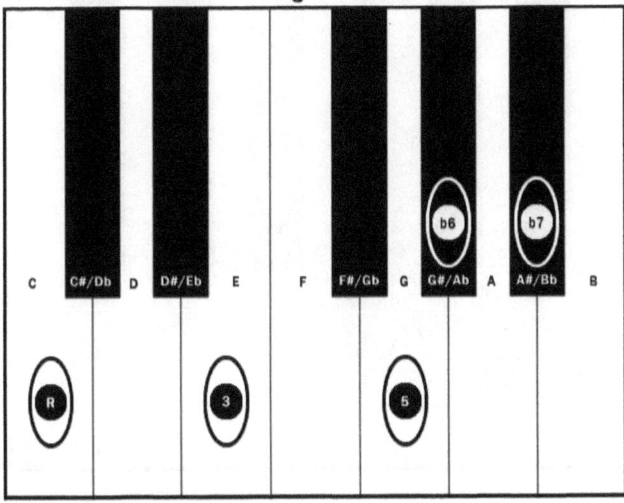

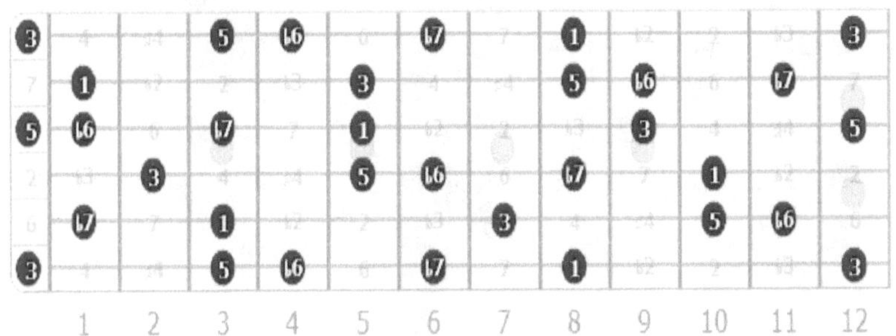

Dominant 9 b5 (R 2 3 b5 b7)

Is in the Melodic Minor Scale on the 5th
Is in the Whole Tone Scale Event on the 1st

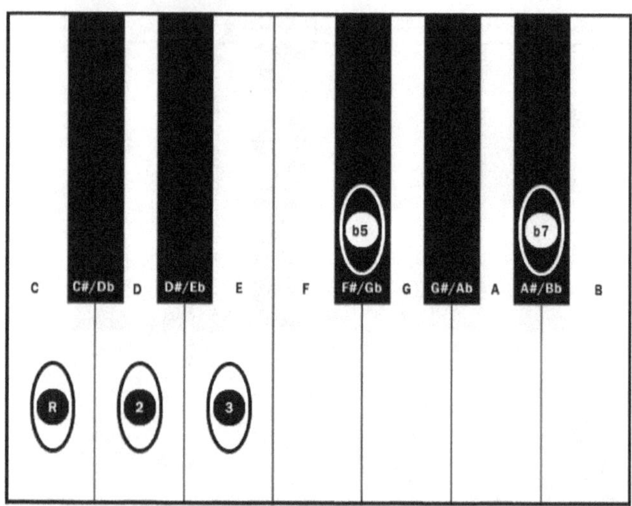

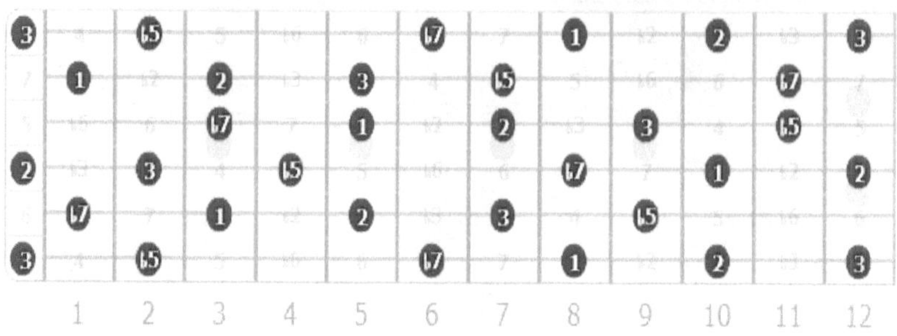

Dominant 7 Add 11 (R 3 4 5 b7)

Is in the Major Scale on the 4th
Is in the Augmented Major Scales on the b6th
Is in the Melodic Minor Scale on the 4th
Is in the Harmonic Major Scale on the 4th

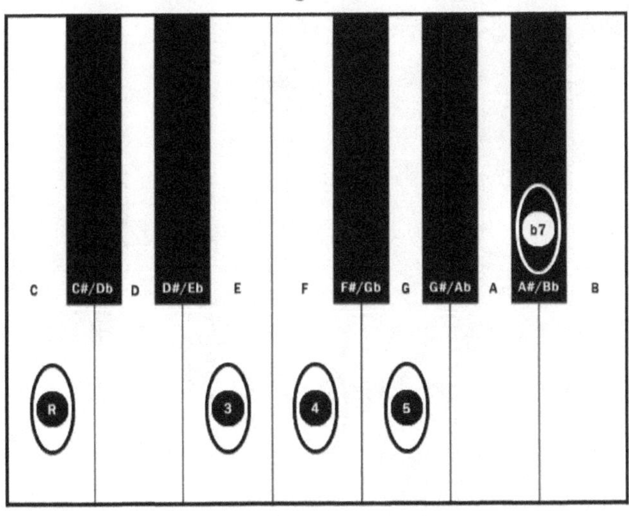

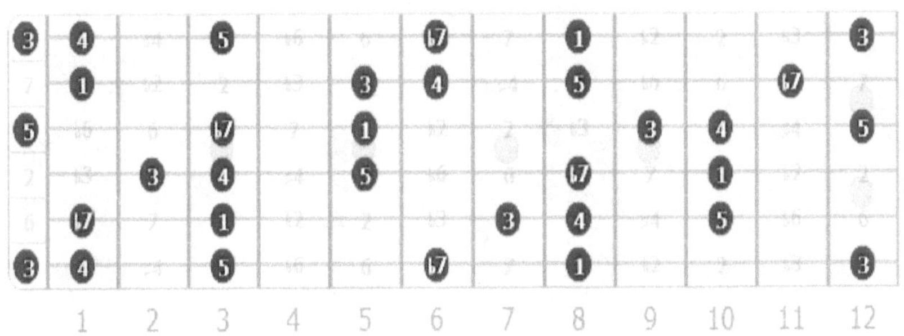

Minor7 Add 11 (R b3 4 5 b7)

Is in the Major Scales on the b3rd, b6th and b7th
Is in the Melodic Minor Scale on the b7th
Is in the Pentatonic Major Event on the b3rd
Is in the Pentatonic Minor Event on the 1st
Is in the Blues Event on the 1st

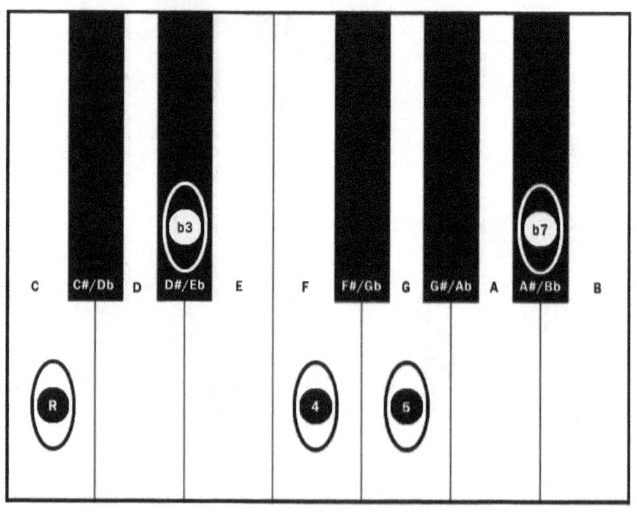

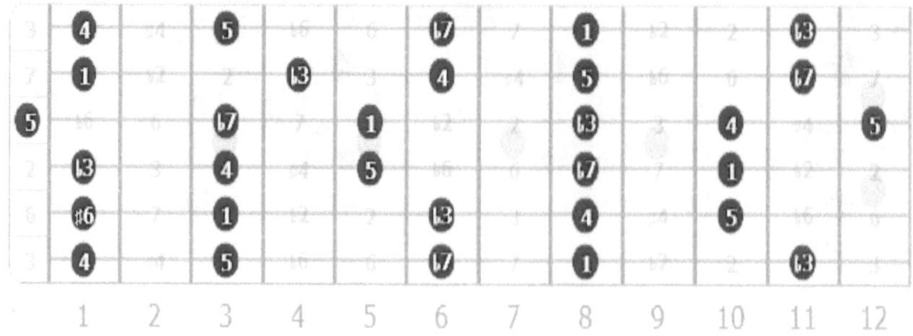

Minor 7 Add #11 (R b3 #4 5 b7)

Is in the Augmented Major Scale on the b7th
Is in the Blues Event on the 1st
Is in the Diminished Scale Event on the 1st

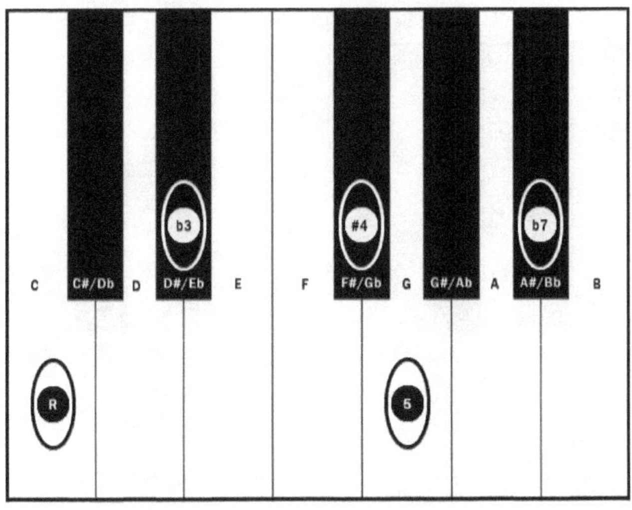

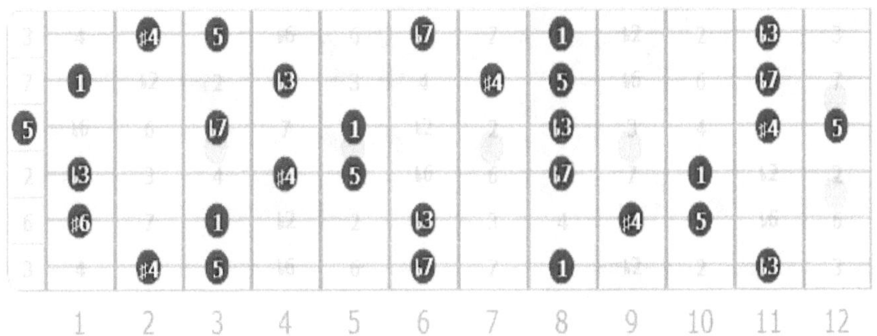

Minor 7 Augmented 4th Add 13 (R #4 5 6 b7)

Is in the Augmented Major Scale on the b7th
Is in the Melodic Minor Scale on the 5th
Is in the Diminished Scale Event on the 1st

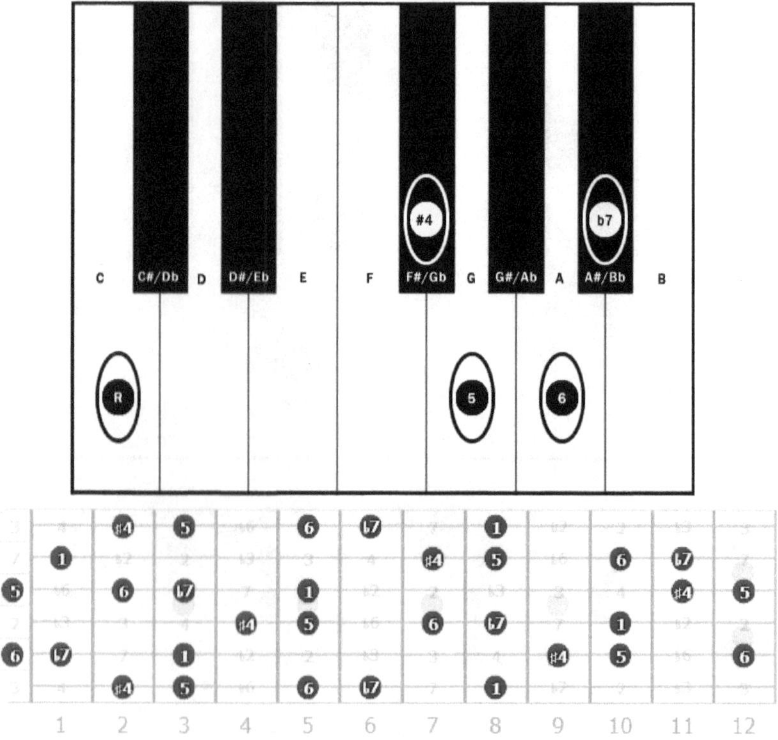

Minor9 (R 2 b3 5 b7)

Is in the Major Scales on the b3rd and b7th
Is in the Augmented Major Scale on the b7th

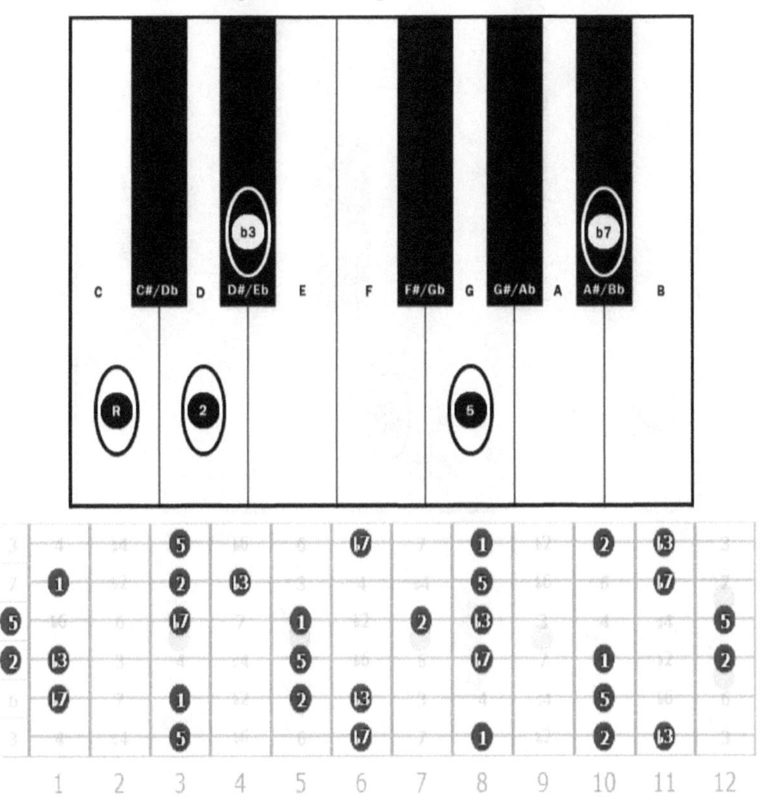

Minor Add 9 Add 11 (R 2 b3 4 5)

Is in the Major Scales on the b3rd and b7th
Is in the Augmented Major Scale on the b3rd

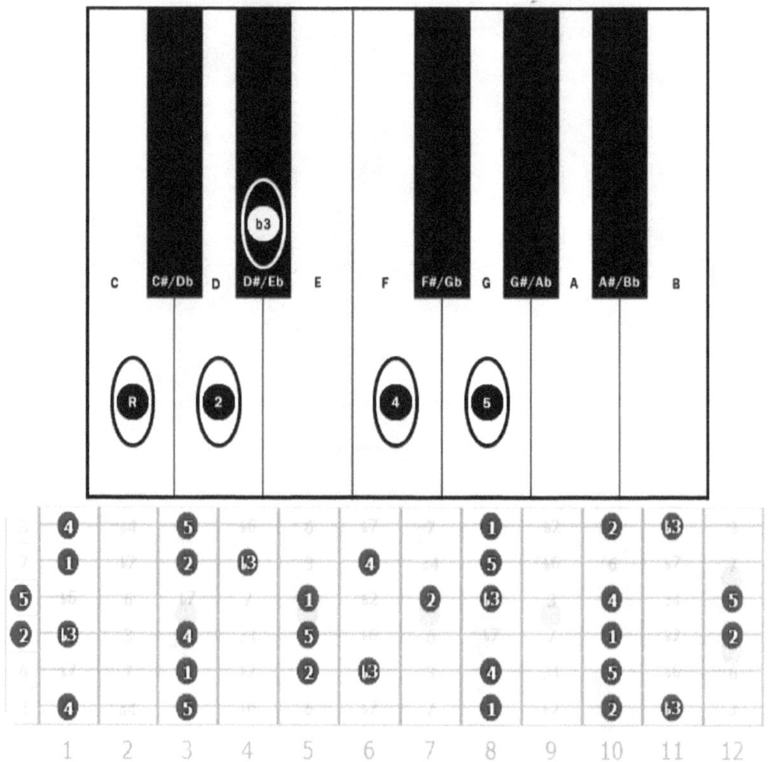

Minor Add 9 Add #11 (R 2 b3 #4 5)

Is in the Augmented Major Scale on the b7th
Is in the Harmonic Major Scale on the 5th
Is in the Hungarian Minor Scale Event on the 1st

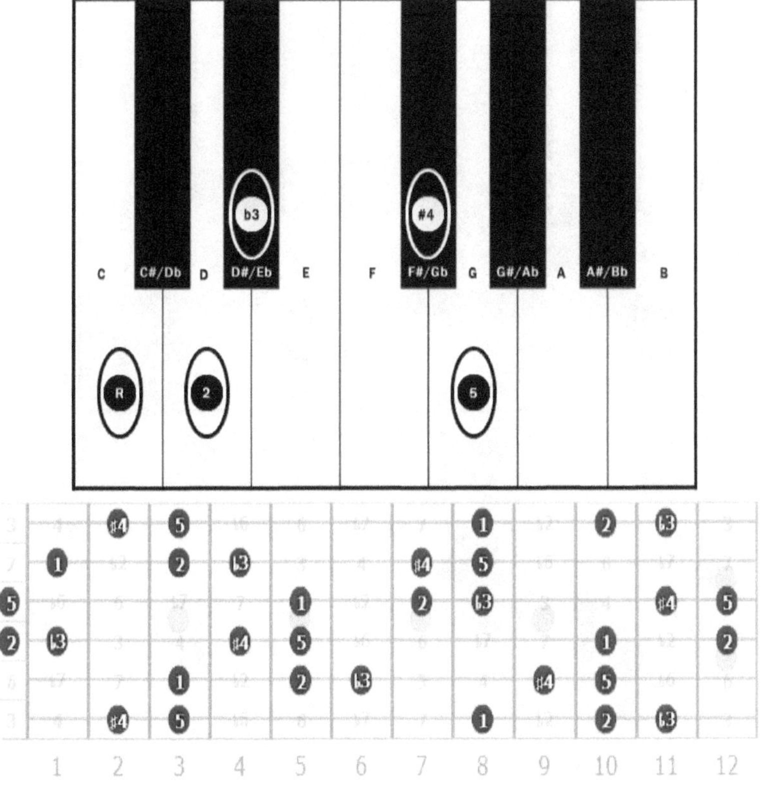

Minor Add b9 Add #11 (R b2 b3 #4 5)

Is on the Diminished Scale Event on the 1st

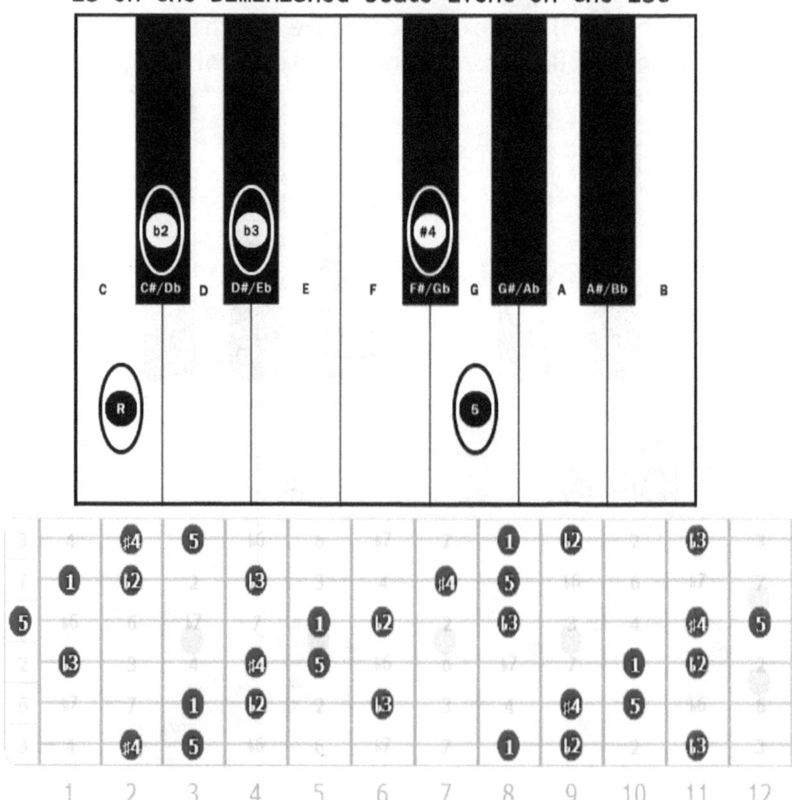

Minor-Major7 Add 11 (R b3 4 5 7)

Is in the Augmented Major Scale on the b3rd
Is in the Melodic Minor Scale on the 1st
Is in the Harmonic Major Scale on the 1st

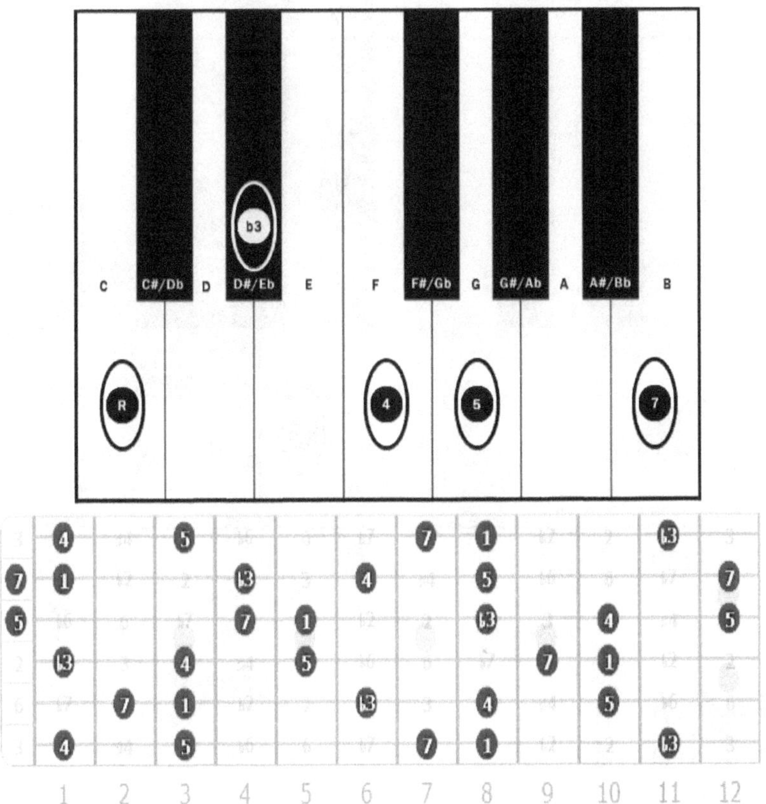

Minor-Major7 Add #11 (R b3 #4 5 7)

Is in the Augmented Major Scale on the 5th
Is in the Harmonic Major Scale on the 5th
Is in the Hungarian Minor Scale Event on the 1st and 3rd

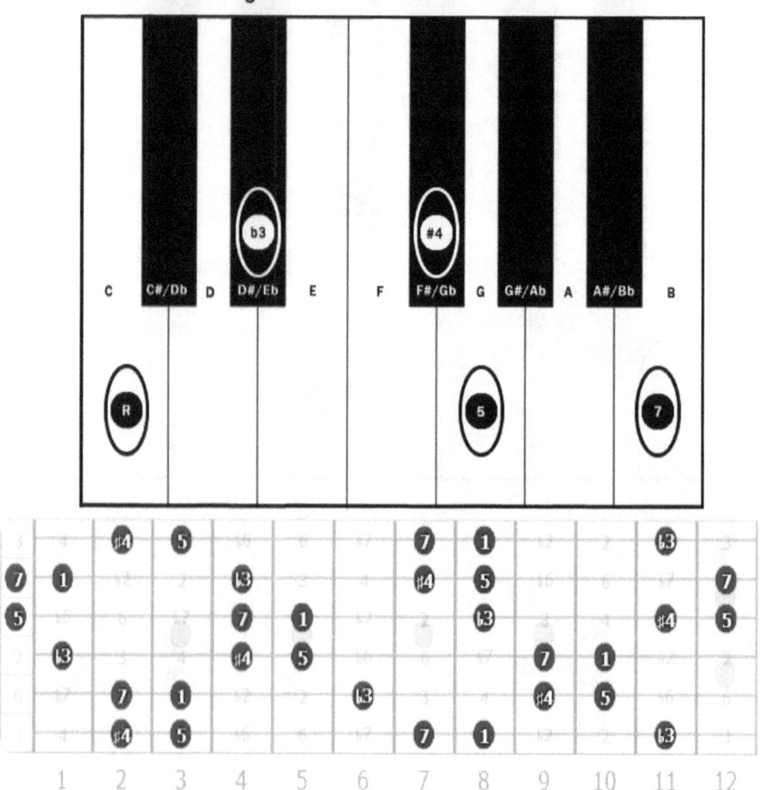

Minor-Major9 (R 2 b3 5 7)

Is in the Augmented Major Scale on the b3rd
Is in the Melodic Minor Scale on the 1st
Is in the Harmonic Major Scale on the 5th
Is in the Hungarian Minor Scale Event on the 1st

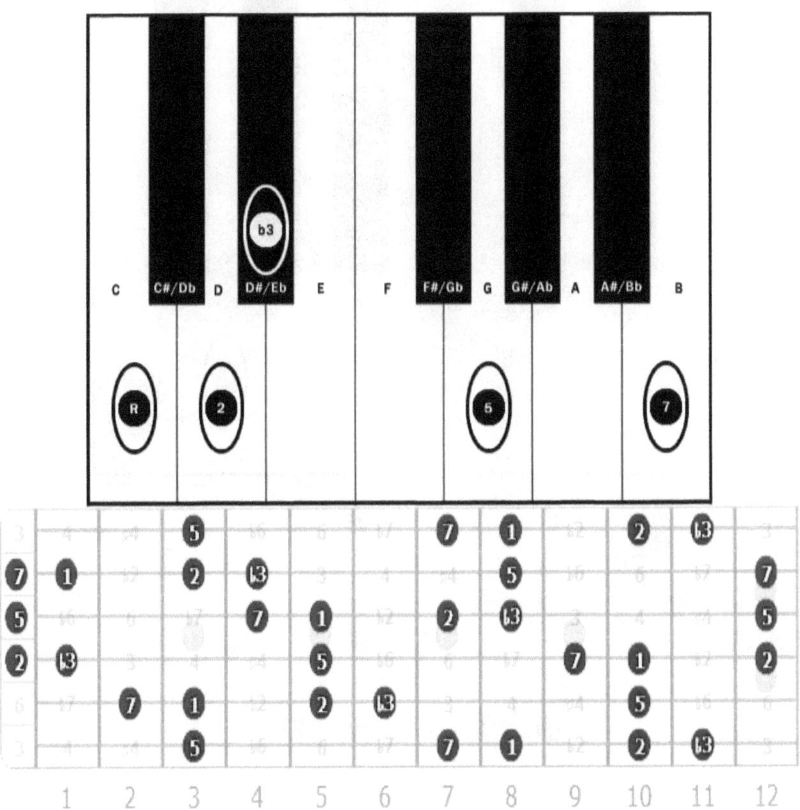

Augmented Minor-Major7 Add 13 (R b3 #5 6 7)

Is in the Harmonic Major Scale on the 3rd
Is in the Hungarian Minor Scale Event on the 6th
Is in the Diminished Scale Event on the 7th

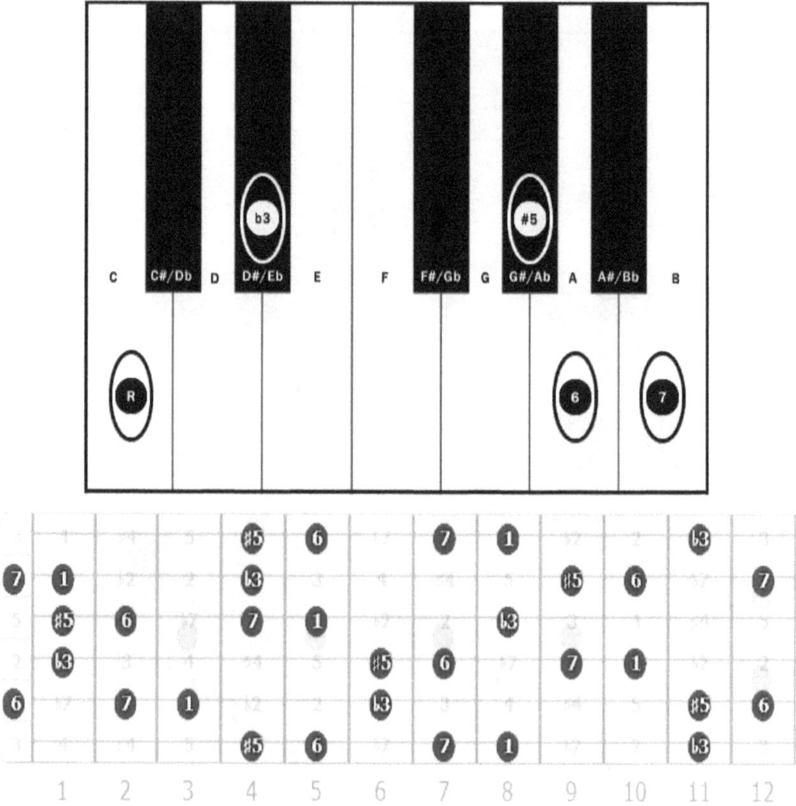

Half Diminished 9th (R 2 b3 b5 b7)

Is in the Augmented Major Scale on the b7th
Is in the Melodic Minor Scale on the b3rd
Is in the Harmonic Major Scale on the b7th

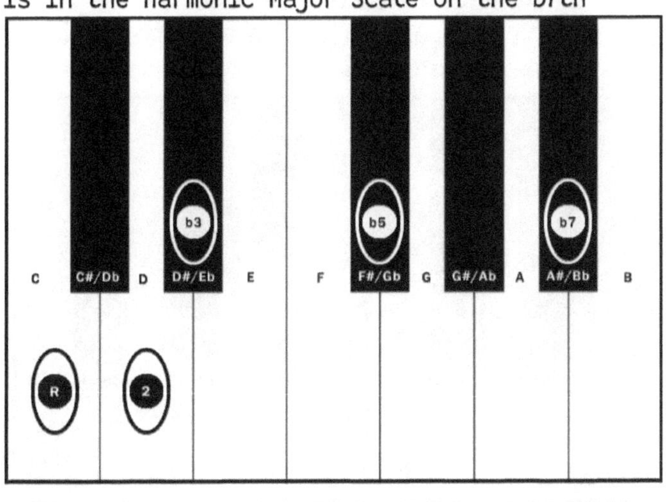

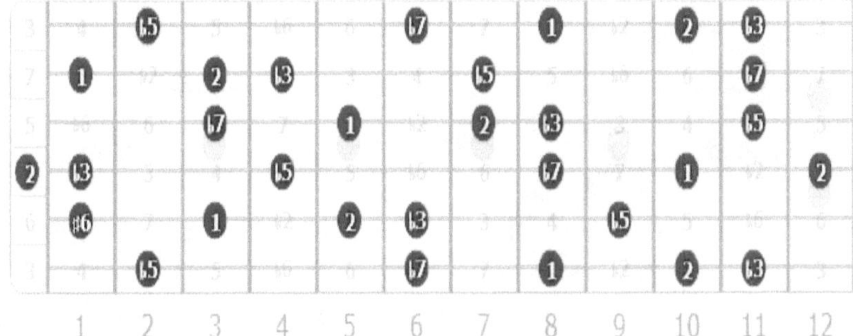

Half Diminished 7th Add 11 (R b3 4 b5 b7)

Is in the Major Scale on the b2nd
Is in the Augmented Major Scale on the b2
Is in the Melodic Minor Scale on the b3rd
Is in the Harmonic Major Scale on the b7th
Is in the Blues Scale Event on the 1st

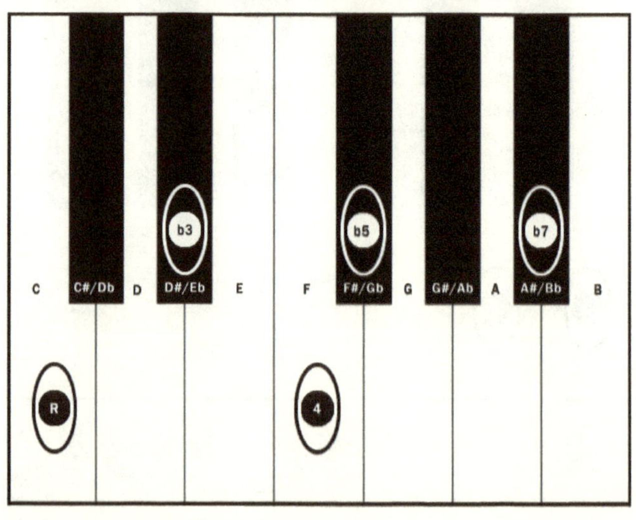

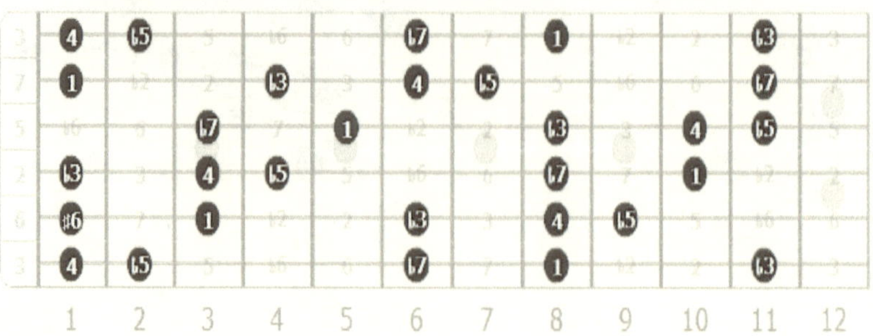

Diminished b9 (R b2 b3 b5 b7)

Is in the Augmented Major Scale on the b2 and 3rd
Is in the Harmonic Major Scale on the b2nd
Is in the Diminished Scale Event on the 1st

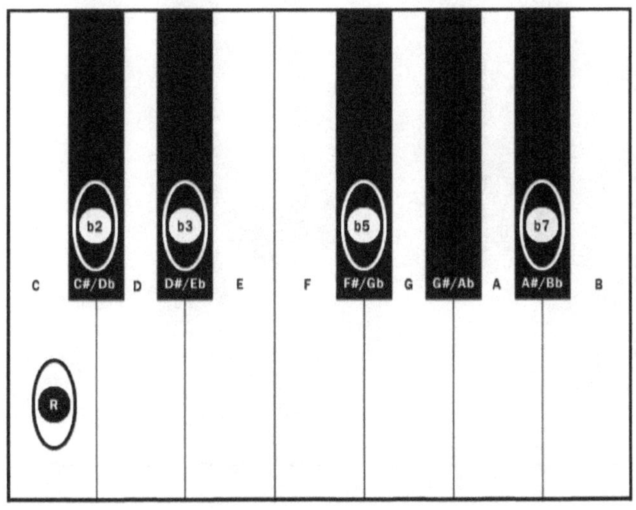

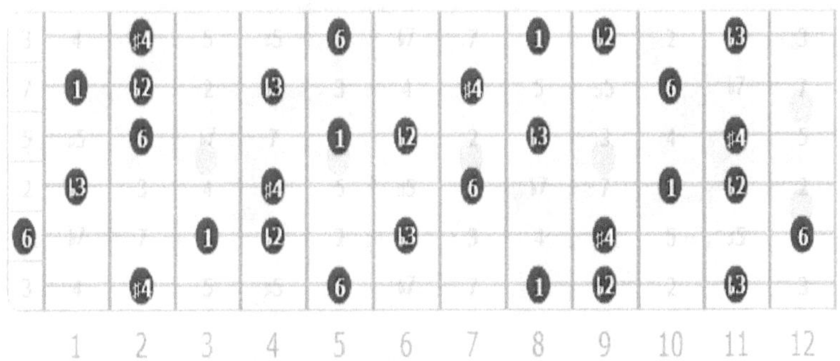

Major 9 b5 (R 2 3 b5 7)

Is in the Major Scale on the 5th
Is in the Melodic Minor Scale on the 6th

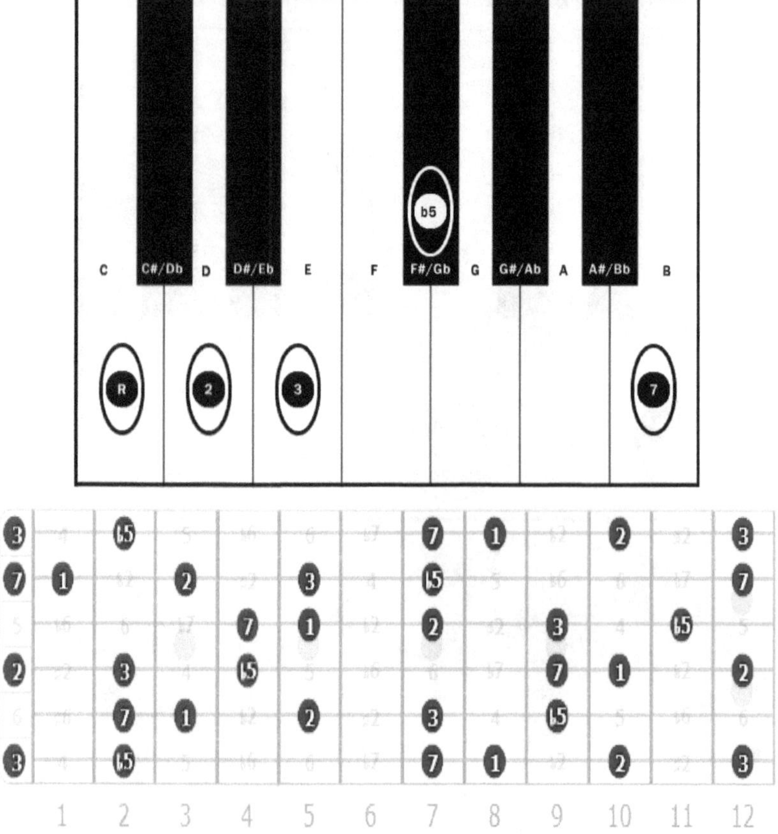

6 NOTE CHORDS

Major #9 Add b13 (R #2 3 5 b6 7)

Is in the Hungarian Minor Scale Event on the 1st

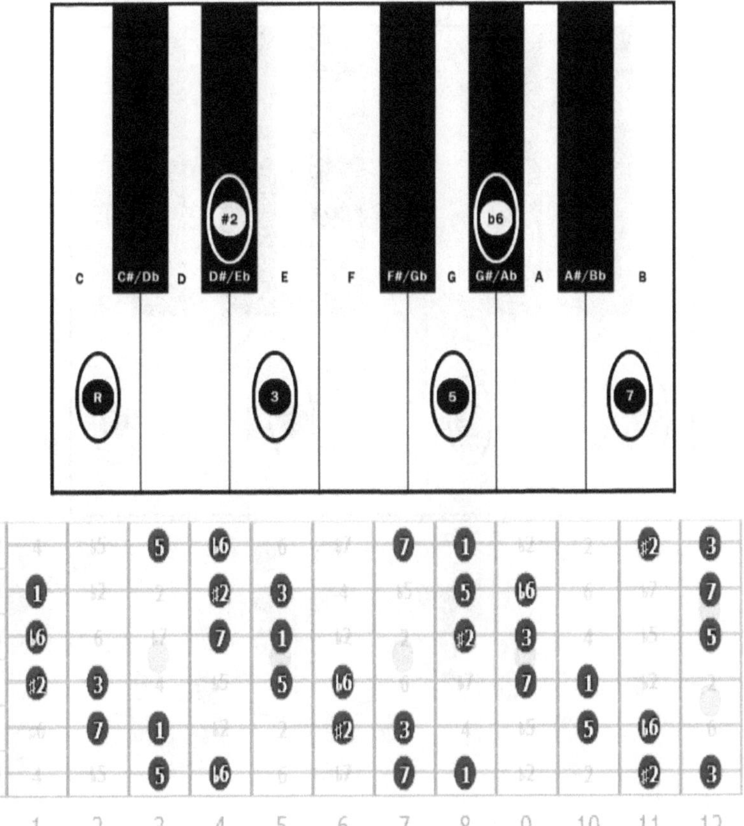

Major #11 #9 (R #2 3 #4 5 7)

Is in the Augmented Major Scale on the 5th
Is in the Hungarian Minor Scale Event on the 3rd

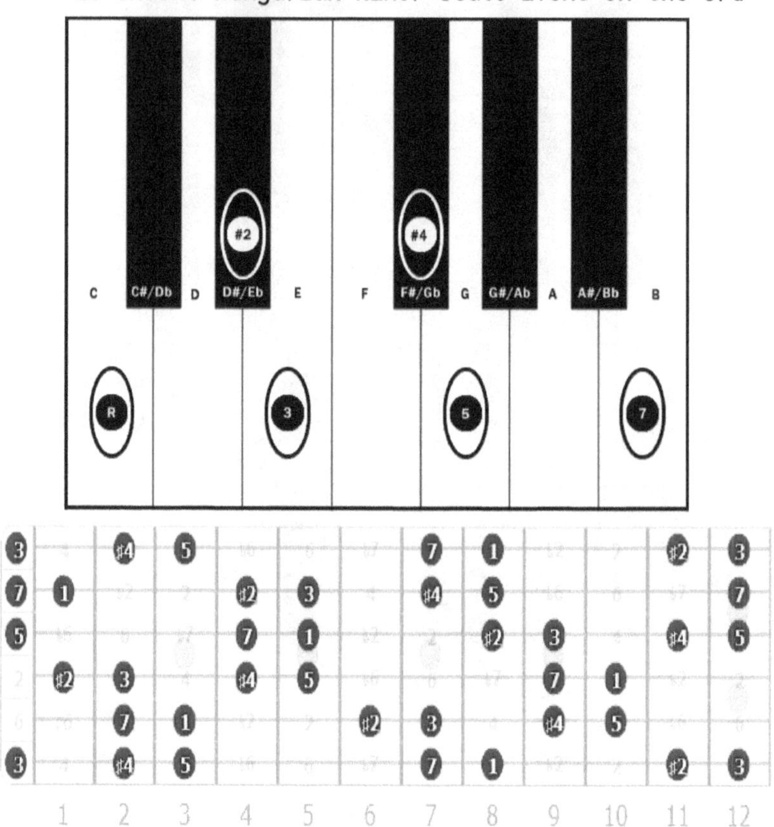

Major 11 (R 2 3 4 5 7)

Is in the Major Scale on the 1st

Is in the Harmonic Major Scale on the 1st

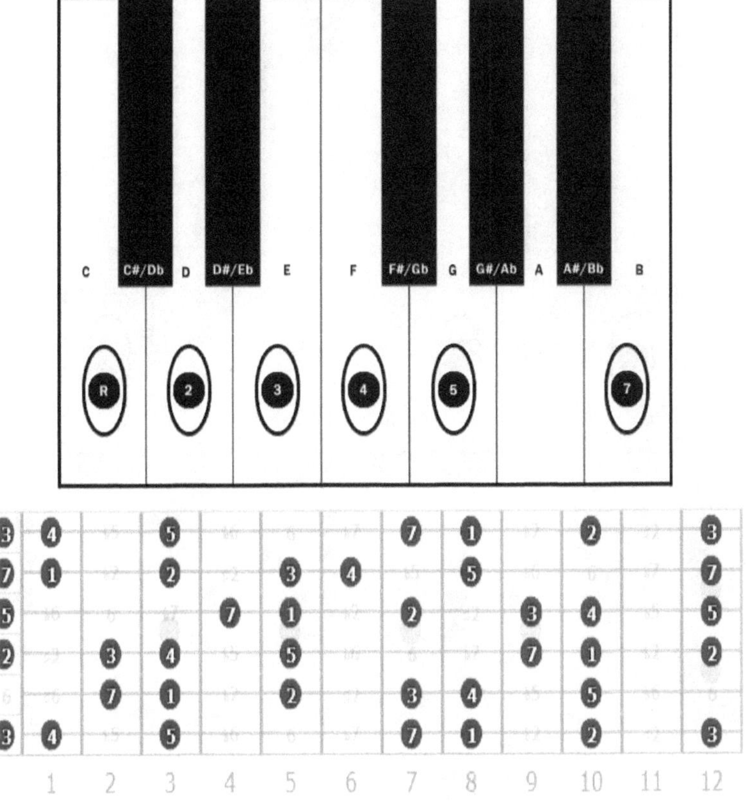

Major #11 (R 2 3 #4 5 7)

Is in the Major Scale on the 5th

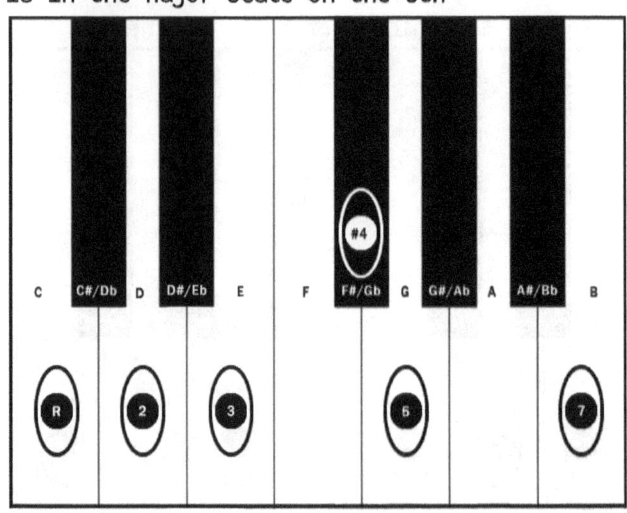

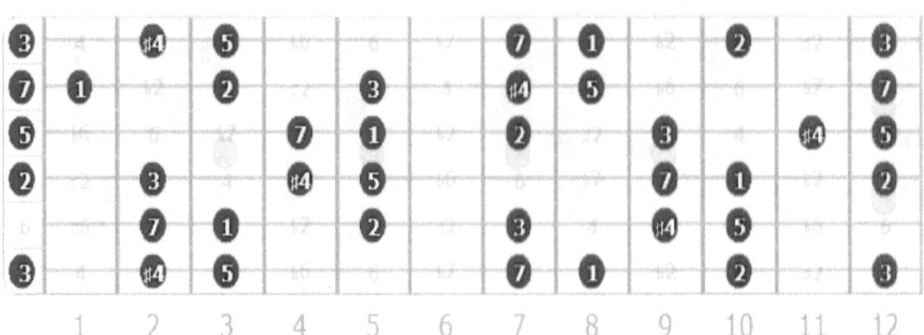

Major 9 Add b13 (R 2 3 5 b6 7)

Is in the Harmonic Major Scale on the 1st

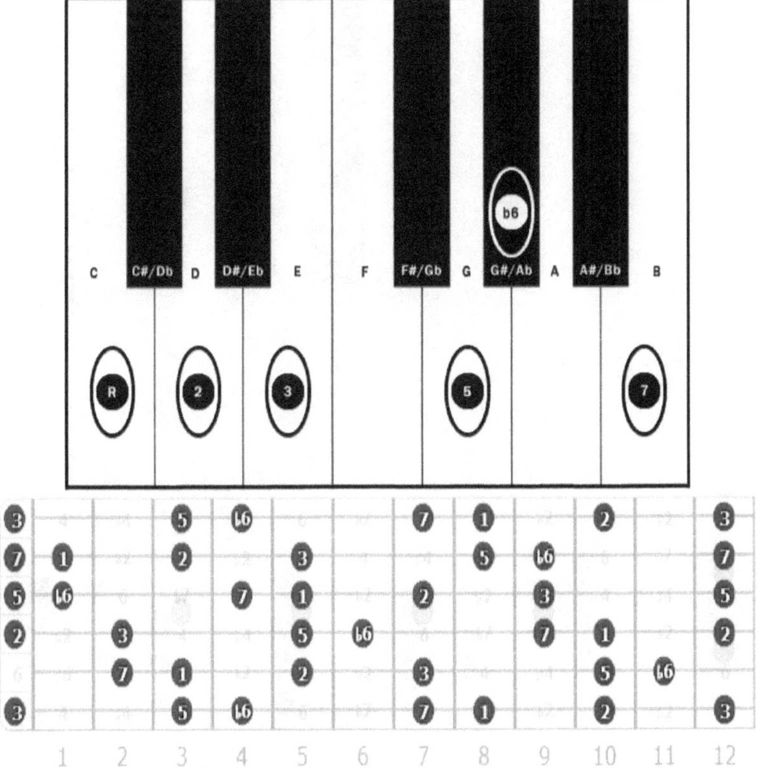

Minor #11 (R 2 b3 #4 5 b7)

Is in the Augmented Major Scale on the b7th

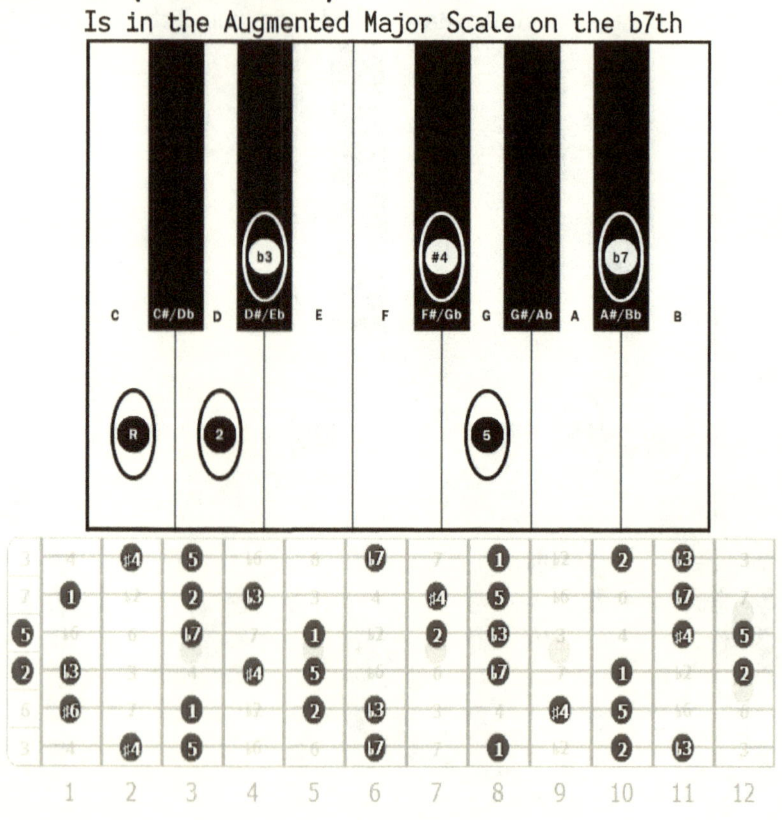

Minor 9 Add 13 (R 2 b3 5 6 b7)

Is in the Major Scale on the b7th
Is in the Augmented Major Scale on the b7th

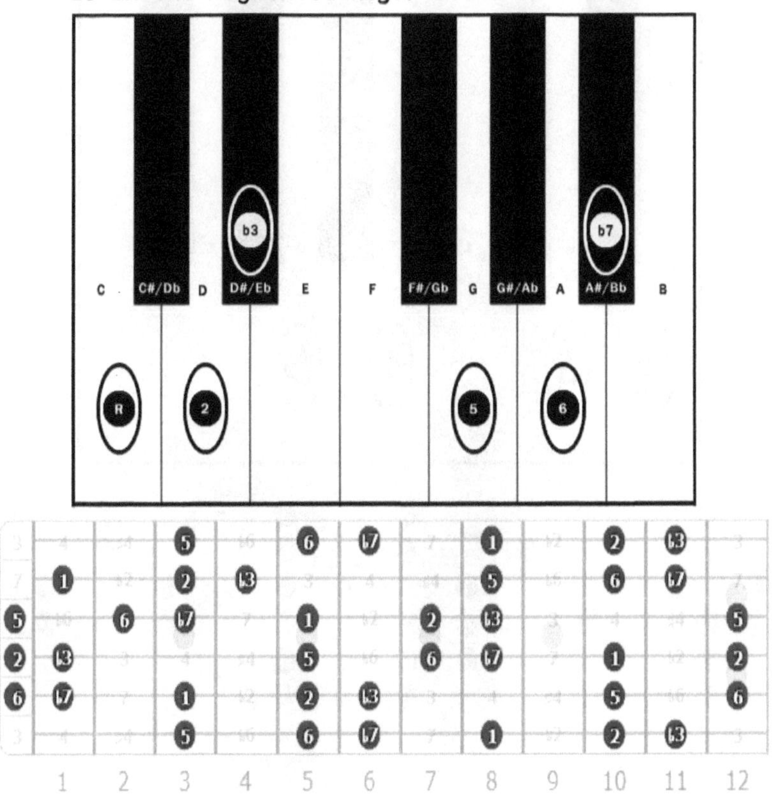

Minor 11 (R 2 b3 4 5 b7)

Is in the Major Scales on the b3rd and b7th

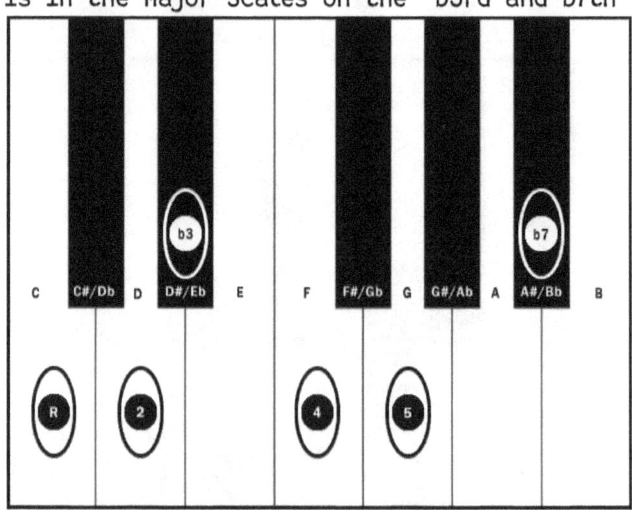

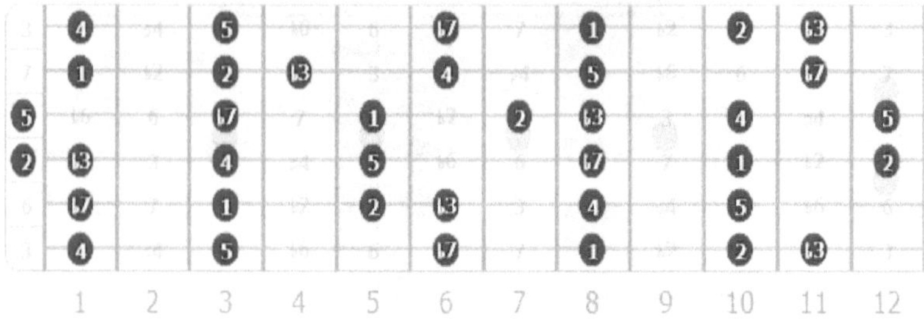

Minor b9 Add 13 (R b2 b3 5 6 b7)

Is in the Melodic Minor Scale on the b7th
Is in the Diminished Scale Event on the 1st

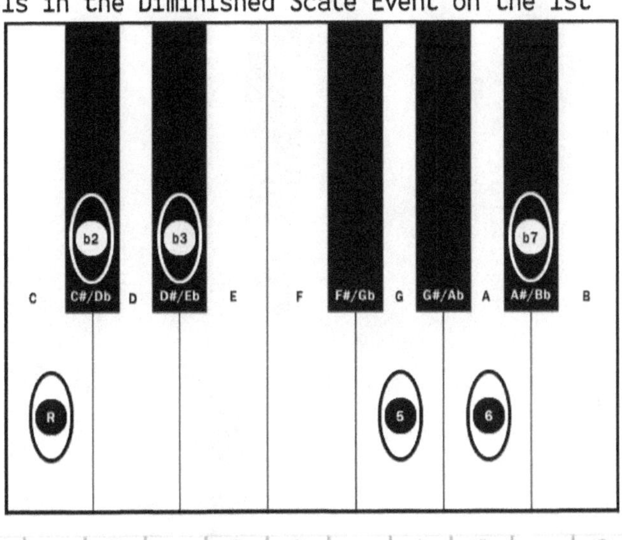

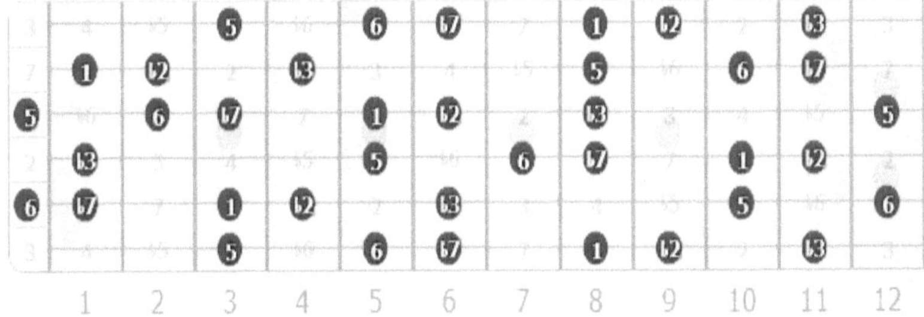

Dominant #11 b9 (R b2 3 #4 5 b7)

Is in the Diminished Scale Event on the 1st

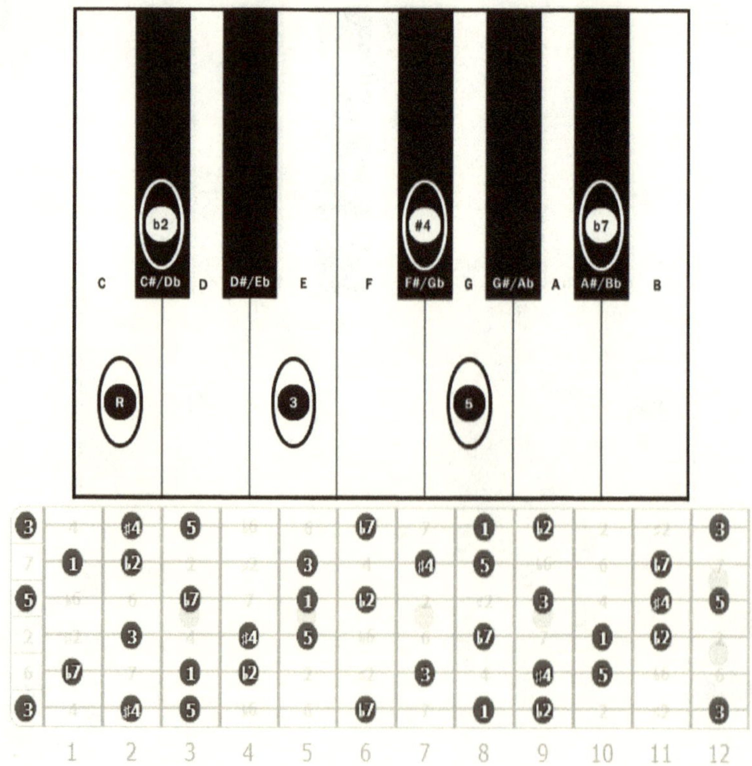

Dominant #9 b5 Add 13 (R #2 3 b5 6 b7)

Is in the Diminished Scale Event on the 1st

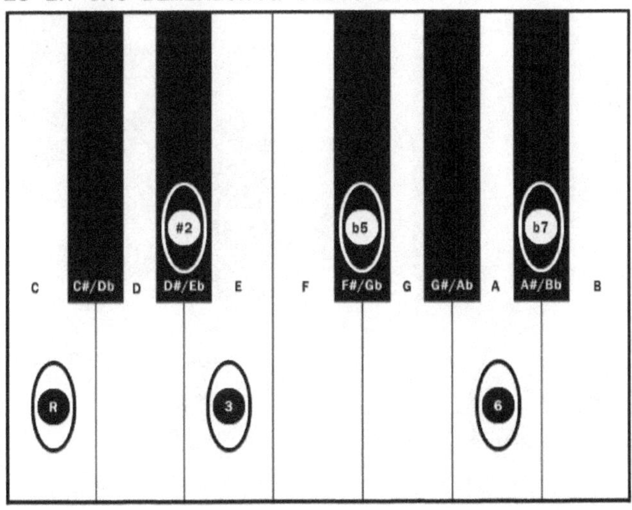

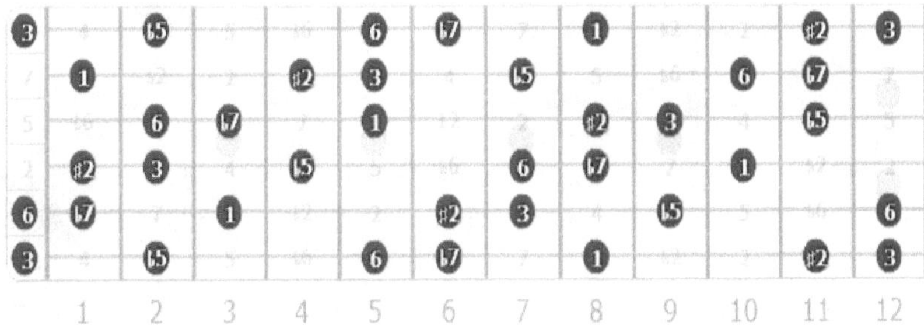

Dominant #11 (R 2 3 #4 5 b7)

Is in the Melodic Minor Scale on the 5th

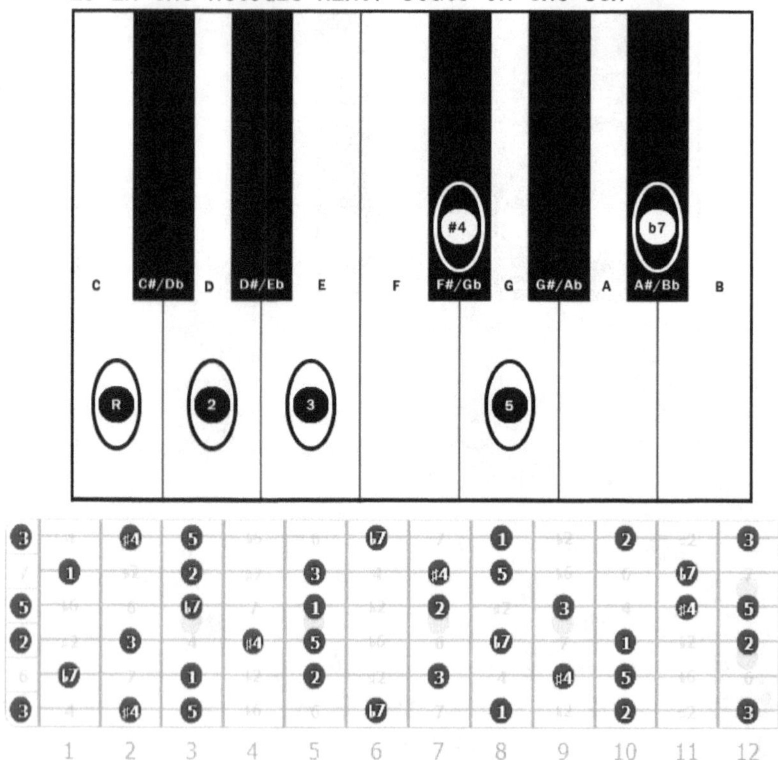

Dominant 9 Add b13 (R 2 3 5 b6 b7)

Is in the Melodic Minor Scale on the 4th

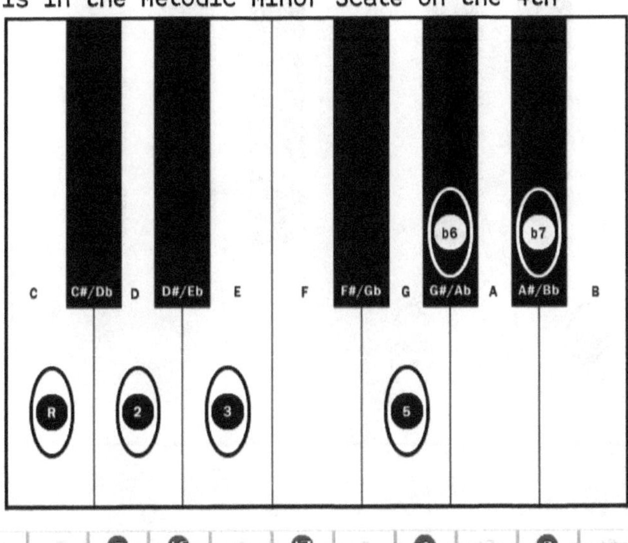

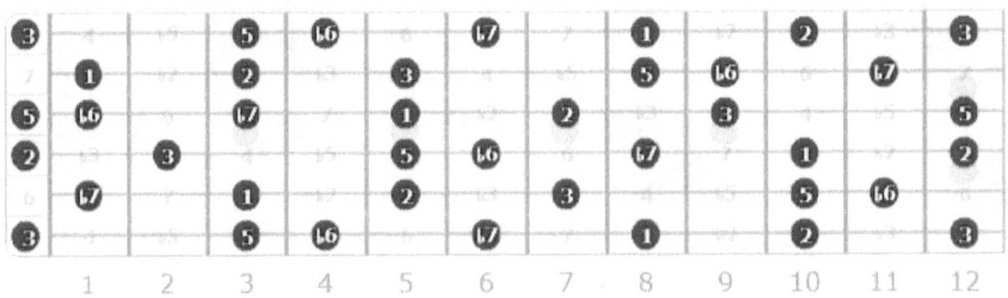

Dominant 9 b5 Add b13 (R 2 3 b5 b6 b7)

Is in the Whole Tone Scale Event on the 1st

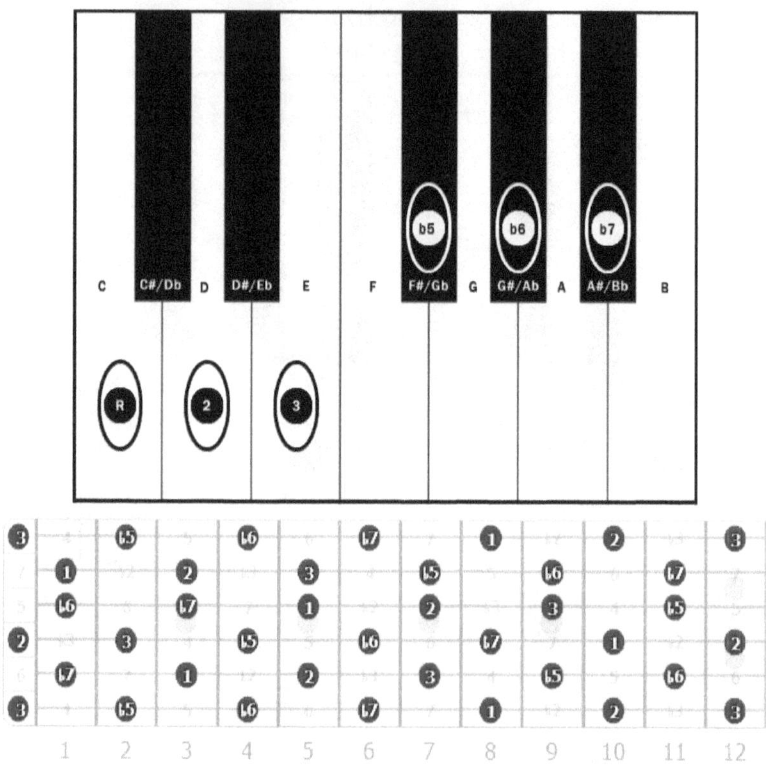

Dominant 11 b9 (R b2 3 4 5 b7)

is in the Augmented Major Scale on the b6th
Is in the Harmonic Major Scale on the 4th

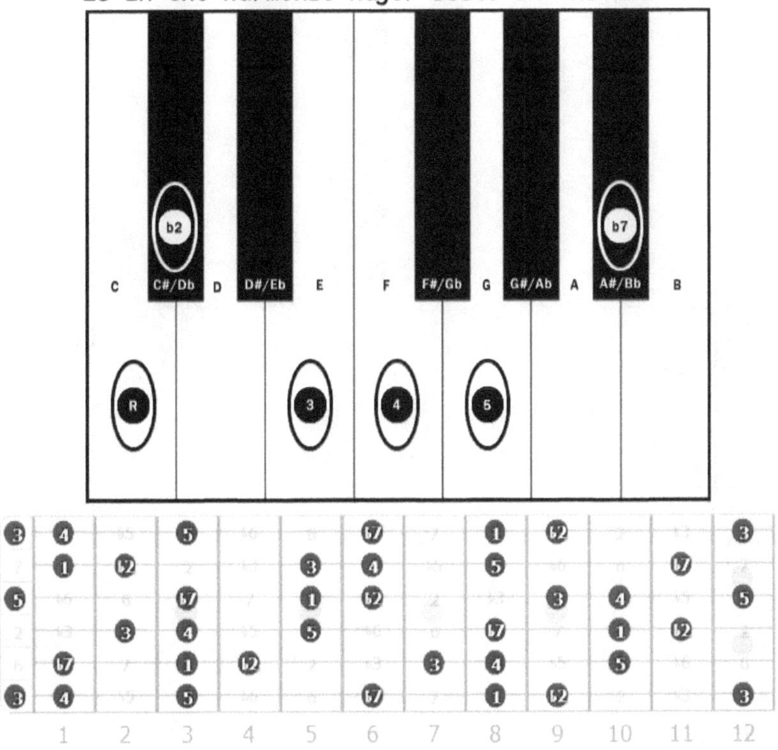

Dominant 11 (R 2 3 4 5 b7)

Is in the Major Scale on the 4th
Is in the Melodic Minor Scale on the 4th

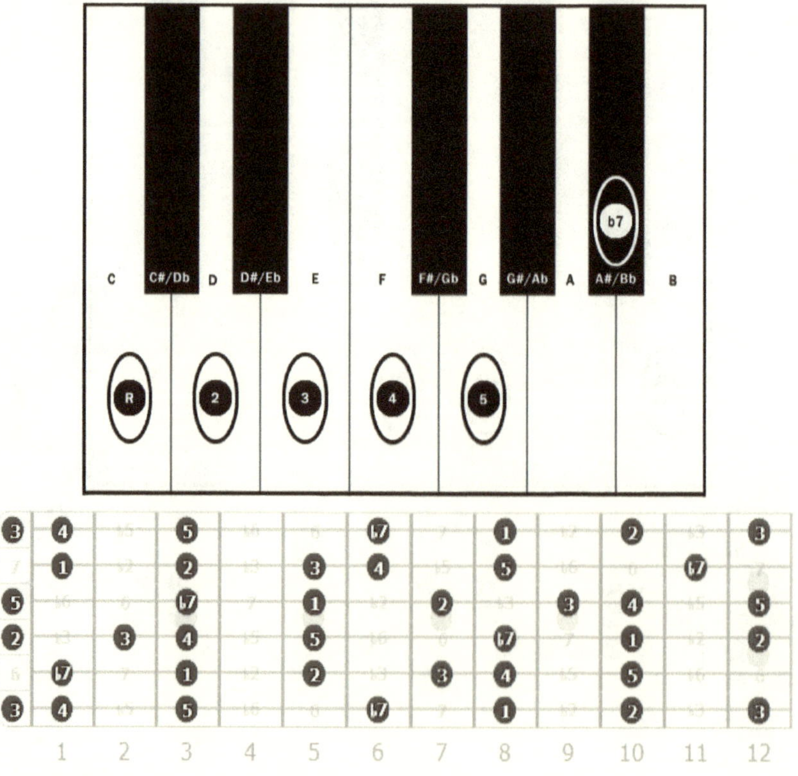

Minor-Major 11 (R 2 b3 4 5 7)

Is in the Augmented Major Scale on the b3rd
Is in the Melodic Minor Scale on the 1st

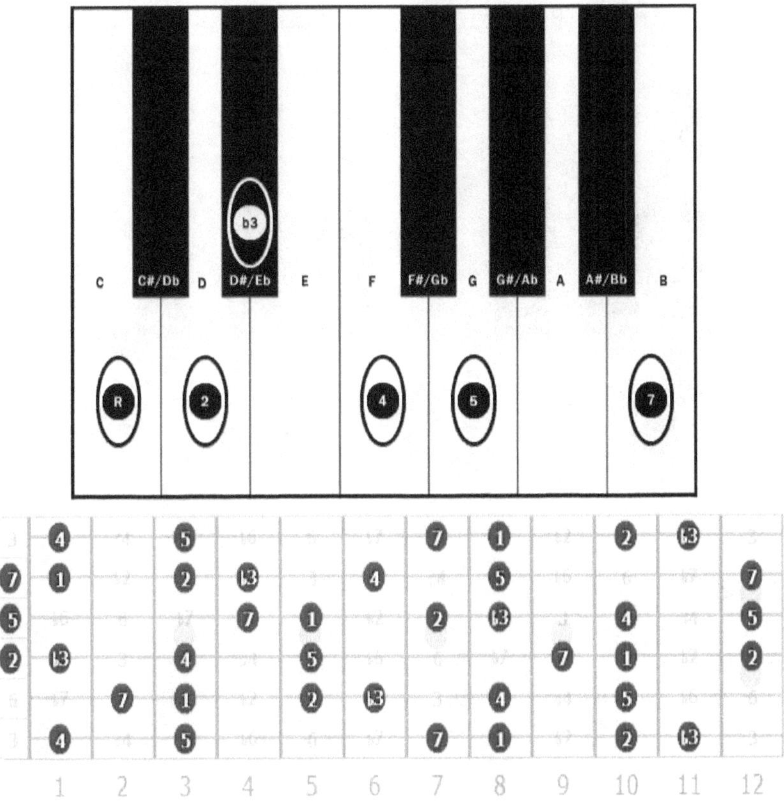

Minor-Major #11 (R 2 b3 #4 5 7)

Is in the Harmonic Major Scale on the 5th
Is in the Hungarian Minor Scale Event on the 1st

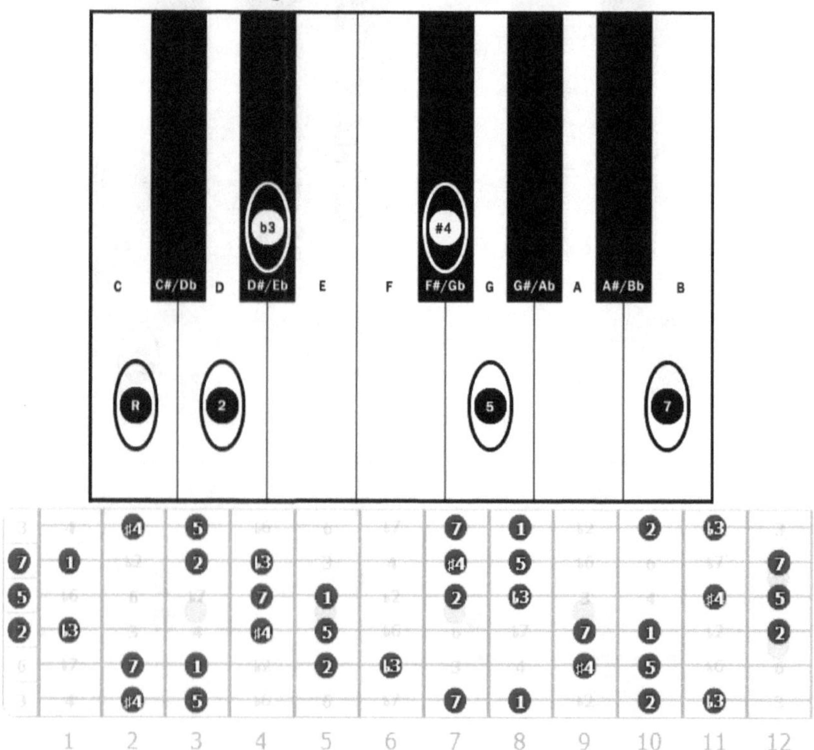

Augmented Minor-Major 9 Add 13 (R 2 b3 #5 6 7)

Is in the Hungarian Minor Scale Event on the 1st
Is in the Diminished Scale Event on the 7th

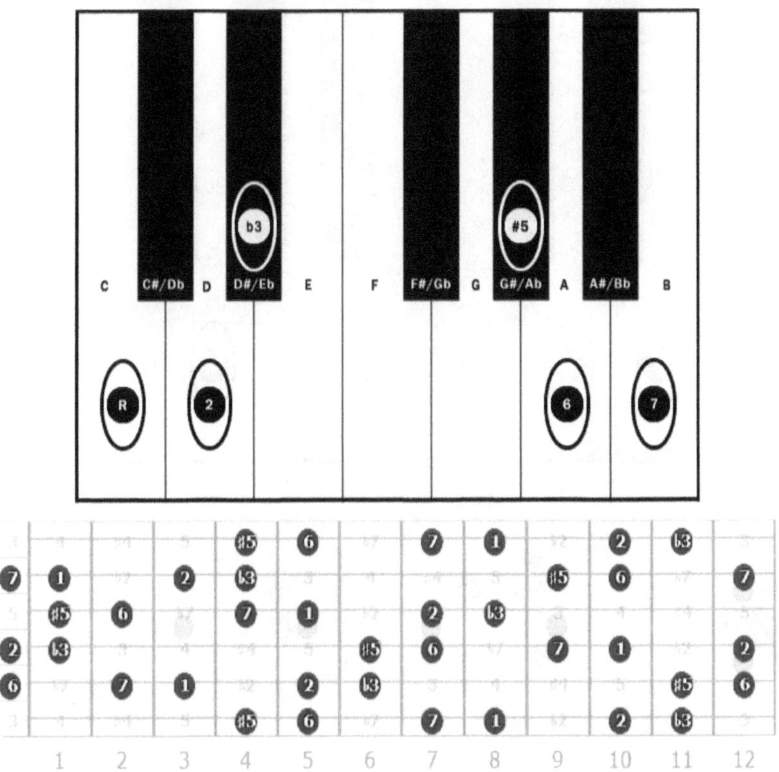

Half Diminished 9 Add 13 (R 2 b3 b5 6 b7)

Is in the Augmented Major Scale on the b7th
Is in the Harmonic Major Scale on the b7th

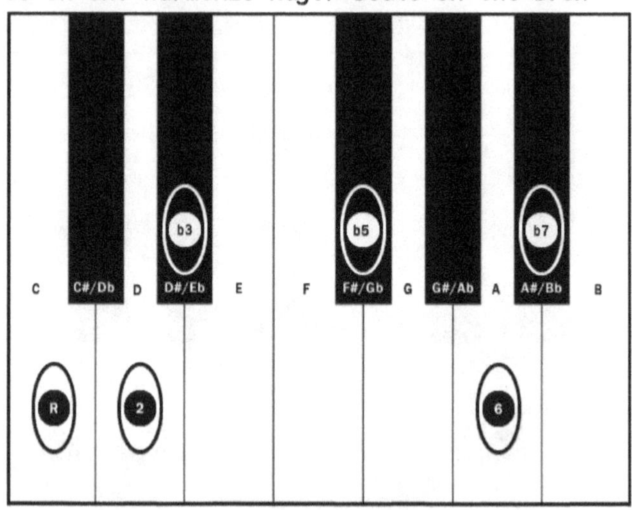

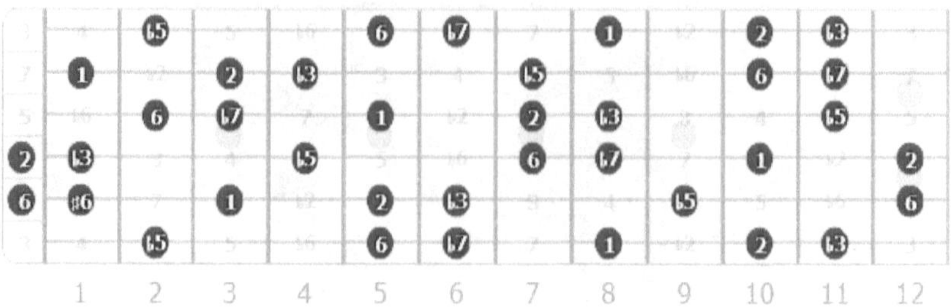

Half Diminished 11th (R 2 b3 4 b5 b7)

Is in the Melodic Minor Scale on the b3rd

Is in the Harmonic Major Scale on the b7th

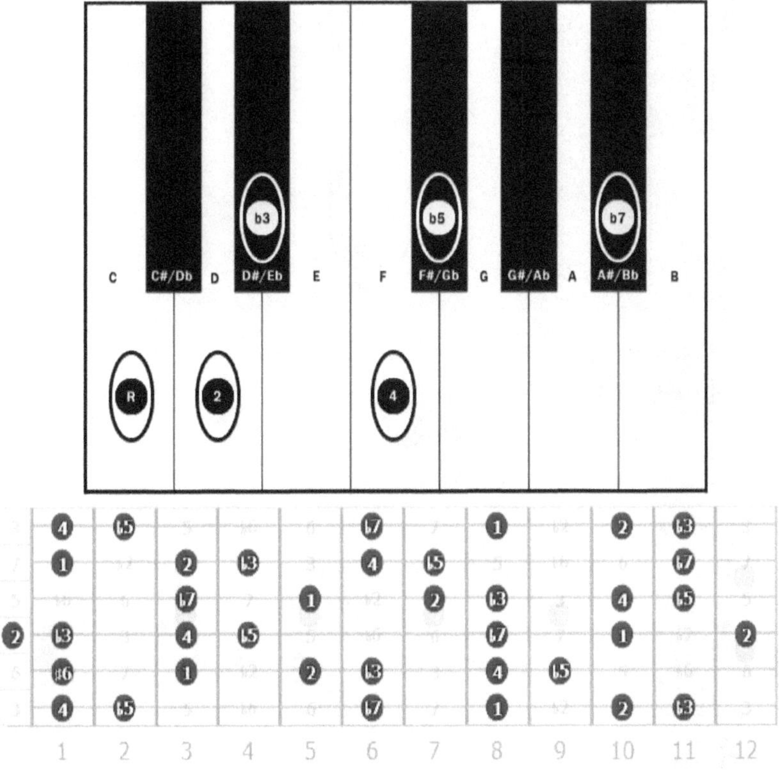

Diminished 11 (R 2 b3 4 b5 6)

Is in the Harmonic Major Scale on the b7th

Is in the Dim Scale Event on the 2nd, 4th, b6th and 7th

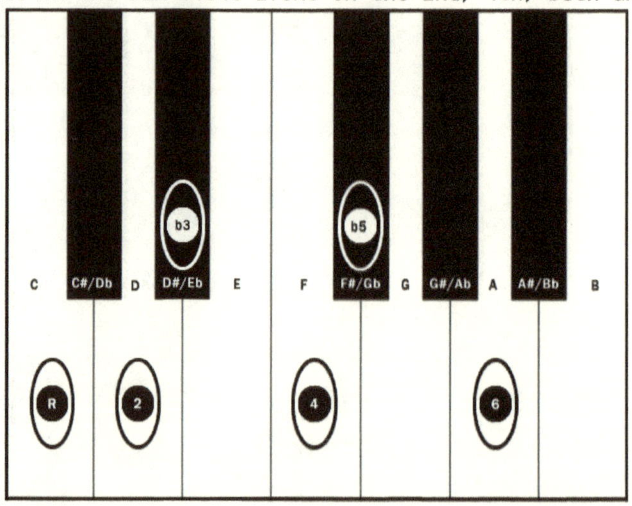

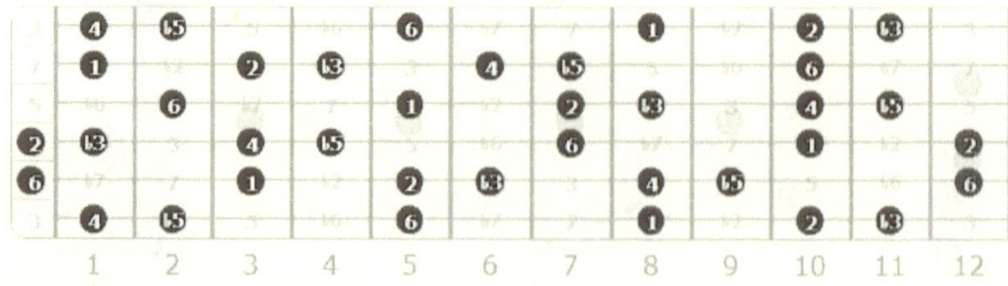

THE OVERTONE SERIES

Why·you·need·to·know·this:

It's the physics behind everything we have learned so far. It validates why a Major Triad sounds "stable" (it matches nature) and why a cluster of low notes sounds like mud. You can just know on the surface level that there is a reason why certain notes sound better together than others.

Nature's Chord

Any time a single note is heard, your brain actually hears a stack of many notes at once. It instantly uses an algorithm to resolve these "Harmonic Overtones" down to one **Fundamental Frequency** to identify the sound.

We likely evolved this trait for survival, quickly determining if a sound is a threat (a growl) or a reward (a bird call).

What is the Overtone Series? It is a predictable pattern of faster, smaller waves vibrating inside the main wave.

1st Harmonic: The Fundamental (The note you "hear").
2nd Harmonic: The Octave (2x speed).
3rd Harmonic: The Perfect 5th (3x speed).
4th Harmonic: The Octave again.
5th Harmonic: The Major 3rd.

The Fingerprint of Sound

Different instruments produce different volumes of these overtones. A flute is mostly the Fundamental (a pure sine wave). A guitar has loud mid-range harmonics (crunch/twang). A piano has a complex, rich spread. This unique "EQ curve" of overtones is called Timbre. It is how you can distinguish a cello from a chainsaw, even if they play the exact same pitch.

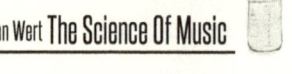

Each harmonic is a smaller and faster wave inside the bigger one.

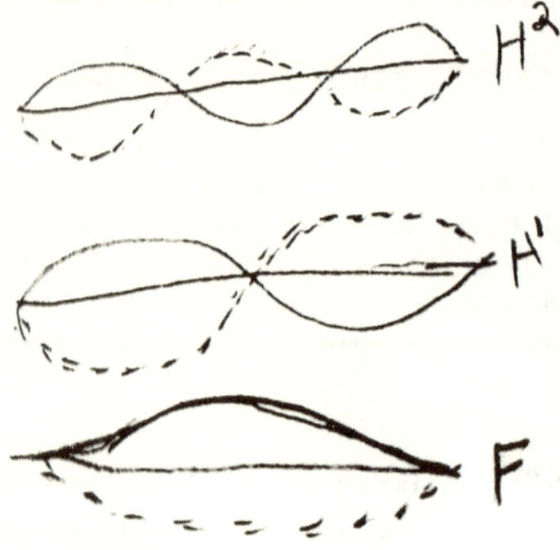

The "Mud" Zone

When a note is very low (like on a bass guitar or piano), the overtones fall squarely within the most sensitive range of human hearing. If you play a low **C** and a low **C#** at the same time, you aren't just clashing two notes. You are clashing two entire towers of overtones. The result is acoustic chaos. Our brains cannot resolve the math, so it sounds "muddy" or "bad." This is because their overtones that fall within our acute range of hearing cause confusion and we have trouble quickly rendering it out to one fundamental frequency. This is why bass players and left hands of pianists usually stick to **Single Notes, Octaves** or **5ths.**

Nature vs. Math

Here is an inconvenient truth about most music: **Our instruments are out of tune with nature.** We use a system called **Equal Temperament**, where we tweak the notes slightly so we can play in all 12 keys. Our "Major 3rd" is actually quite sharp compared to the natural overtone series. Our "minor 7th" is way off.

The Barbershop Effect

When four singers harmonize a Dominant 7th chord, they naturally adjust their pitch to match the physics of the overtone series. When they lock in that chord, they are accessing the Harmonic Series and are in accord with nature.

A vibrating string divides itself into integer sections (1/2, 1/3, 1/4, etc.). When you get to the 7th division (the 7th harmonic), the pitch is a b7th, but it is significantly flatter (by about 31 cents) than what is on a piano.

When the singers hit this exact frequency, the sound waves physically line up. The "beating" (the wobble you hear when things are slightly out of tune) stops completely. The chord "locks" and produces a pleasant phantom "ringing" sound. You are physically aligning with the mathematical laws of the universe. It is a static, perfect column of sound. If we tuned our instruments to do this perfectly to the Overtone Series of **C**, we would sound like angels in the Key of C, but we would sound terrible in the Key of F#. The math wouldn't line up anymore. You would hit what used to be called a "Wolf Interval" or dissonant clash.

To solve this, we created the Matrix (12-Tone Equal Temperament). We took the "comma" (the mathematical error that occurs when you cycle through keys) and spread it out evenly across all 12 notes. On a piano, every single interval is slightly out of tune (except the octave). The Major 3rds are too sharp and the 5ths are slightly flat.

The Matrix

The overtone series is about vertical depth. It is about sitting in one place and building a skyscraper of perfect vibration. But while in the skyscraper, it takes time to get to different floors and rooms, even with an elevator (different keys). So like in the Matrix, you take the pill that gives you the truth and you are then able to hack the system and crush all of the floors into one hallway

with doors for each key. The trade-off is that the keys inside the doors are slightly synthetic and out of accord with the reality people in the matrix experience, but it allows us to instantly modulate anywhere without concern of tuning changes.

We accepted a world that is slightly "false" so that we could access all of the possibilities faster and without needing a bunch of instruments for different keys.

When the Barbershop Quartet sings a Dominant 7th chord, they **instinctively** sing the b7 a little flatter than a piano would play it. They do this because it **"feels right"**. They are briefly locking back into the mathematical perfection of the harmonic series that we are all a part of.

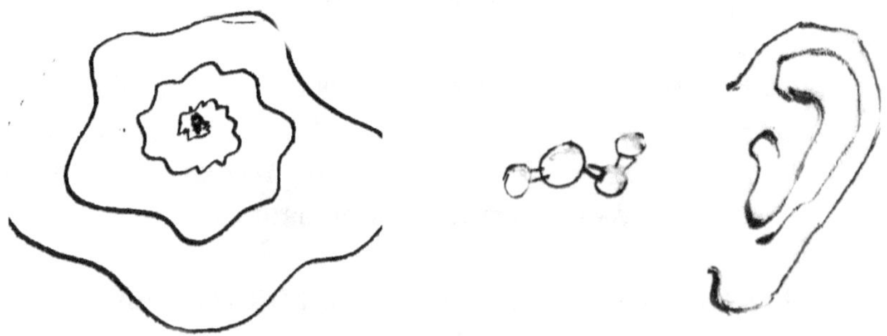

TENSION

Why you need to know this:

It is a primary component of every part of music and how we experience it. You will use tension in music for lead melody composition and improvisation. You will also use it for chord progression construction.

Tension is what we feel when there is an expectation that isn't met. It can be a rhythm that doesn't change when expected, an instrument that suddenly drops out or notes in the melody that clash with the harmony.

The Golden Ratio (75/25)

Tension has varying degrees of strength. If you change everything at once, it just sounds like disconnected random noise. The continuity that works in most successful music is retaining about **75%** of the familiar elements and introducing **25%** tension.

As an Exercise:

- Create a 4-measure loop.
- Make the melody resolve perfectly on measures 1, 2 and 4.
- On **Measure 3**, deliberately fail to resolve. Play a wrong note or an unexpected rhythm.
- Notice how much more powerful Measure 4 feels when the resolution finally happens.

The "V Chord" Secret

In traditional classical and jazz oriented music theory books, you will find ideas about scales, licks and alterations designed to be played specifically over the V chord. But, the V chord is just a placeholder for "Tension." Where you place a V chord is the same spot you could place a **bII** chord or a **vii** chord. The specific notes don't matter as much as the function. We are simply placing a "Question Mark" in the music that sets up an "Exclamation Point."

The Van Halen Mindset

Look at the pre-chorus of "Panama" by Van Halen.

- Eddie walks down completely out of key.
- The rhythm feels disjointed and "wrong."
- But he lands perfectly on the **V/V** just before the chorus.
- **What happens** is the chorus feels massive because the tension before it was so chaotic.

How I think

Don't obsess over which specific scale to play over the V. Just create tension. Play outside notes. Play contrasting rhythms. Do anything that sounds "unstable," then resolve it cleanly on the next chord.

Tritone Substitutions (Simplified)

Jazz musicians talk about **Tritone Substitutions**, but I see it as just taking the normal chord you might default to but instead, using a similarly tense chord in its place.

The V Chord (G7): pulls to C from a **5th** away.

The bII Chord (Db7): pulls to C from a **half step** away.

Both chords create a similar amount of tension because they both want to resolve to the same target. Even more importantly is to look at each note of each chord and how they move from the tension to a resolution.

The "Future Note" Hack

Here is a cool trick to exploit tension and push your chords forward. Take one of the notes from the next chord you plan to play. Adjust a note in your current chord so it sits exactly one half step away from that future note.

Example: G Major → C Major

We're moving from **G Major** (G - B - D) to **C Major** (C - E - G).

- Target the **C** of the next chord.
- The note **B** is already a half step below C. (Good but we can also jump it up above C to C# for ten sion).
- Let's change the **D** to a **D#** (half step below the tar get E).
- And target the **G** of the next chord by playing **G#** in the current chord.

Try this progression: (B-D-G) → (C#-D#-G#) → (C-E-G)

Or this: (B-D-G) → (C#-D#-**G**) → (C-E-G)

You will hear the inner voice smoothly drop from D to C# to C. In the second option you keep the G for continuity in the melody the whole time.

As an exercise, keep the B in the first two chords and resolve it to the C in the target chord. See what other options you can come up with that you like. Try different inversions and voicings.

The Child's Mind

You could study every fancy "Neapolitan 6th" chord in classical theory or every "Altered Dominant" in jazz books, but it is always just this same fundamental thing happening. Remember that the music doesn't know what we call it. Some children can do this naturally because their brains resonate with the simple idea of tension. They don't need to memorize hundreds of examples; they just feel the gravity of the notes. They basically destabilize the harmony and move to nearest neighbor notes from the current chord that lead to the next chord. Making sure it won't fall next to another note also being played where they land on the target chord. I was one of those children apparently, but I just assumed everyone did this like me.

MELODY

Why·you·need·to·know·this:

Melody is the single most memorable part of music for non-musicians. Instead of what people think of as an expression of 'innate talent', melody is actually just physics and probability.

The Zoetrope

My dad used to have a program on our Amiga computer called Zoetrope. He pronounced it Zoethrope and I remember this animation program where you would make individual images and it would play them in sequence. Man this makes me sound really old. It was in 1992 or so. He used to make animations of fireworks for hours and stare at them on that little CRT monitor. I later found out he was smoking pot all the time. On one of his last days with us I snuck him outside of the hospital and while cops kept going by and my mom kept yelling that we are gonna get caught (never rob a bank with this woman), I gave him a ton of pot and lit and held it for him and after about a half hour of this he said "I feel wonderful, Allen is the only one who loves me."

Anyway, melody reminds me of this. Melody is something we notice as a single entity moving along a path in pitch at various distances. It is an illusion but a very important one to understand. While we often think of "melody" as the singer's voice, **everything** in music is melodic. The notes inside a chord and the movement of a bass line are all individual melodies weaving together.

The Physics of Movement

Melody loves **Half Steps**. Moving by the smallest possible distance usually sounds "good" to our brains because it is efficient. **However, context is king.** Moving a half step but landing on a **non-chord tone** on a **strong beat** creates massive tension. Imagine every musical choice adds weight to a scale.

Landing on a chord tone = **Resolution (-5 weight).**
Landing on the tonal center = **Resolution (-10 weight).**
Landing on a non-chord tone = **Mild Tension (+5 weight).**
Landing on a non-scale note = **High Tension (+10 weight).**

If you stack too many "heavy" choices together, the music sounds chaotic. If you make every choice perfectly resolving (<0 weight), it sounds boring and predictable (like a nursery rhyme).

The Sweet Spot

You want enough tension to keep the ear interested, but enough resolution to keep the brain safe. Melody follows a sort of **Gravity.**

- **Linear Motion:** Melody tends to move in small steps up or down the scale.

- **The "Rubber Band" Effect:** When a melody jumps a large distance (more than a 3rd), it almost always wants to move back in the opposite direction immediately after. This balances the energy.

Even non-musicians notice contour. They hear the line go "up, then down a little, then up higher." Practicing sequences (repeating patterns) helps you master nested contours. This is where there is a small repeating pattern inside a larger overall movement.

The rhythm of your melody controls the "importance" of the notes.

- **Duration:** Long notes draw more attention.
- **Placement:** Notes on the "1" count are perceived as more important than notes on the "and" of 4.

The Continuity Rule (75/25) To make a melody feel like a coherent story, you need **Continuity.** Just like I mentioned in the

Tension chapter, try to retain about **75%** of the elements (rhythm, contour shape, scale) from one phrase to the next. Change only about **25%**. This makes the listener feel like they are following a logical narrative.

The "Bones" of a Strong Melody

Just remember this skeleton:

1. **Strong Beats (1 & 3):** Play **Chord Tones.**
2. **Weak Beats (2 & 4):** Play **Scale Tones** (connecting the chord tones).
3. **Subdivisions (e & a):** Use **Chromatic Passing Tones** (out-of-key notes) to slide into the target notes.

Intuition

Our brains are wired for this. If you hum or whistle over a chord progression right now, you will likely automatically hit the chord tones on the strong beats without even trying or thinking about music theory options. This is likely why many improvisational musicians don't "need" theory in their opinion. But theory goes much deeper than their innate safe surface level dictates as their only options.

Exercise in Algorithmic Composition

Let's strip away the "magic" for a moment and build a melody using pure science and logic. In C Major with the chord progression of I - vi - IV - V **(C - Am - F - G).**

Chords: C: (C - E - G), **Am:** (A - C - E), **F:** (F - A - C), **G:** (G - B - D)

Step 1: The Anchors: Place a **Chord Tone** on beat 1 and beat 3 of every measure.

- Measure 1 (C): **C** (beat 1) ... **E** (beat 3)
- Measure 2 (Am): **E** (beat 1) ... **C** (beat 3)

Step 2: The Connectors: On beats 2 and 4, place **Scale Tones** that bridge the gaps between your anchors.

- Measure 1: **G** ... **D**(beat 2) ... **G** ... **B** (beat 4) -> Note: B leads nicely into the next C (Tonal center) on the strongest beat.

Step 3: The Spice: Add **Chromatic notes** (out of key) on the weak subdivisions ("e" or "a") to slide into the anchors.

- Measure 1: **Eb** ... Measure 3: **F#** (the "and" of 2)

By following this simple algorithm, you have created a melody that sounds intentional, grounded and harmonically correct without waiting for "inspiration" to strike.

Here is that example

My Beethoven Experiment

Create a melody using the steps above, but do it ***deaf***. Use blank notation paper, or use the Piano Roll/Staff view in your DAW with the volume muted. Strictly follow the "Strong Beat/Weak Beat" algorithm. Once you are finished, turn the volume up and listen to your creation. It is a fun reveal that proves a powerful point: **The logic of music holds up, even when you can't hear it.**

BASSLINES

Why-you-need-to-know-this:

The bassline will strongly influence how the rest of the music feels. It forces context more than any other part besides rhythm.

The Root of the Tree

Basslines are typically the lowest note in a chord, but they are also experienced by the listener as a moving melody of their own. Bass is powerful because it strongly influences the Tonal Center due to it having overtones that fit with primary chords in our acute range of hearing, (you know this because we covered it in the overtone series chapter).

If a guitarist plays a **C Major chord** (C-E-G), but the bassist plays an **A** under it, the audience hears an **Am7.** You can change the entire emotion of a song just by moving the bassline, without changing a single chord above it.

The "Hidden" Progression

I view bassline movement as its own independent version of a chord progression. While most people focus only on the harmony of the chords, the bassline often follows its own common theme such as a I-IV-V movement even if the chord progression above it is doing something else. I identify specific intervallic movements (like a Half Step or a Perfect 4th) as important entities to account for. This creates a separate layer of tension and release. When the bass follows its own logic, it grounds the song even if the chords are flying around in their "own world".

Composing with Bass

I often compose music by writing only the top melody and the bassline first. This establishes the "ceiling" and the "floor." Once those are locked, I fill in the middle space with chords that fit both.

Just because you compose something on one instrument (like piano) doesn't mean it stays there. You can split that middle harmony between a guitar and an organ for the final recording. I usually make the music sound good with only shitty midi piano sound on the computer and then break it off into actual instruments.

Slash Chords (Inversions)

If the lowest note in a chord isn't its Root, we use a **Slash Chord.** [Chord]/[Bass Note]. E/G# would be E Major (E - G# - B) with a G# bass note (The 3rd of the chord)

Case Study [Hotel California]

The famous progression from Hotel California uses slash chords to create a "Walking Bassline" that moves down in half steps.

- **The Progression: B**m - F#**/A#** - **A** - E**/G#** - **G** - D**/F#**
- **The Bass Movement:**
    1. **B** (Root of Bm)
    2. **A#** (3rd of F#) a step down
    3. **A** (Root of A) a step down
    4. **G#** (3rd of E) a step down
    5. **G** (Root of G) a step down
    6. **F#** (3rd of D) you guessed it...a step down

If the bassist just pounded the root notes (B, F#, A, E...), the melody would jump around jaggedly. By using the **3rd** in the bass on every other chord, the bassline creates a smooth, melodic descent. That causes melodic tension and release back and forth to draw you in and tell an interesting story while maintaining continuity in the melodic contour (of the bass itself). Even with outside chords it all feels deliberate and fitting due to that continuity.

Here is another example of bass moving independently of chords

Bass isn't just harmony, it's also **Percussion.** Because low frequencies carry more energy than high frequencies, the simple binary of a bass note being held or stopped creates massive rhythmic power. Bass usually locks to the Kick Drum. In Latin music, the bass often plays on the "and" (upbeats) to create syncopation. When the bass stops, the track loses weight. When it comes back in, it hits hard.

Exercise: The "Ghost Key" Experiment

Let's take a basic progression: **C - Am - F - G.** Now, let's manipulate the bass to create tension. The trick to making a chorus do the big magic chorus thing, is to make it a big payoff where you finally get what you want. This sort of idea works great for building tension in a verse or pre-chorus.

Variation 1: Inversions (Smoothness)

- **Bassline:** G - E - F - B
    - **C/G:** (C chord over 5th)
    - **Am/E:** (Am chord over 5th)
    - **F:** (Root)
    - **G/B:** (G chord over 3rd)

Variation 2: The "Ghost Key" (Advanced Tension)

Try avoiding the root note (C) entirely in the bassline and the chords. **Bassline:** E - E - F - B. **Harmony:** Remove all C notes from the upper chords. Even though you are never playing a C, the listener's brain fills it in. We are used to the structure of the Major Scale, so the brain assumes C is home. By withholding the C, you build massive tension. When you finally hit a low C Bass and a C chord in the chorus, the resolution feels explosive because you made the listener wait for it.

The "Scale Jump" Effect

If you played a **C#** instead of a C in that tension section, you would briefly shift the ear to **D Melodic Minor** (A Mixolydian b6).

- **C** - D - E - F - G - A - B (C Major)
- **C#** - D - E - F - G - A - B (D Melodic Minor)

The Chords: C/C - A/C# - F/D(Dm7) - G/E(Em7)
This creates a bassline that walks upward at the same time. With how much you can control with the bassline the options are fun to explore. This shows how playing between two adjacent scales (scales that differ by only one note) allows you to blur the lines of tonality before resolving home.

Simplicity Wins

You can enhance the chorus simply by reserving certain low frequencies only for that section. There is no need to overcomplicate it. Less is more, or in Yngwie Malmsteen speak: "*More space is more better like more donut ya kno. Unleash the fukin fury.*"

I like to start by allowing complexity in my intention and play with extremes, then begin removing what isn't needed. You are often left with fewer notes, but they are the *right* notes. More about why this works in the next chapter I bet no one expected a shred guitarist to include in his very nerdy but hopefully fun and very enlightening music theory book.

LESS IS MORE

Why·you·need·to·know·this:

Doing less works best and is more impactful.

For composing, having fewer notes in your chord progression gives the melody more room to explore. In chemistry, a solvent (like water) can only hold a certain amount of solute (sugar) before it becomes saturated. Your song's frequency spectrum is the water. The notes are the sugar. If you keep adding sugar (notes) beyond the saturation point, it stops dissolving and turns into a gritty, cloudy sludge at the bottom.

For production, fewer instruments fighting for space allows for a louder, more dynamic, and punchier song. After a neuron fires a signal, it enters an "Absolute Refractory Period", The brief window of time where it literally cannot fire again, no matter how strong the stimulus is. (Kind of like trying to swallow three times in a row quickly.) It needs that "space" to reset its ion balance. If you stimulate a nerve too fast without space, the information jams and the signal degrades into a sustained contraction or simply stops registering. This is exactly what happens in a mix if you add too much shit. The "solution" becomes opaque and "muddy," and nothing is distinct anymore. More space keeps the solution clear. If you bombard the human eardrum (which is basically a transducer and tympanic membrane) with non-stop transients without space to reset, the brain stops perceiving the "impact" and starts perceiving it as a flat, tiring drone (listener fatigue). Space allows the brain to "reset" so the next hit feels explosive.

For songwriting, Less clutter allows the listener to actually remember the hook. Repeating the exact same melody while changing the harmony underneath it is one of the most powerful tricks in songwriting. It keeps the familiarity (the hook) while providing variety (the context). Less complex melody but changing context. Neil deGrasse Tyson, the nerdy but fun Astrophysicist (who blocked me on TikTok when I jokingly claimed that HE in fact is an alien), knows that astronomers cannot observe faint stars from a city because of "light pollution" there is too much background information (photons) flooding the sensor. "Space" in music is the black sky. By removing the background clutter (unnecessary notes), the remaining notes shine brighter.

Something I noticed when I caught myself overplaying
When composing without a drumbeat, I have a tendency to overplay. I feel the need to hammer the downbeat because there is no kick drum already providing that for the music. I learned to always write with a beat. When you record with a drum loop, you naturally start making more interesting rhythmic decisions against the static beat. Playing in the gaps between the drums as a counter rhythm leads to more interesting parts. I like to leave space for the snare drum. I often mute my instrument right before the snare hits to create anticipation for the crack. Bass players famously avoid playing on the snare for this exact reason, it lets the backbeat cut through. I learned this by noticing how Quincy Jones did this for Michael Jackson. Also worth noting, Michael Jackson composed music with his voice and the producer and musicians translated it into a song. By only have a monophonic compositional technique like he did, it makes the songs have small trade off complimentary parts that don't overlap. (Think B.B King vocals and lead guitar taking turns on phrases.) You can't argue with that many hit songs.

Withholding the Key
Doing less by saving one specific note for a special targeted moment (like the chorus) can make the song deeply fulfilling. If you only use **C - D - E - G - A - B**, and avoidany type of F (**F** or **F#**). The listener doesn't know if you are in **C Major** (needs F) or **G Major** (needs F#). The listener's brain fills in the gaps with whatever they

prefer to hear. They are subconsciously co-authoring the song.

I think this is why **Pentatonic** based music is so universally loved. Because it fits over three different keys, the listener can project their own imagination and expectation into it until you force them to hear a specific one.

Books vs. Movies

Think of this strategic use of ambiguity like a book vs. a movie. A **movie** shows you exactly what the character and the setting they are in look like and there's nothing to imagine. But a **book** describes things vaguely, letting you imagine the most personally interesting version in your head because the reader parses in their own memories and this places them right in that book as if they are living there. When you leave space in music (harmonic or lyrical), it is like the book where the listener projects their own life experience into the gaps.

The Physics of a Speaker

Recorded music eventually has to come out of a speaker. That transducer can only vibrate in two dimensions (in and out). Everything in a mix is fighting for the same sonic space to push the polarity either in or out to vibrate the air. Hit songs tend to have fewer things happening at the same time. If you have a massive bassline, you don't need a massive piano chord in the low-mids. It is a good idea for you to try to keep only four or five elements happening at the same time.

Start treating "Space" as an instrument. If you mute a guitar part for four bars, that silence is just as loud as the solo that comes after it.

Light and Dark

When you want a chorus to sound big, make the pre-chorus sound small. You need the contrast. If you want a wide stereo image, you need to contrast it with narrow or mono sounds.

CHORD PROGRESSIONS

Why·you·need·to·know·this:

Being able to quickly identify chord progressions by ear or common use will help in many ways.

Data Clusters

Chord progressions are simply a way of categorizing movement. In reality, music is just a stream of individual notes (frequencies) happening in linear time. However, Rhythm forces these notes to group together into clusters.

When notes happen at the same time (or within the same rhythmic window), our brain takes a "snapshot" of them. We give that snapshot a name (e.g., "G Major chord").

A "**Chord Progression**" is just a list of these snapshots in the order they appeared.

The Classics (Common Groupings) Key of G Major

I-IV-V-IV	**(G - C - D - C)**	Rock / Folk / Pop
I-vi-IV-V	**(G - Em - C - D)**	50s Progression
vi-IV-I-V	**(Em - C - G - D)**	Modern Pop
I-V-vi-IV	**(G - D - Em - C)**	Most Pop Songs
vi-V-IV-V	**(Em - D - C - D)**	Moody Rock
I-V-IV	**(G - D - C)**	Classic Rock
V-IV-I	**(D - C - G)**	Alabama
ii^7-V	**(Am^7 - D)**	Santana
ii^7-V^7-I	**(Am^7 - D^7 - G)**	The Jazz Standard
IV-V	**(C - D/C)**	Lydian
I^7-IV^7-I^7-V^7-IV^7-I^7-V^7	**(G^7 - C^7 - G^7 - D^7 - C^7 - G^7 - D^7)**	12 Bar Blues

Here are some fancy chord progressions that use key changes/ borrowed chords/secondary dominants:

I-I⁷-IV-iv	**(G - G⁷ - C - Cm)**	Gravitational pull
I-III-IV-iv	**(G - B - C - Cm)**	Creep
I-II-V-I (aka IV-V-I-IV)	**(G - A - D - G)**	Lydian Lift
VI-IV-V-VI	**(E - C - D - E)**	Picardy Mixolydian-b6
I-bII-V-I	**(G - Ab - D - G)**	Neapolitan

Some people use chord progressions to generate melody (Jazz) and some people already have a melody and try different chord progressions that support or enhance the melody (Pop). For the sake of analysis and a more focused learning experience in this section, we will be using chord progressions on their own in isolation.

Hacking the Code

Most books just list these progressions and tell you to memorize them. We are going to fix that. We can analyze why one chord flows into the next. It comes down to three things:

1. **Internal tension** of the chord itself? (e.g., G7 has a tritone interval within it).
2. **Melodic Gravity** of notes in Snapshot A sitting just one step away from the notes in Snapshot B and their melodic tendency leading them in this direction?
3. **Bass Movement** in short steps (Smooth). Vs. jumping by a 4th or 5th (Strong).

The "G7 to C" Example

Why does **G7** pull so hard to C?

- **Bass** jumps a perfect 4th (G → C). Strong.
- **Melody** from **B** leads up to **C** and **F** leads down to **E**.
- **Tension** between B and F within that G7 is a tritone which is unstable and demands resolution.

The "Mad Scientist" Substitution

You can use this underlying universal logic to hack new progressions. Instead of using **G7**, let's find another grouping of notes that has the same amount of tension and melodic gravity.

The Chromatic Slide Experiment

Let's take a **Db Major** chord (Db - F - Ab). Add a **b9 (D)** to it. Now you have a cluster of tension.

- Does it resolve to **C Major**?
  - **Db** falls to **C**.
  - **F** falls to **E**.
  - **Ab** falls to **G**.

It works perfectly. It has the same "gravity" as the G7, but a totally different color.

Visualizing the Story (Voice Leading)

Let's look at a sequence: **Dm → Db(add b9) → C Major.**

Dm	**D**	**F**	**A**	Start
Db Major	**D**	**bF**	**Ab**	Slide Down
C Major	**C**	**E**	**G**	Resolution

Notice the story? It is almost entirely **downward linear motion**.
The Trick: Change the C Major to a **Csus4** or **Cm** to delay the satisfaction. This is misdirection. You can use this to **"hack"** the idea of chord progressions and begin to come up with your own using the same basic understanding.

Newton's First Law of Melody ***"An object in motion stays in motion."***

If you start moving notes down by half-steps, the listener expects that motion to continue. If we change that F note to an E in the middle chord, we get **Db minor** (Db - E - Ab). Now every note is sliding down.

Dm	D - F - A	Tension
Dbm	Db - E - Ab	Momentum (Half step down)
Cm	C - Eb - G	Momentum (Half step down)
Bm	B - D - F#	Arrival

Classical Name: Neapolitan 6th (ish).
Jazz Name: Tritone Substitution (ish).
My Name: Melodic Momentum (No name needed).
We don't need the fancy names. We just need to know that sound follows a path.

Why not continue? Rhythm allows an escape from the path of constant one directional motion in these cases. We expect a certain looping point or changing point. If the expectation isn't met, it would cause tension or eventually boredom. Anything that has been repeated enough becomes background noise for our brain. In classical music theory once the music resolves tension, the expectation is to go somewhere new. It is because of how our brain works.

Relative Substitutions (The "Backdoor")
Chords that share notes can often be swapped.
The minor iv In the key of G, we often see **G → C → Cm → G.**

- That **Cm** (C - Eb - G) provides a beautiful, emotional lift.
- Now look at **Eb Major** (Eb - G - B).
- They share two notes (Eb and G). If you combine them, you get **Cm7**.

Instead of playing **Cm**, try playing **Eb Major. Progression:** G - C - Eb - F. It gives you the same "emotional logic" because it hits the same sensitive notes (specifically that Eb), but with a different bass context.

Exercise 1:
Take a song you love. Keep the melody exactly as it is. Change the underlying chords. Reharmonize it. First, Isolate the melody note (e.g., **E**) that happens on a chord change or strong beat. For instance, if the song had an **Am** (A - C - **E**) with an E in the melody over it. Find any other chord that contains the note **E** and use that instead of the original chord.
A Major (A - C# - E) → Bright shift.
C Major (C - E - G) → Safe shift.
F Maj7 (F - A - C - E) → Dreamy shift.
Db Minor (Db - E - Ab) → Dark/Weird shift.

Be a mad scientist! No one will die from a bad chord choice. Test the crazy combinations and see how they completely alter the emotional context of the melody.

Exercise 2:

Testing the stability of a single note against chaos. One melody note ringing constantly over every chord you make. Find 5 different chords where that note is in the chord (as the Root, 3rd, 5th, 7th, 9th, etc.).

Example: Keep an E note in the upper melody. E Major (**Root**), C Major (**3rd**), A Major (**5th**), F Maj7 (**7th**), Dadd9 (**9th**).

This teaches "Common Tone" connection and how to make complex progressions sound smooth by keeping one "Anchor" note static.

Exercise 3:

Assign the numbers 1–6 to six random chords (1=C, 2=F#, 3=Bb, etc...). Roll a die 4 times to generate a random progression. Your job is to make it sound "good" using voice leading by finding the half-step connections between the chords to glue them together.

There are no "wrong" progressions, only lazy voice leading.
You can connect anything if you build the right bridge.

Exercise 4:

Start with a C Major chord and with less than five chords get to the F# Major chord. (The Tritone is a far distance so it can be challenging). This forces us to look ahead and plan a route, rather than just playing shapes. Try to connect chords with voice leading and shared notes so it has some continuity.

CYCLE OF FOURTHS

Why-you-need-to-know-this:

This is musical alphabet listed in order of adjacent keys. Music modulates in many ways, one of those is in 4ths. This shows exactly that along with six of the chords within a key around it.

Not on my stage

The Circle of Fifths might seem like a good visual cheat sheet for a beginner piano player sitting in a classroom, but for a modern guitarist or composer, it is often just a wall decoration.

A Broken Compass?

I am including this topic because it is taught in almost every music theory class, but I feel it is limiting and a slight waste of time.

The Logic (The One-Note Rule) You don't need a diagram to find a neighbor scale; you just need to change **one note**!

- **To go up a 5th** raise the 4th note of the current scale. For example **C Major** (C-D-E-**F**-G-A-B) becomes **G Major** by raising the **F** to **F#**.

- **To go down a 5th** lower the 7th of the current scale. For example: **C Major** (C-D-E-F-G-A-**B**) becomes **F Major** by lowering the **B** to **Bb**.

The problem is that the diagram only shows this specific "One Note" change. But real music changes in many ways. Memorizing a wheel that only describes one type of movement is limited. The **Circle of Fifths** (or **Cycle of 4ths**) is a graphical wheel designed to help beginners see which Major Scales are "neighbors" (scales that differ by only one note). And what chords are in each scale (in a weird way most won't even notice).

The Problems?
Limited Scope of only accounting for the **Major Scale** and **Limited Movement** in assuming music only modulates by perfect 4ths or 5ths.

But in real life we modulate by other intervals like **Major 3rds** (Coltrane changes). We change scales by **altering a single chord** (making a minor chord Major). We **modulate by other intervals to different scales.**

If we made a diagram for every possible modulation (Cycle of 3rds, Cycle of Seconds, etc.) compounded by every scale and every key of every scale all connected in a gigantic wheel graphic or 167,452 graphic wheels, it would create infinite complexity. This would make the point of graphical wheels well... pointless. Because, they are. In my opinion, **It was a beginner teaching tool taken way too far.** Instead of memorizing a wheel, remember that **most modulations involve changing just ONE or TWO notes from where we already are.**

The Guitarist's "GPS"
On guitar, you don't need a paper diagram. You have the Circle of Fifths built directly into your fretboard geometry. You can instantly find your "Neighbor Scales" (scales one note apart) by looking at the strings vertically on the **same fret**. (This is for any instrument tuned in 4ths like a guitar, bass and ukulele.)

My simple visual method:

1. **Find your Root on the A-String.** (e.g., **C** on the 3rd fret).
2. Look at the **Low E-string** on the same fret.(its **G**, your **5th**).
3. Look at the **D-string** on the same fret. (This is **F**, your **4th**).

- **C Major** (Center)
- **G Major** (Neighbor 1: One sharp difference)
- **F Major** (Neighbor 2: One flat difference)

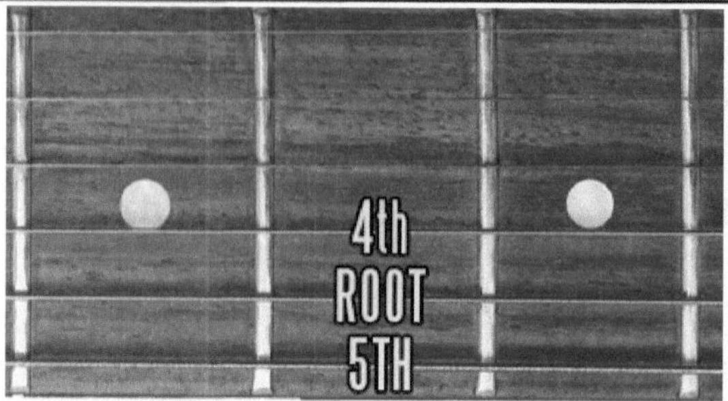

Finding the Chords: This same shape reveals the **Three Major Chords** in your key. In the key of **C**, the I, IV and V chords are physically sitting right next to each other on the 3rd fret.

This image shows the C minor chord is contained in the G#, D#, and A# Major scales using my visualization trick!

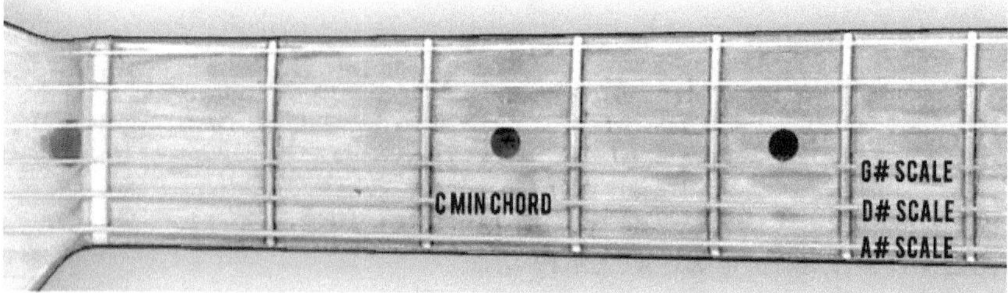

To find the relative minor, move that entire shape **down 3 frets**.

- In C Major (3rd Fret), move down to the **Open Strings**.
- **A-String:** A Minor (vi)
- **E-String:** E Minor (iii)
- **D-String:** D Minor (ii)

Now you have physically mapped the entire skeleton of the key (I, IV, V and vi, iii, ii) without drawing or looking at a single circle.

Reverse Engineering (Finding the Parent Scale)
Use the same logic to find which scales a chord belongs to. Lets say you have a **C Minor Chord** and want to know which major scales contain it?

Find the C on the A-string (3rd fret). **Look 3 frets up** (6th fret). Apply the "Stacking" method on the 6th fret.

A-String (6th): Eb Major Scale
E-String (6th): Bb Major Scale
D-String (6th): Ab Major Scale

In reverse the **Eb Major** contains Cm (as the **vi**), **Bb Major** contains Cm (as the **ii**) and **Ab Major** contains Cm (as the **iii**).

On the cycle diagram, if you take the seven notes on the outside starting from B going around to F, it is the notes of the C major scale. Chords are B dim, E, A and D minor and G, C and F major.

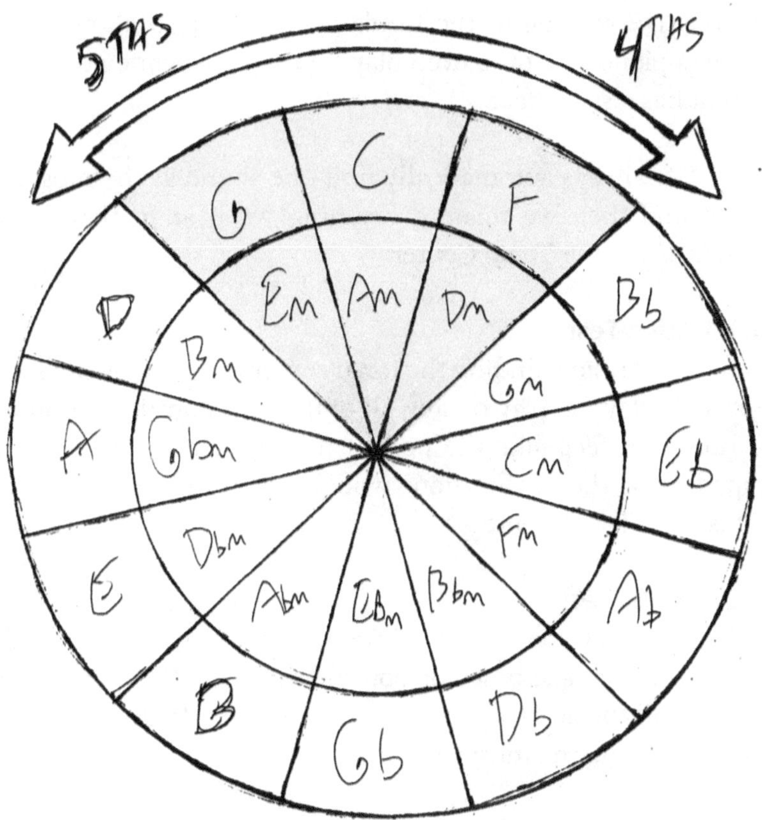

TONAL CENTER

Why you need to know this:

> The tonal center is what gives context to the rest of the sound we hear. Being able to understand this and use it will allow you to compose and improvise with more control. Your reality will match your intention. This is the bridge between "Science and Theory" and "Magic and Psychology".

Finding "Home"

Our evolution is based off of survival, we have evolved to discern if a sound is something we should run either away from or to within milliseconds. This allows us to render down overtones and their relative volume to the fundamental but also allows us to identify a piano vs a flute even playing the exact same note. This shortcut has a side effect...

We always automatically find one sound as the most important and then we relate everything we hear to that sound which is called the Tonal Center.

The Intuitive Test

On the human side, finding the tonal center is easy. Play the song, then as it's playing, play or sing all of the notes until you find the one note that feels like the perfect note to end on. If the song stopped right there, that note would feel completely resolved. That is your Tonal Center.

The Scientific Test

On the technical side, the Tonal Center isn't magic, it's a calculation our brains make based on specific variables. We quickly render down all the auditory information into one "Master Note" to make processing the music easier.

The "Importance" Weights

Think of your brain as a scale weighing different factors. The note with the most total weight takes over as the Tonal Center.

Here are the factors that add importance to a note:

1. Pitch Depth (Low Frequencies)
Lower notes feel more important than higher
notes (up to the point where it's so low that the pitch becomes indiscernible). The bass provides overtones in our acute range of hearing that affect the other things we hear the strongest.

2. Frequency of Occurrence (Repetition)
The more often a note happens, the more important it becomes. Also how long it has been established and reinforced as the tonal center. If a note appears in the bass, melody, and chords constantly, that all raises the likelihood of it being the tonal center.

3. Rhythmic Placement (Strong Beats)
Notes that land on strong beats (especially beat 1 of a measure or a chord change) carry more weight. Our brains prioritize information that happens on the "grid." Anything on a strong beat is extra whatever it was already.

4. Loop Position (The "Start")
The note that starts a primary loop (usually a 4 or 8-bar phrase) is often perceived as the anchor. Our brain tries to make sense of sound by finding looping points in data it hears.

5. Historical Expectation (Genre)
We are conditioned by genre. In a 12-Bar Blues, even if the scales change over every chord, our brain expects the "I" of the bassline to be "Home" due to historical conditioning causing an expectation.

Understanding the Tonal Center is vital because the **Tonal Center controls the MODE.** The Mode is simply where the Tonal Center sits within the scale structure. If you can predict the Tonal Center, you know the Mode.

Sometimes, the Tonal Center can shift often like an optical (or in this case, sonic) illusion. In the song "Sweet Home Alabama" for instance:

Chord Progression: D - C - G - G
Parent Scale: G Major (all chords fit into G Major).

It starts the loop on the **D** chord and is the first chord heard. (strong weight), but **G** is the lowest root note in the progression and happens twice as often as the others. (also a strong weight).

This resulted in a song where the Tonal Center flips back and forth between D (Mixolydian) and G (Ionian). If forced to choose, **D** often wins because it starts the phrase, establishing the initial context.

The tonal center is something that your brain is always automatically noticing. In most cases, it tends to last for a long time or the entire song. It seems to be talked about as only a brief mention and I feel that we accidentally missed its importance in the history of music theory. My findings about this are one of the reasons I needed to change or nudge traditional theory to better fit our reality. The system in place didn't seem to notice how important the tonal center was or describe how it works for our brain. Or if they did, they described it incorrectly.

MODES

Why·you·need·to·know·this:

It controls emotion and vibe. The listener will always experience a mode so you should understand how to control and apply them so you can craft and narrate an experience for them.

I never gave up on my intuition and I am happy that I finally have the evidence with many years of testing to prove that my definition and explanation of what modes are is the simple and scientific reality.

What exactly is a mode?

Modes are your brain noticing **WHERE** the **TONAL CENTER is** within the collection of sounds (The Scale) it is hearing. That's it!

You have the set of notes we call a scale and any of those can be the tonal center. Depending on which one sounds the most important to your brain in the scheme of things (for most of a song usually), you will experience a different mode. It will make things sound and feel different in your perception depending on where that tonal center is within the scale. You can change the scale by using different notes in the chords, melody and bassline or you can change the tonal center within a scale by changing which note sounds most important to the listener. (previous chapter)

The "Starting Note" Lie

You will find thick books and thousands of youtube videos telling you things like "Dorian is when you start the scale on the 2nd note." **This can be false when tested in actual music. Melody** has the least influence on the mode. **Harmony (chord progression) and Bass** have the most influence. With limited information, your brain will still pick a tonal center, in an example with only an isolated melody that starts and ends on a specific note, that note will be the most important sounding by default. This has misled the teacher and student into believing that is what modes are. The issue is, as soon as you drop that same exact example into music that has a bassline or chord progression that cause a different tonal center, their example fails to cause the intended mode.

Imagine learning about colors by studying a single paint swatch. You might know "Blue," but until you see it on a canvas next to "Yellow," you don't understand how it interacts. Teaching modes in isolation (just the melody) is like looking at a paint swatch. A mode only exists in context. You need the full painting including the harmony (chords), bass and rhythm) for an accurate representation of what a tonal center will be.

If you play a **C Major Scale** but you start your melody on **D**, you are not always or automatically playing Dorian. You are just playing the C Major scale starting on a different note. **Unless** the bass player hits a big low **D** and the chords switch to **Dm**. Then (and only then) does the tonal center shift to D, creating the Dorian sound. There is also no use in renaming it as a new scale or considering it an extra scale. That would cause an infinitely nested loop and that would be illogical and needlessly complex.

The Seven Modes of the Major Scale

So, to make sure you understand this, If the scale you are playing or hearing notes from has what we traditionally identify as the first note as the tonal center, we will experience Ionian. The second note as the tonal center causes us to experience Dorian. The third note as the tonal center sounds like Phrygian. The fourth note as the tonal center sounds like Lydian. The fifth note as the tonal center sounds like Mixolydian. The sixth note as the tonal center sounds like Aeolian. The seventh sounds like Locrian.

Here they are in order of the Tonal Center's location:
Ionian (Eye-Oh-Nee-In): **The 1st Note**. (Happy and Safe).
Dorian (Door-Ee-In): **The 2nd Note**. (Santana).
Phrygian (Fridge-Ee-In): **The 3rd Note**. (Exotic/Spanish sound).

Lydian (Lid-Ee-In): **The 4th Note**. (Dreamy/Movie score).
Mixolydian (Mix-Oh-Lid-Ee-In): **The 5th Note**. (Rock/Hendrix).
Aeolian (Ay-Oh-Lee-In): **The 6th Note**. (Dark Stable).
Locrian (Loke-Ree-In): **The 7th Note**. (Unstable/Dark).
(Major scales would be **C** in **Ionian**, **Bb** in C **Dorian**, **Ab** in C **Phrygian** etc...)

Chromesthesia and Auditory-Tactile Synesthesia (sort of)
Each mode has a certain sound to them that we remember almost like you remember a color or flavor. It might be tough to describe to others but you can sense what you are feeling/hearing. As you become more experienced you will usually hear the mode based on the notes that stand out in the scale as important when compared to the tonal center as an intervallic relationship or combination of a few notes.

Comparing Colors in Parallel
You can compare the modes from the same root note (e.g., C Ionian vs. C Dorian) to hear exactly which intervals change in relation to the tonal center. Have a bass note hold down the "**1**" and while it plays, play these modes over it. I list the modes starting from the same note so you can compare and hear their unique qualities.

Ionian	1 - 2 - 3 - 4 - 5 - 6 - 7
Dorian	1 - 2 - **b3** - 4 - 5 - **6** - b7
Phrygian	1 - **b2** - b3 - 4 - **5** - b6 - b7
Lydian	1 - 2 - 3 - **#4** - 5 - 6 - 7
Mixolydian	1 - 2 - 3 - 4 - 5 - 6 - **b7**
Aeolian	1 - 2 - **b3** - 4 - 5 - **b6** - **b7**
Locrian	1 - **b2** - b3 - 4 - **b5** - b6 - b7

You can either change the scale around the tonal center so it occupies a different spot in the scale being used or you can change the tonal center within the same scale you have been using. Or both at the same time, but it's just different ways of doing that same thing. So the definition doesn't change and accounts for both. **Where the tonal center is within the scale is the mode either way.**

These modes still hold true when you change the scale to a modification such as the Melodic Minor version of the Major scale (Major scale but with a b3rd). They will sound slightly different but the base name is what I retain except I then connect it to the other scale name. So the Phrygian mode of the Augmented Major scale. This would historically be called Phrygian Dominant and people historically consider it a scale of its own. It isn't really. It is just the Phrygian mode of the Augmented Major scale. (1 2 **3** 4 #5 6 7). Yet another mistake we have made in the naming convention of music theory. I dislike the renaming of the modes into new scales because it adds complexity in the form of redundancy and causes students to believe there is more to memorize than there actually is.

My "Time Travel" Experiment

I devised this experiment as a way to prove to students that what I am saying about modes is exactly the truth. They will hear a different mode without being able to go back in time to change their position or starting note or emphasis in the melody. It is almost as if they went back in time to re-record their melody. This directly contradicts the traditional definition and lessons often given for modes. (This part is fun for me because proving the established "expert" way as wrong allows people to start thinking more critically. As a bonus, I also get to watch other teachers squirm when their lesson no longer works and undeniably reveals them as a fraud when it comes to knowing about modes.)

1. Record yourself playing a simple, wandering melody using **ONLY the notes of C Major** (C-D-E-F-G-A-B).
2. Play that recording on a loop. Now, play these bass notes/chords underneath it to force the Tonal Center to shift.
    - **C** - F - G - F is C **Ionian**
    - **D**m7 - G7 is D **Dorian**
    - **E**m - F - Em - Dm is E **Phrygian**
    - **F**add9add#11 - G/F is F **Lydian**
    - **G** - F - C is G **Mixolydian**
    - F - G - **A**m - **A**m is A **Aeolian**
    - **B**m7b5 - Am is B **Locrian**

The Result of my experiment

The melody notes never changed. But the mode and feeling did because the tonal center moved. If you are having trouble with this you can repeatedly play a low note while listening to your melody recording. You will start to hear the low note you repeat as your tonal center and the mode will be experienced. It is really that simple.

If your chord progression and bassline are missing or avoiding a specific note, that note can be selected in the melody which can change the mode we hear due to it changing the scale. This won't change the tonal center but will change where it is in relation within the scale being used. The less information we have in the chord progression, the more options we have with lead melody to control the scale.

Modes actually existed before Major/Minor scale stuff we are told to believe. They defined modes as individual scales instead of **one scale with different tonal centers**

Remember what modes are and aren't:

1. **Melody does not dictate the mode.** (Their starting/ending notes don't matter nearly as much as previously taught by scholars).
2. **Fretboard or piano hand position isn't a mode.**
3. **Mental focus does not change the mode.** (You can't "think" a mode into existence and magically make others hear it). The order you write it on a page also means nothing.
4. **Modes are NOT their own separate scales.**
5. **The Mode is simply experiencing the Tonal Center** within the scale heard. (It is a relationship, not a pattern).
6. **Modes apply to ALL scales.**
7. **Modes are not up for interpretation.** (It is physics, not opinion and we all hear them the same).

If you hear a teacher say "just play the scale but start it on a specific note to ~use modes~"... **run.**

SECONDARY DOMINANT CHORDS

Why·you·need·to·know·this:

It helps to be able to understand how music moves. This will help you to identify and predict patterns of resolution within chord progressions.

Artificial Gravity

It is a common lesson in music theory textbooks to become aware of something called a Secondary Dominant. Firstly, a dominant chord is rooted on the 5th note of the major scale (**the V chord**). This chord makes you feel tension that would be resolved to the **I chord**. So, If G, G7 or maybe a G9 was the V chord then C is the I chord. It pushes your ear to want to hear the C due to harmonic encapsulation (My fancy way of saying that the notes of the first chord are adjacent to the notes of the second chord you are resolving to or preparing to resolve to.) Why does this work? It isn't magic, it's physics. When you play a dominant chord, the notes are physically adjacent to the notes of the target chord.

But, the **Secondary** dominant is where you set up **ANY** other chord (besides the I chord) with **its own "personal" V chord**. You are creating temporary "Artificial Gravity" to pull the listener toward a specific target. The functionality of this isn't hard coded into the major scale only. It is the other way around actually.

Here is what happens for example **G7 to C:** The **F** in G7 falls to **E** of the C chord. The **B** rises to the C chord root, **C**. This "encapsulation" (surrounding the target note from above and below) creates a pull like a magnet.

Example: The "V of V" (**V/V**) to add to a I to ii move.

- **Without it:** C - Dm (I to ii). That is the direct move.
- **With Gravity:** C - **A7** - Dm (This is a roundabout way that makes Dm feel more like home).

Analysis: A7 is the V of D. Even though A7 has a C# (which is not in the key of C), that note pulls strongly to D. You can chain these together in a long journey. **Progression:** A7 - D7 - G. In this example A7 pushes to D. D7 pushes to G. This is a II7 - V7 - I movement.

Now let's take a standard progression and inject it with secondary dominants to see how it changes the effect and feel of it. **(Key of C)** C - Am - F - G.

1. **To target the Am** (the vi chord). We need the V of A so count up 5 notes in the A major scale: A-B-C#-D-**E**. So the new chord is **E7.** This gives us: C - **E7** → Am
2. **Target the F** (The IV chord of the C major scale)
   We need the V of F. Count up 5 notes in the F major scale this time: F-G-A-Bb-**C**. The new chord is then **C7.** So it re sults in C - **E7** → Am - **C7** → F. The song is in C Major, but we are turning the home chord into a Dominant 7 temporarily to force a pull toward F.
3. **Target the G** (The V chord of the C major scale)
   We need the V of G. Count up 5 notes: G-A-B-C-D. So the new chord will be D7. This results in C-**E7**-Am-**C7**-F-**D7**-G7

The Tritone Hack (Tritone Substitution)

Remember, you can use a variety of chords to cause the same effect of tension to resolution? Instead of playing the V of the target, play a Dom 7th chord one half-step above the target. **For example:** C Major. The normal V chord would be G7. Tritone Sub is the **Db7.** Why does this work? Because Db7 and G7 share the same internal tension notes (F and B), just flipped. **They both create the same gravitational pull to C.**

Exercise 1

Take a song you are working on. Before every chord change, try inserting the V7 of the next chord. Do some sound sophisticated? Do some sound too busy? You decide. The magic is in how you use the science.

Exercise 2

Try to find how each chord relates to the next chord and why it is there. **C - A7 - Dm - Ebdim - Esus4 - E - E7 - Am - Adim7 - D7 - G7 - (C)**. First, try to path out what scale we are using for groups of chords, then notice how each chord maintains continuity while causing tension that pulls it to the next chord.

There are usually a bunch of specific examples in text-books with these but I see them as all doing the same thing of taking a chord we plan on moving to and then sounding adjacent notes to that chord's notes just before it happens so the ear hears a stronger pull to that target chord. This is just tension and release due to melody sounding good in small movements. Also, playing a chord outside of the scale will draw attention to it and it will generate more tension which will of course resolve when we play the target chord to release some of that tension.

Lowest Common Denominator

There is something outside the usual information that I want to share with you. It is how my own brain works. I don't want to use old standby options where people talk about how a certain chord "functions" within a key or any of that boring stuff. Instead, I like to take whatever chord I am looking to move to next and I modify my current chord to start doing things to make that next chord feel like a big payoff. I move the target chord's notes a half step out of place to upset the stability and then I keep a note from my current chord to provide continuity.

For example, if I were playing an A Major chord while already in the A major scale and wanted the music to go to a G major chord (not in key). I would take G B D into my thoughts and then select something like Gb and D# because those notes are a half step away from notes in the **NEW HOME** of G. A C# E were the starting notes in the A chord. I would keep the C# and put it with the Gb and D#, creating a C# - D# - Gb chord. I don't need to know what it might have been historically named, or which person did it often. That is the topic of history. I don't care that some dead composer used it for some special "function" nerds will argue about online instead of making their own music. I don't care how that chord sounds in isolation much either. I only concern myself with how this combination of sounds makes the G chord **FEEL** when we get to it.

When I do it with specific inversions of the chords it might look like (C# E A) - (C# D# Gb) - (B D G). I could also try to keep the A instead of the C# for the middle chord that connects them. Maybe I even try different tension notes preparing to move us to the notes in the G chord. There are a lot of options to try. Some of them will be named extra fancy names in old music theory books written by guys who feel smarter than other people. I want to feel exactly as regular and dumb as other people and want to hide away in a cabin deep in the forest remaining totally unknown while somehow helping others tap into the magic of creativity. Maybe this chapter in this book will help us do that.

Now you have the tools and understanding to create gravity on demand. You can now make a chord sound like home and feel more important. You gain power with understanding. So, instead of teaching you a huge list of historically used chord progressions and effects from classical music, as I promised, I teach the universal causes that were the reasoning behind those existing in the first place.

RHYTHM

Why-you-need-to-know-this:

> Everything in music is rhythm in some form. Rhythm causes us to hear things in different contexts and heavily influences the feel of music. You also need to understand how where sounds are placed changes their effect to a listener. This is important for improvisation and composition.

The Timeline of Perception

Rhythm isn't just "when" you play, it dictates "what" you are actually playing. Where a note falls on the grid gives it either more or less power.

- Notes on **Strong Beats** feel important and intentional

- Notes on **Weak Beats** feel fleeting, transitional or decorative.

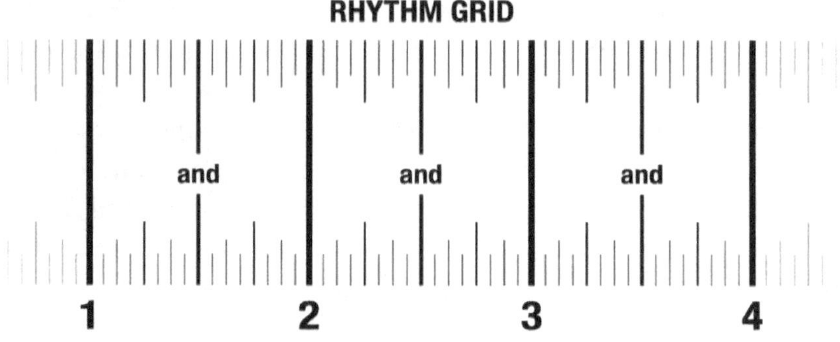

Strongest beats are usually where a kick and snare hit like the 1 and 3 beat. The other strong beats would be the 2 and the 4 beat. So generally the 1234 are strong. The weak beats are the in-betweens, so if you counted 1 ee and ah / 2 ee and ah / 3 ee and ah / 4 ee and ah. The "and" are weak and the "ee" and "ah" are the weakest. The further you subdivide the beat and further those are off the grid, the weaker they get. The closer you get to a strong beat without being on it, the weaker the note. Anything half way between strong beats is half as strong as the strongest it divides.

Sound that you place on a strong beat makes it EXTRA whatever it already is. The opposite is true for whatever note is placed on a weak beat. So a note that is tense placed on a strong beat is EXTRA tense. We usually place chord tones on strong beats. This anchors the ear. Weak Beats get scale tones and the weakest are sometimes chromatic notes not fitting the scale or chord at all.

The "Blind Spot" Hack (Chromaticism)

You can take advantage of the listener's perception "blind spots" by using the weakest rhythmic subdivisions (like the "ee" or "ah" of a 16th note). You can play Chromatic Notes (outside the key) without sounding "wrong." As long as it resolves to a chord tone on the next strong beat, it sounds like a brilliant moment rather than a mistake.

InTENSIONal

If you deliberately place a Non-Chord Tone on a Strong Beat, you create massive tension. The listener's brain becomes alert, anticipating the resolution. This is where art lives. You are controlling the listener's attention using rhythmic placement and note choice.

You can change the entire emotional meaning of a melody simply by shifting it forward or backward in time.

Figure 1. (On the Grid): The melody lands on the beat. It locks with the bass. It sounds consonant and safe.

Figure 2. (Displaced Back): Shift that same melody back by one 16th note. Now, the "wrong" notes (the Minor 2nds or tension notes) are landing on the strong beats. The melody sounds tense, unstable, and "outside," even though the notes are identical to Figure 1.

Figure 3. A lick played on the beat. The accents land on C so it-sounds like the C Ionian mode.

Figure 4. The exact same lick, displaced forward by one 8th-note triplet. Now the accents land on A and the ear re-contextualizes the entire phrase as the A Aeolian mode. This shows that rhythm even influences the mode due to it emphasizing specific parts of the harmony.

Figure 5. The melody and bassline stop abruptly without any rhythmic setup. It sounds like a mistake. A sudden, unpunctuated stop that leaves the listener confused.

Figure 6. The bass locks into the rhythm of the melody. They stop together on a tense note (not the root). Silence. The tense note lingers in the listener's mind during the silence. The empty space creates massive anticipation. When you finally hit the resolution chord after that pause, it feels like it hits ten times harder.

Improvising

When you are improvising, instead of only thinking about "notes" or thinking about which notes to use first, try thinking of what rhythm to put them on. Rhythm is the sketch showing structure of the image. Notes are the color you fill it in with.

On the more scientific side, pitch is also rhythm. We often think of Pitch and Rhythm as separate things, but they are the same element of physics. Rhythm is events happening over time like a drum beat at 120 Beats Per Minute. Pitch is also events happening over time... just much faster. An A note (440Hz) is just a static rhythm of 440 cycles per second. Everything in the universe has rhythm.

Rhythm is the most important part of music.

There is a lot of depth to rhythm and you can analyze accenting and ghost notes along with many other drummer-specific components. There are textures that you can remember for different rhythm feels that are historically common but I didn't intend to make a section on this part of rhythm study. I do feel that it can be fun for non-drummers and composers to look into how rhythm can interact and affect how we interpret things. Syncopation for instance can make the same four notes all feel like the most important note at different times. This is a subset of strong and weak beats.

The rhythm itself changes the overall feel of music. The same notes applied to a polka feel | a swing jazz | a metal gallop | a dotted 8th feel | will imply different genres of music and emotional intention.

Tempo changes not only the overall energy of music but the subdivisions start to mean less or more depending on the overall speed. Once you speed up enough, the strongest beats start appearing on the 1 and 3 instead of the 1 2 3 4. With a slower tempo, the ANDs can be included as strong beats.

TIME SIGNATURES

Why·you·need·to·know·this:

It helps to know how music loops on a timeline and be able to identify the differences in each time signature

It looks like math, but it isn't

You don't divide the numbers or anything like that. It's just a way to easily show how many beats we consider a measure to be. A measure is just an arbitrary segment of time we put notes into. It is very simple and also limited. The top number is **how many** of whatever the bottom number is per measure. In other words, the bottom number is the **length/type** of note we are using to count and the top number is HOW MANY of THAT TYPE OF NOTE per measure.

HOW MANY: 4
OF THIS LENGTH: 4

Bottom number types:

2 IS HALF NOTE
4 IS QUARTER NOTE
8 IS EIGHTH NOTE
16 IS SIXTEENTH NOTE

4/4 means there are 4 beats. The bottom number 4 is code or shorthand for "Quarter Note". Quarter notes counts as one beat and the top number says there are 4 of those Quarter note beats per measure.

We notate or verbally associate certain looping patterns as time signatures. This helps us communicate and remember the basic structure of music along a timeline.

We decide what a measure should notated as based on what feels like a natural looping point for our brain in the context of what we are listening to. Sometimes there are a few ways to hear things but whatever seems the easiest for the majority of humans to read will be what we indicate or name as the time signature.

Here are some other examples:

So, 4/4 is 4 quarter notes. 2/4 is two quarter notes. 3/4 is three quarter notes. 5/4 is five quarter notes. 2/8 is two eighth notes. 4/8 is four eighth notes. 3/8 is three eighth notes. All per measure/bar/block of music.

If you see a C in the time signature area it stands for **common time** (4/4). C with a line (¢) **Cut Time** (2/2). This feels like a march.

Popular music is usually 4/4, but understanding other feels expands your toolkit.

- 3/4 The Waltz. (ONE-two-three, ONE-two-three).
- 5/4 The Limp. Money by Pink Floyd.
- 7/8 The Rush. Common in Progressive Rock and Metal.
- 2/4 The March. Left-Right-Left-Right.

"6/8 or 3/4"

I am sometimes asked the difference between 6/8 and 3/4, since they technically contain the same amount of time (6 eighth notes = 3 quarter notes). Drum teachers say that accents fall differently (6/8 is two groups of three; 3/4 is three groups of two). I somewhat disagree because accents are an independent element. You can accent whatever you want. The only real difference is **readability**. One version will simply be easier to read or count depending on the song's phrasing. Don't let tradition limit where you put your accents.

Swing & Shuffle

Swing/shuffle feel is basically taking a triplet and not playing the middle note of three notes. Sometimes I see people attempting to describe different variations and I have seen people mention that it is a secret feeling only certain jazz musicians can understand or perform properly. I disagree. Pairs of 8th notes are played with the first longer, the second shorter. When performing fast the swing feel tends to fall into less of a strict distance in time. This is likely due to the challenge physically and mentally. It isn't a spiritual awakening. It's just a triplet grid where you skip the middle note. Swing and Shuffle are simply triplets. Take a group of three triplets. Don't play the middle note. You play the first note (long) and the third note (short).

SWING AND SHUFFLE = 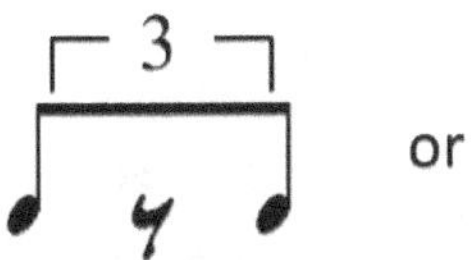 or 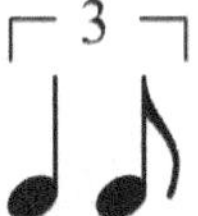

The Drummer's Definition:

- Shuffle: The drummer plays the snare on every beat (ghost notes) but accents the backbeat.

- Swing: The drummer skips the "and" of beats 1 and 3 on the ride cymbal.

Shuffle is swing but is only strict triplets. Shuffle for drummers also means they will tend to play the swing feel but will play on every 8th. Swing to them means they don't play on the "and" of 1 or 3.

Jazz musicians have at times claimed that "swing" means a mystical vibe that only some can attain and it means the music is locked into a pocket that isn't perfectly on time but is better sounding than being perfectly in time with the metronome. Jazz people tend to romanticize things and enjoy pretending things are more complex than they really are. Swing and Shuffle are the same thing and are simply not playing a triplets middle note. If you do that slightly off time that is your option and maybe an underlying issue with your skill level.

MURDER

"Chordlumbo" and the Case of the Missing Scale

This is going to be a fun learning and testing experience. I have been testing students in a fun way where I uncover clues like a murder mystery. I am a big fan of Columbo and enjoy watching him play dumb, scratch his head, ask "just one more thing" and drive the suspect nuts with constant annoyances while he solves the mystery.

In this section you can also be the detective. We are going to look at a "crime scene" (a chord progression) and determine who the killer is (the Scale).

Here's the progression we found at the scene of the crime:
Am-Dm-G7-Cmaj7-F-Dm-E7-Am-A7-Dm7-G7-C-Am-Dm7-G7-C-E

Those chords are the witnesses and evidence we will be using to solve this mystery. The evidence is in order so we will go chord by chord to determine what options we have. You can use the section called Every Chord In Music to determine every option as a reference or you can use the scales you already know to come up with options. I would try it each way for more fun.

Chordlumbo scratched his head, his cigar dangling precariously. "You see, folks," he began, squinting at the sheet music. "Music is like a puzzle. Each chord is a clue, and the key it belongs to might just unlock the mystery."

The Usual Suspects

We start by examining the first three chords **Am**, **Dm** and **G7.**

Am is composed of the notes A, C and E. This could be the vi of C Major, the ii of G Major or even the iii of F Major. **Dm** is a 4th away from Am. They are close friends. **G7** looks to be the Smoking Gun. Dominant 7th chords are almost always the V chord. We can deduce that if G7 is the V then C Major must be the I.

Let's check the neighborhood...The **C Major** scale contains: **C, Dm, Em, F, G, Am** and **Bdim.** Looking at our evidence list of Cmaj7, F and Dm... These guys, they all live in the C Major neighborhood. It looks like an open-and-shut case. C Major is our guy.

The Alibi

But wait... just one more thing. As we look further down the evidence list, we find a couple of characters that don't fit the C Major profile, the **E7** and **A7.**

Chordlumbo leaned over the piano, one finger poking at the keys. "I spoke to Mr. C Major earlier, he claims he was with Am and F all night. But these other chords... E7?... A7? They have notes that Mr. C Major doesn't know. E7 has a G#, and A7 has a C#. Someone is lying."

In C Major, the E chord is supposed to be minor (Em). Here, it is Major (E7). A Disguise? This E7 acts as a "V" chord pushing us back to Am. To play this, we need to change the G to a G#. That makes it the A Harmonic Minor scale.

Chordlumbo interjects, I think the A Harmonic Minor scale is also called C Augmented Major scale ever since the Science of Music book came out, My wife loves that book, I tell ya, I can never pull her away from it. Now she keeps correcting me about the names of scales that have been around for centuries. What do I know, My piano teacher said I hurt her ears so I stuck to baseball, but I just cant seem to understand the difference between all those modes like she does.

The A7 Clue

Later, we see an A7 resolving to Dm7. In C Major, A is supposed to be minor (Am). Another Disguise because this is a Secondary

Dominant (V of ii). It's an imposter trying to pull us toward Dm. To play over this, we need to raise the C to a C# now (so we can fit the A7 chord).

The Verdict

Chordlumbo paced the room, cigar smoke trailing behind. "Now, the real question is, which scale fits this whole progression? We're not just playing 'Chopsticks' here. It's mostly one guy, but maybe he keeps putting on fake mustaches."

To look into each chord we would see a large variety of scales they belong to. We can then see what scales match the highest number of times. That is your likely killer. The underlying "Killer" here is the C Major Scale. You can use this scale for 90% of the song. Over the E7 the killer puts on an egyptian looking wig. Change the note G to G#. (A Harmonic Minor). Over the A7 the killer puts on fake glasses. Change the note C to C#. (D Harmonic Minor / A Mixolydian b6). Instead of memorizing three completely different scales, just think in a way where you can gradually adapt what you need to fit the next chord that appears out of the current key. "I am playing C Major." "Oh, here comes the E7, I'll sharp the G." "Oh, here comes the A7, I'll sharp the C."

And so, with a final note, the case was closed.
The killer's alibi fell flat like a poorly resolved cadence. With the sleeve of his raincoat trailing atop the piano, Chordlumbo tapped his cigar ashes into the waiting candy bowl then stepped out into the rain whistling "This Old Man Came Rolling Home" in the key of C.

Fade to black.

NOTATION

Why·you·need·to·know·this:

You might need to understand notation to play examples from books that use it.

Recording Music as Images

This chapter isn't "Theory." It is simply the method people use to record sound as images. This wasn't something I wanted to add to this book because I feel it isn't music theory as much as handwriting or spelling doesn't belong in a book about literature or creative writing. It is often what people expect when they hear the words "music theory" because it starts out every music theory book for hundreds of years now.

Notation has changed over time and I am not totally convinced that some virgin named Guido around the year 1000 created the best system for music notation. It's the same guy who took the first two letters of a hymn and used them instead of numbers to indicate sounds. (Do Re Mi Fa...) Tablature has been around since 1300-1450 or so depending on if you count pipe organ vs lute versions. It is often regarded as a lesser form of notation due to it being specific to instruments. I think it is a better system in certain ways. Especially for things like guitar.

But if you come across notation (such as a few examples in this book itself) and you get upset saying, "Oh no, not this crap again...I can't understand this". I will show you the basics in this chapter.

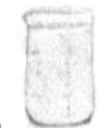

Here are the note names on the (not so) grand staff in various ways you might see them. Remember that it's **just the alphabet** in order from A to G looping upward.

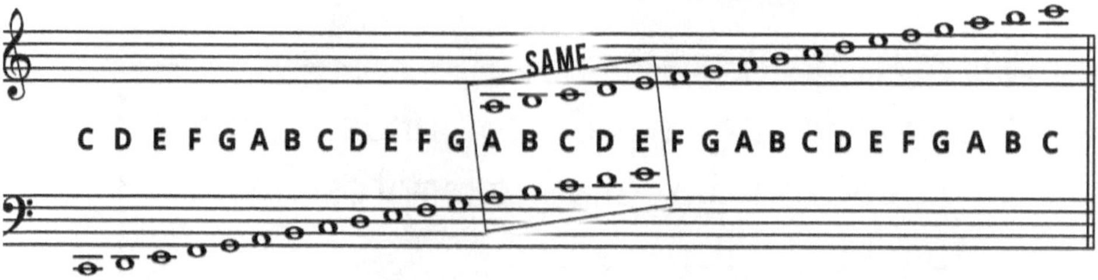

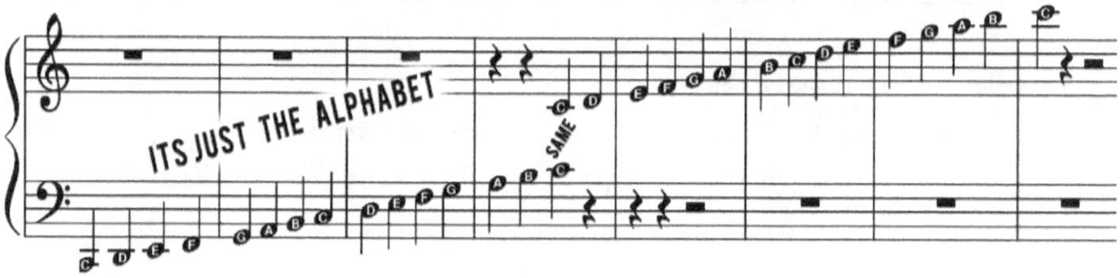

SAME
C D E F G A B C D E F G A B C D E F G A B C D E F G A B C

ITS JUST THE ALPHABET
SAME

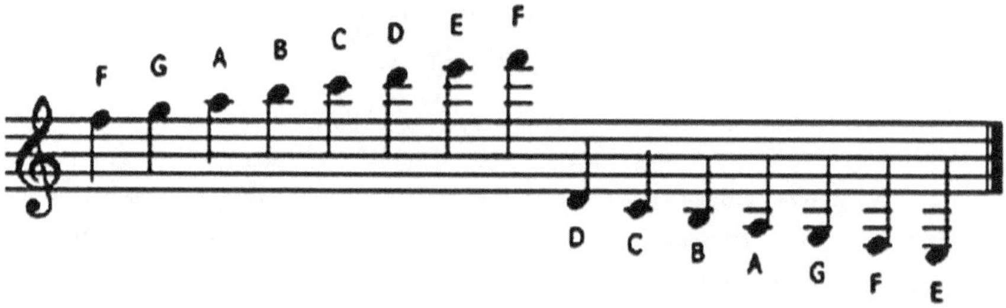

F G A B C D E F
D C B A G F E

Here is a blank set of measures. The measures will contain notes or rests of specific lengths. Each measure is separated by a barline. These measures will have 4 quarter notes per measure or notes of equal value. No more, no less. It has to be exact. Look back to the time signature section for review if needed on how this works.

measure 1
measure 2
barline

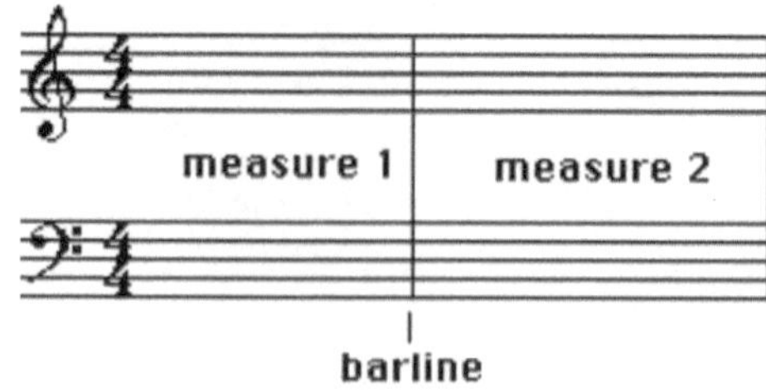

Next up, here are the clef types. They simply point out what line is what note so instead of an arbitrary array of lines and spaces, we have a reference to what one of the lines are as a note/frequency/pitch.

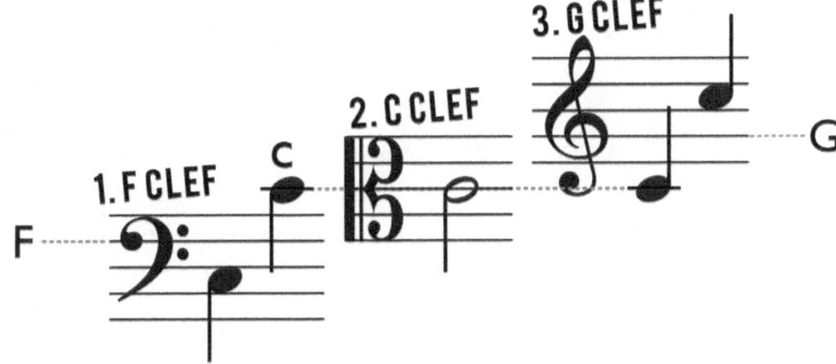

1. The F clef has the shape of the letter F and if you look between the two dots to the right of it you will see they are centering around the line that will hold the value of F for a note. If you lowered this down to the next line, then that next line instead would be the F.

2. The C clef looks nothing like a C shape but the middle of it has an arrow sort of curve that points directly to whatever line we want the C note to be on.

3. The G clef is tough to draw by hand and is in the shape of the letter G. The middle of the swirly circular part points out what line the G note is going to be on.

You count up and down from whatever clef line is shown and know what notes are on the line or space using this "system". I think it should be locked to one clef always without any deviation because that would be easier but again, some virgin named Guido and his pals from the church might not be the best scientist or logical thinker.

Here are sharp, flat, and natural note indications. Sharp raises it one half step from natural, flat lowers it one half step, and

natural changes it back to the normal note without a flat or sharp. When a note is already # or b from the key signature at the beginning of the song or in a spot where we put a new key signature in the middle of the song, we remember it is adjusted up or down and we don't mark it as # or b every time. We just remember it still is until we say otherwise. Also, when we do say otherwise and put a # or b in a measure somewhere, any notes regardless of the octave they are in will continue to be adjusted as such until that measure ends and they go back to whatever the last key signature stated.

Here are the key signatures. I just see them as a way to shove all of the expected sharps or flats into one measure to make it easier on the person writing it. Not always when reading it though (at least for me, but I suck at sight reading... guitarist).

Go one note above the last # to see the key

F Bb Eb Ab Db Gb Cb

Go one b before the last b to see the key

For sharps, just go to the last sharp shown on the right and go up one half step from it, that's the Key.

For flats, go to the second from the last flat on the right and that is the Key.

You don't need to memorize notes of the Major scales or the number of sharps or flats in each Major scale. When reading music, you just need to know what notes are on what line or space, how long they last and, if they are adjusted to be sharp or flat.

Here is a flow chart of sorts. This is one of the ways we shorten the length of notation and save some trees for Guido and his virgin friends from the church to breathe easier while living in sin but trying their best before the internet or even toilet paper existed. Yuck Guido. (Did he use his hand? nm)

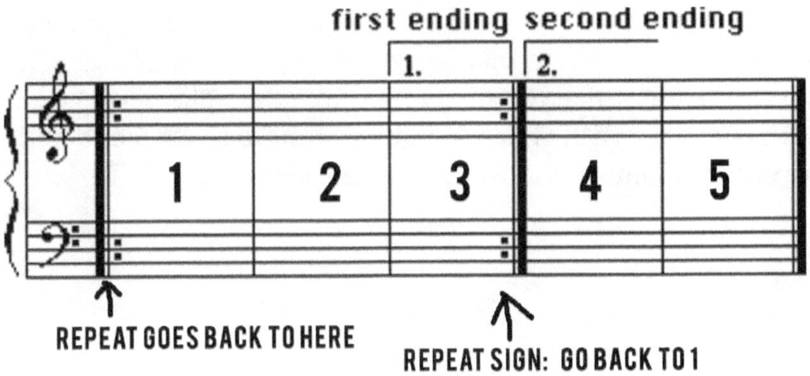

You would play measures 1-3 and then consider the first ending to be finished, then you would go back from 1-2 then skip to the second ending on 4-5.

Here are other signs and extra fancy Italian words Guido and his daft friends used to save some trees.

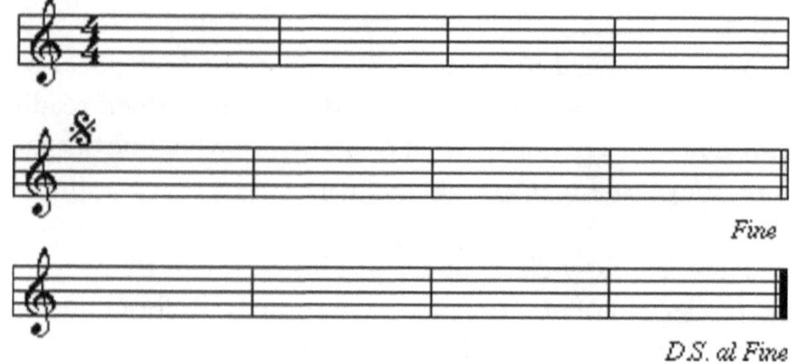

You play until the "**D.S. al Fine**" at the end, then that is telling you to go back to either the beginning OR if you have a very fancy looking "**S**" symbol like we happen to notice on measure five, you go back to that fancy looking "S" symbol and play until the "**Fine**". I like to remember it like this. The very proud Italian (aren't they all) Guido, is telling us to **Go to Da S and al D way until it's Final.** Or until you feel fine I suppose.

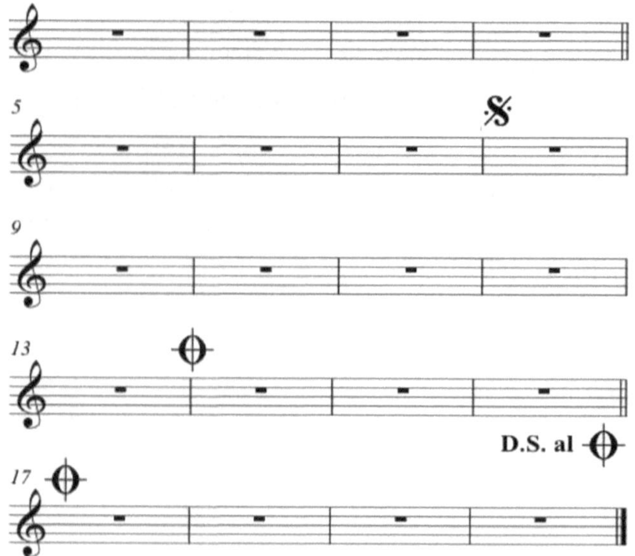

Now here is a more complex one to save even more paper and allow for more secret elitist fancy symbols. Now we see that Guido is telling us to play until the "**D.S. al coda**". It looks like a target and we all know how very excited Italians and Christians are about firearms (at least here in the United States) so this should be easy to remember. We will **TARGET** the coda after the **fancy "S" Sign**. I like to see them as a portal though. So when you get to the **portal/target/coda sign**, you warp to the next one on measure seventeen in this case. It is also perhaps a way to confuse triangle players who have 26 measures of rests and fall asleep through the very proud religious music about the original sin that Guido has been composing with his virgin pals.

So the flow from this example is that you would play **1-16** then go back to **DA FANCY ASS S SIGN** at **measure 8** and play until the **portal/target/coda sign** at **measure 14**. (so 8-13) then skip directly to **measure 17**, do not pass go, and play until the last **measure at 20**. However, you wouldn't be playing anything since we don't have any notes in any measures as this is just a flow example.

Here are all of the notes and rests with their length indications..

On top, are notes telling you when and what to play and how long, and on the bottom the rests of equal length telling you to not play and wait.

Here is a tree showing the breakdown of how the length is cut in half as you start filling in the notes and adding stems and flags to them. More trinkets and ornamentation the shorter the note basically.

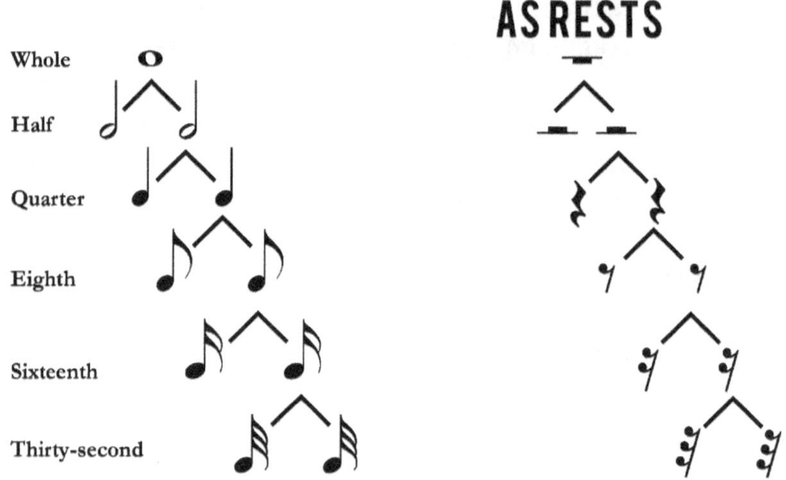

You can see how two half notes equal a whole note and two quarter notes equal a half note. So four quarter notes equal a whole note. Next up are dotted notes. They are confusing to some but I will explain them to you. The dot tells us the note is equal to whatever the original length is plus half of that. So a dotted half note is equal to a half note and half of a half note, which is a quarter note. So three quarter notes.

The second one is a dotted quarter note. So it is a quarter note plus half of that which is an 8th note so three 8th notes.

The third one shows a Double Dotted quarter note. That means it is the quarter plus half of the quarter.. plus half of THAT. So Quarter note + eighth note + half the 8th note which would be a 16th note. So it adds up to seven 16th notes.

On the left of this text are **Triplets.** They are to be played as three notes per one subdivision longer. So three 16th triplet notes are the same length as two straight 16th notes or one 8th note. Three eighth note triplets are the same length as two eighth notes or one quarter note. A set of three quarter note triplets are the same length as two quarter notes or one half note. A set of three half note triplets are equal in length to two half notes or one whole note.

These can be visually tricky so it's much easier to listen to them while looking at them to get a feel for it. Sextuplets are basically the same as triplets but are expected to get no accents besides the first of 6 notes. Triplets are therefore expected to have an accent every three notes. Drummers feel this way but I leave accents to the notation, specifically the marks for accents. Here they are:

•	Staccato	Short
–	Tenuto	Long
>	Accent	Hard
Λ	Accent	Harder
>̣	Accent with staccato	Hard and short
≥	Accent with tenuto	Hard and long

Those accents are what you might see above notes and will forget which one is which and come back to check this book someday.

I told my daughter Rylie that I would use her drawing of notes in the book. So, here is her hand drawing of some notes and rests. See if you can name each of them as the final assignment.

GOODBYE

Remember to have fun creating music and don't fall into a trap where you use music theory in place of creativity for inspiration. It is best to do what feels right and then perhaps analyze it later on. I tend to use music theory as a tool when I want to look at various options. These options are usually out of the ordinary because they can be more fun and give unique results.

This theory stuff is all just a way to name and remember things that happen often enough to seem important with music. It won't replace your intuition.

Thank you for reading,

Allen Van Wert

You can visit AllenVanWert.com

Guitar players looking to train their picking can go to UltimatePicking.com

To generate random rhythms visit Randobeat.com

EXERCISE ANSWERS

MUSICAL ALPHABET:

Half Steps

Fill in the missing notes low to high (left to right) as half steps (one fret apart for each of the three)

A A#/Bb B	C C#/Db D	Eb E F
G G#/Ab A	A Bb B	E F F#/Gb
B C C#/Db	Bb B C	C#/Db D D#/Eb
F F#/Gb G	G G#/Ab A	D#/Eb E F

Whole Steps

Fill in the missing notes low to high (left to right) as whole steps (two frets apart for each note)

A B C#	C D E	Eb F G
G A B	Ab Bb C	D#/Eb F G
A#/Bb C D	Ab Bb C	C D E
D#/Eb F G	C D E	G A B

Half and Whole Steps mixed

Fill in the missing notes low to high (left to right) as a mix of half and whole steps (h = half and w = whole)

A - w - B - h - C	D - w - E - h - F	E - w - F# - h - G
B - w - C# - h - D	G - w - A - h - Bb	A# - h - B - h - C
E - h - F - w - G	Eb - w - F - w - G	F# - h - G - w - A
G# - w - A# - h - B	B - h - C - w - D	D# - w - F - h - F#
C - w - D - h - D#	Bb - w - C - h - Db	D# - h - E - w - F#
C - h - C# - w - D#	G - w - A - h - Bb	C# - w - D# - h - E
F - w - G - h - Ab	G - h - G# - w - A#	

MAJOR SCALE EXERCISES:

Build these Major Scales

1. A B C# D E F# G#
2. B C# D# E F# G# A#
3. E F# G# A B C# D#
4. D E F# G A B C#
5. E F# G# A B C# D#
6. F G A Bb C D E
7. G A B C D E F#
8. A# B# Cx D# E# Fx Gx
9. C# D# E# F# G# A# B#
10. D# E# Fx G# A# B# Cx
11. F# G# A# B C# D# E#
12. G# A# B# C# D# E# Fx
13. Ab Bb C Db Eb F G
14. Bb C D Eb F G A
15. Db Eb F Gb Ab Bb C
16. Eb F G Ab Bb C D
17. Gb Ab Bb Cb Db Eb F
18. A B C# D E F# G#
19. B C# D# E F# G# A#
20. Ab Bb C Db Eb F G
21. G A B C D E F#
22. C# D# E# F# G# A# B#
23. F# G# A# B C# D# E#
24. D E F# G A B C#
25. G A B C D E F#
26. Bb C D Eb F G A
27. Eb F G Ab Bb C D
28. C D E F G A B

TRIAD EXERCISES:

Build these triads

A Major: A C# E
B minor: B D F#
C minor: C Eb G
D Major: D F# A
E minor: E G B
F diminished: F Ab Cb(B)
G Major: G B D
A# minor: A# C# E#
C# diminished: C# E G
D# minor: D# F# A#
F# minor: F# A C#
G# diminished: G# B D
Ab minor: Ab Cb Eb
Bb minor: Bb Db F
Db diminished: Db E G
Eb diminished: Eb Gb A
Gb diminished: Gb A C

Reverse work

Name these triads

E G# B = E Major triad
F A C = F Major triad
G# B D = G# Dim triad
A C# E = A Major triad
B D F = B Dim triad
G Bb Db = G Dim triad
A C Eb = A Dim triad
Bb Db Fb = Bb Dim triad
D# F# A# = D# Min triad
C Eb Gb = C diminished triad
F# A C# = F# Min triad

Name the Major Scale (also known as the Key) using the chord progression

1. Dm - G - C is in the key of C Major.
2. E° - C - Gm is in the key of F Major.
3. Am - G - C is in the key of C Major or G Major.
4. Dm - Am - Em is in the key of C Major.
5. Am - Em - Bm is in the key of G Major.
6. A - B is in the key of E Major.
7. C - Bb is in the key of F Major.
8. Dm - Am - F - G is in the key of C Major.
9. C - Bm - Am is in the key of G Major.
10. Em - Am - G is in the key of G Major and C Major.
11. Dm - Em - F is in the key of C Major.
12. G - A - F#m is in the key of D Major.

INTERVAL EXERCISES

Name these intervals

1. E - C = m6th
2. F# - Db = 5th
3. G - A = 2nd
4. A - Gb = 6th
5. B - E = 4th
6. C# - D = m2nd
7. D - A = 5th
8. F - Bb = 4th
9. G# - C = 3rd
10. A - E = 5th
11. C - F = 4th
12. D - Bb = m6
13. E - C# = 6th
14. G - E = 6th
15. B - E = 4th

Name the note at the interval shown

1. Minor 3rd above E = G
2. Minor 6th above B = G
3. Major 3rd above D = F#
4. Minor 7th above C = Bb
5. Perfect 4th above F = Bb
6. Perfect 5th above D = A
7. Major 2nd below G = F
8. Minor 3rd below A = F#
9. Minor 2nd below F = E
10. Perfect 4th below A = E
11. Perfect 5th below D = G
12. Minor 6th below C = E
13. Minor 7th below G = A
14. Major 7th above F# = F (E#)
15. Diminished 5th above Bb = E

7TH CHORD EXERCISES:

1. E Major 7: E, G#, B, D#
2. F# Minor 7: F#, A, C#, E
3. G Dominant 7: G, B, D, F
4. A Major 7: A, C#, E, G#
5. B Minor 7: B, D, F#, A
6. C# Minor 7b5: C#, E, G, B
7. D Dominant 7: D, F#, A, C
8. F Major 7: F, A, C, E
9. G Minor 7: G, Bb, D, F
10. A Dominant 7: A, C#, E, G
11. C Major 7: C, E, G, B
12. D Minor 7: D, F, A, C
13. E Dominant 7: E, G#, B, D
14. G Major 7: G, B, D, F#
15. B Diminished 7: B, D, F, Ab

1. A Major 7: A, C#, E, G#
2. C# Minor 7: C#, E, G#, B
3. D Dominant 7: D, F#, A, C
4. F Major 7: F, A, C, E
5. E Minor 7: E, G, B, D
6. G Dominant 7: G, B, D, F
7. B m7b5: B, D, F, A
8. A# Major 7: A#, C##, E#, G##
9. D# Dominant 7: D#, F##, A#, C#
10. E Dominant 7: E, G#, B, D
11. C Major 7: C, E, G, B
12. F# Minor 7: F#, A, C#, E
13. G# Dominant 7: G#, B#, D#, F#
14. A Diminished 7: A, C, Eb, Gb
15. B Major 7: B, D#, F#, A#
16. D Minor 7: D, F, A, C
17. G Dominant 7: G, B, D, F

Name the key(s) that the chords all belong to

1. Dm7 - G7 - C = C Major scale
2. Em7b5 - C - Gm7 = F Major scale
3. Am7 - G - C = C and G Major scale
4. Dm - Am7 - Em = C Major scale
5. Am - Em - Bm7 = G Major scale
6. AMaj7 - B7 = E Major scale
7. C7 - Bb = F Major scale
8. Dm - Am7 - F - G = C Major scale
9. CMaj7 - Bm7 - Am = G Major scale
10. Em7 - Am - G = G and C Major scale
11. Dm7 - Em - F = C Major scale
12. G - A - F#m = D Major scale

9TH CHORD EXERCISES:

1. B Major 9: B, D#, F#, A#, C#
2. C minorMajor 9: C, Eb, G, Bb, D
3. B minor 9: B, D, F#, A, C#
4. E add 9: E, G#, B, F#
5. E dom 9: E, G#, B, D, F#
6. Fm9: F, Ab, C, Eb, G
7. AΔ9: A, C#, E, G#, B
8. G# minor 9: G#, B, D#, F#, A#
9. C# halfdim b9: C#, E, G, B, D
10. D# minor add 9: D#, F#, A#, C#, E#(F)
11. A#m9: A#, C#, E#(F), G#, B#(C)
12. D# add 9: D#, F##(G), A#, E#(F)
13. Gb major add 9: Gb, Bb, Db, Ab
14. Bb dom 9: Bb, D, F, Ab, C
15. Ab min9: Ab, Cb, Eb, Gb, Bb
16. Fb(E) half dim b9: Fb(E), Abb(G), Cbb(Bb), Ebb(D),Gbb(F)
17. Eb9: Eb, G, Bb, Db, F

1. Cmaj9: C E G B D
2. Dm7b9: D F A C Eb
3. E9: E G# B D F#
4. Fmaj7b9: F A C E Gb
5. G7#9: G B D F A#
6. Am9b5: A C Eb G B
7. Bb7b9: Bb D F Ab Cb(B)
8. Cm9: C Eb G Bb D
9. D7b9b13: D F# A C Eb Bb
10. E7b9: E G# B D F
11. F#m9: F# A C# E G#
12. Gmaj7#9: G B D F# A#
13. A7b9b5: A C# Eb G Bb
14. Bbmaj9: Bb D F A C
15. C#dim9: C# E G A# D#

Name the key(s) that the chords all belong to

1. F Major: Bbmaj9 - C9
2. G# Major: D#7 - Fx(F##) halfdim9
3. C Major: Dm9 - G7 - Bm7(b5 b9)
4. F Major: Dm9 - Gm7
5. B Major: F#7 - Bmaj9
6. Eb Major: Fm9 - Gm7
7. B Major: G#m9 - C#m9 - D#m7
8. G Major: Am9 - D7 - F#m7(b5)
9. D Major: A7 - Bm9
10. B Major: C#m9 - F#7
11. Bb Major: Ebmaj9 - F9 - Gm9
12. Eb Major: Fm9 - Gm7b9
13. C# Major: D#m9 - G#7
14. A Major: E7 - F#m9 - G#m7(b5)
15. Gb Major: Abm9 - Db7 - Fm7b5b9

OTHER SCALES EXERCISES

Build these scales

1. C Harmonic Major: C D E F G Ab B C
2. D Harmonic Minor (F Augmented Major): D E F G A Bb C#
3. C# Melodic Minor: C# D# E F# G# A# B#
4. E Hungarian Minor: E F# G A# B C D
5. F# Augmented Major: F# G# A# B Cx D# E#
6. C Major Pentatonic: C D E G A
7. C# Minor Pentatonic: C# E F# G# B
8. A Melodic Minor: A B C D E F# G#
9. B Augmented Major: B C# D# E Fx G# A#
10. D Augmented Major: D E F# G A# B C#

Reverse work - Name these scales (They may not be in order)

1. Eb F G A B C D = C Melodic Minor
2. B C D# E F# G A = G Augmented Major (E Harmonic Minor traditionally)
3. D E F G A B C# = D Melodic Minor
4. F G Ab B C D E = C Harmonic Major
5. C D# E F G# A B = A Hungarian Minor (C AugMajor#2)
6. G A Bb C D E F# = G Melodic Minor
7. A B C D Eb F# G = G Harmonic Major
8. G A B C# D# E F# = E Melodic Minor
9. B C## D# E F## G# A# = G# Hungarian Minor (B AugMajor#2)
10. C D# E F# G A B= G Augmented Major (E Harmonic Minor traditionally)

HARMONIZING OTHER SCALES EXERCISES

What scale is the chord progression using?

1. E - AmMaj7 = C Augmented Major scale (A Harmonic Minor)
2. Eb Aug - A Dim - Cm = C Melodic Minor scale
3. C Dim - Dbm = E Augmented Major (Db Harmonic Minor)
4. Fm - Ab Aug - B Dim = C Harmonic Major
5. Bb maj7 - A7 - DmMaj7 = F Aug Major (D Harmonic Minor)
6. D7 - E7 = A Melodic Minor
7. G AugMajor9 - B Maj #9 = G Harmonic Major
8. C# Dim - Emb9 = D Melodic Minor
9. BminMaj9 - D AugMaj7#9 = F# Harmonic Major
10. Ebm7b5 - Fm7b5 = Gb Melodic Minor

www.ingramcontent.com/pod-product-compliance
Lightning Source LLC
Chambersburg PA
CBHW030923120626
46554CB00001B/255

9798990789807